Guide to
Companion
Parrot
Behavior

Second Edition

Mattie Sue Athan

Dedication

For Gale Whittington whose efforts have so shaped my life, and for Monique Skotarek for her ongoing support and inspiration.

All inquiries should be addressed to:
Barron's Educational Series, Inc.
250 Wireless Boulevard
Hauppauge, New York 11788
www.barronseduc.com

ISBN-13: 978-0-7641-4213-0
ISBN-10: 0-7641-4213-5

Library of Congress Catalog Card No. 2009014984

Library of Congress Cataloging-in-Publication Data
Athan, Mattie Sue.
  Guide to companion parrot behavior / Mattie Sue Athan.
    p. cm.
  Includes bibliographical references and index.
  ISBN-13: 978-0-7641-4213-0
  ISBN-10: 0-7641-4213-5
  1. Parrots. 2. Parrots—Behavior. I. Title.
SF473.P3A845   2009
636.6'865—dc22   2009014984

Printed in China

9 8 7 6 5 4 3 2 1

About the Author

Mattie Sue Athan is a founder in the field of companion parrot behavior management. Since 1978, her study and practice has focused on the home environment and its role in the development of independence in producing easy-to-live-with parrots.

Photo Credits

Mattie Sue Athan: pages 2, 59, 75, 171 (bottom), 179; Joan Balzarini: pages vi, 4, 6, 14, 17, 25, 28, 30, 37, 38, 45, 49, 50, 57, 65, 70, 71, 76, 78, 80, 83, 84, 89, 91, 97, 98, 107, 112, 116, 117, 120, 121, 124, 138, 145, 147, 148, 151, 159, 161, 162, 163, 164, 165, 172, 173 (top right), 173 (top left), 173 (bottom), 175, 176 (top), 180, 181, 182, 187, 192, 196, 199, 198, 200, 201 (top left), 201 (top right), 202, 205, 214; Gerry Bucsis and Barbara Somerville: pages 3, 10, 11, 15, 27, 69, 100, 103, 133, 153, 230, 185, 193; Isabelle Francais: pages 5, 23, 42, 67, 72, 82, 86, 155, 157, 183; Susan Green: pages 66, 141, 156, 158; Paulette Johnson: pages 9, 13, 16, 20, 24, 32, 35, 36, 46, 51, 52, 61, 87, 92, 108, 118, 126, 129, 130, 137, 154, 168, 170, 171 (top), 176 (bottom), 177, 178, 143, 195, 209, 218; Pets by Paulette: page x.

Cover Photos

Front cover, back cover, inside front cover, inside back cover: Shutterstock.

Important Note

While every effort has been made to ensure that all information in this text is accurate, up-to-date, and easily understandable, neither the author nor the publisher can be responsible for unforeseen consequences resulting from the use or misuse of this information.

Poorly socialized or unhealthy parrots may be a danger to humans in the household. Escaped non-native species represent an environmental threat in some areas.

Outdoor release or unrestricted outdoor flight is absolutely condemned by the ethical parrot keeper. This book recommends that a parrot's wing feathers be carefully trimmed at least three times per year.

Contents

Foreword

The first edition of *Guide to Companion Parrot Behavior* was arranged to be used like a dictionary—a resource for specific details—with redundancies benefitting those who chose not to read from cover to cover. The resulting book was over-long, a less-than-easy read, and included a few obvious "owies," including an upside down photo of a hyacinth macaw hanging by its toes with a peanut apparently defying gravity over its head. I appreciate this opportunity to both update and restructure this important information.

Over the years, I've often been asked how this book differs from *Guide to a Well-Behaved Parrot,* winner of Amazon.com's Best-selling Bird Care Book Award. While a certain amount of basic information appears in both, the following issues are covered more thoroughly in one than the other.

Guide to a Well-Behaved Parrot
- Passive games birds like to play
- Preventing unwanted behavioral issues
- To shoulder or not to shoulder
- How to pet a parrot

African Grey parrot

- When a parrot spends the day alone
- Disaster preparations
- Parrots and children
- Parrots and other pets
- Potty training a parrot

Guide to Companion Parrot Behavior
- Finding the right bird
- Modifying existing behavioral issues
- To fly or not to fly
- Specific wing-feather trims for particular issues
- Selecting and training a talking parrot
- Eliminating screaming and foul language
- Stimulating the reluctant talker
- Feather chewing, snapping, and plucking
- How access to choice fosters freedom and independence

Additionally, I'm often asked how these books differ from *Parrots: A Complete Pet Owner's Manual,* winner of the Oklahoma Writers' Federation's Best Non-Fiction Book Award. *Parrots* is targeted to anyone considering a first parrot. It includes basic information about accommodations, accessories, anticipated needs of different species, feathers, molting, grooming, safety issues, and things a parrot should be able to expect from a person providing care. Any of these books should be a pleasurable read at this time—whether beside the pool, in a luscious bubble bath, or in a cramped airline seat.

For those who love the stories following the important practical considerations provided here, I'm pleased to offer Frankly Scarlet, a fictional story—a first among these publications—based on fact. Only the ending is changed. At this moment, that gorgeous bundle of red feathers is happily flapping atop her cage in my dining room. Troubling behavioral issues—which led to her being thrown out a window—were left behind many years ago. She's perfect, perfectly loved, perfectly cherished.

Again, thank you Barron's Educational Series for the commitment to keeping these texts contemporary, relative, and actively involved in the world of companion parrots—a very political place at this time. I appreciate the contributions of Dianalee Deter, Jean Pattison, Zoie Howland, and a galaxy of other "stars" (you know who you are) in my personal and professional universe.

—Mattie Sue Athan

Preface

When *Guide to a Well-Behaved Parrot* came out, I was already involved in the retail sale of parrots. Many customers wanted a book to help them raise their birds. There were many articles around, many techniques; but when someone had a problem, it was a challenge to dig up the answer. Mattie Sue Athan's first book received criticism for not being anything new. These techniques had been used by many people for many years. When I asked my veterinarian what he thought of the book, he said it wasn't earth-shaking stuff, but it sure was nice that someone finally put it in a book.

It was a place to start. While many of those techniques have been revised and expanded, the book was one of the focal points for revolutionizing parrot training and letting everyday parrot owners access the wisdom of professionals.

Now this book is in the same category. Many of my customers ask for a book to help them choose a parrot, a book that will help them know what is involved in taking care of the birds before they make the commitment that will often be for a lifetime. The author has again taken a leap. She has worked very hard to gather information, sometimes about species she knew little about. This placed her at the disadvantage of having to trust the opinions of others, and possibly being criticized for doing so. But active critique is the good part. This is the part that helps get more people talking and writing and presenting the information to the people who will use it.

This book might be considered "incomplete," for no one book can completely cover the complex field of companion parrot behavior. However, this book covers many of the questions that prospective parrot owners have. This book needed to be written. Thank you, Mattie Sue.

—Dianalee Deter, Consulting Editor

Chapter One

People Who Live with Parrots

The human companions of parrots differ from those living only with dogs or cats. Friends, coworkers, and family might not understand how *anyone* could enjoy the company of an animal that may occasionally draw blood, sometimes screams for its supper, and can be more intent on commanding attention than sharing it. To top it all off, that "stupid" bird might chew up the furniture or cuss in front of the minister!

It's all part of their fascination. The parrot in the living room is increasingly farther from the wild, but is not yet considered domesticated. To the uninitiated, the human/parrot relationship may appear odd, curious, perhaps even masochistic. Those "clueless" people can't possibly understand the delights of a gorgeous animal that talks with association (in human language and voice), is always ready to surprise even the most jaded colleague, and excels at being goofy. A well-accommodated parrot brings joy the way sunlight brings warmth.

Blue-and-gold macaws

"She was not quite what you would call refined. She was not quite what you would call unrefined. She was the kind of person that keeps a parrot."

Mark Twain
Following the Equator;
Pudd'nhead Wilson's
New Calendar

A parrot-oriented human may even prefer the company of birds to that of other people, but anyone who doesn't like people might not like a parrot either. Like humans, some parrots are more enjoyable companions than others. We all relish kindness, courtesy, respect, and trust; but parrots have to learn these behaviors just as people do.

Indoor and Outdoor Life Quality

A parrot is quite unlike a dog or cat. It's considered an "undomesticated exotic" animal with wild

Bodini Amazon

don't just use words; they might bark like and with the dogs, meow like a cat, sing like a canary, caw like a crow, crow like a rooster, cry like a baby, beep like the microwave, and/or squeak like the door.

Most of the time, a parrot's sexual instincts take a backseat to social ones, leaving little need to surgically remove the bird's sexual organs—a procedure so risky that it simply isn't done. Sometimes even the parrot's instinct to fit in can seem self-motivated, selfish. A parrot will compete for attention—the pleasure of your company—with other humans, other pets, babies, the telephone, and television. Therein lies the "undomesticated" side of the parrot personality. In a human, this behavior might be called simply "rude" or "unschooled." Or it might be called "jealous."

Somewhere there's a line between social bonding expressed by parrots and the overzealous guarding of treasured humans to the point of driving away every other living thing. This is when bonding becomes sexual. If it is new or transitional rather than habitual behavior, it's just part of life with Paco.

Like humans, parrots cannot rely merely on instinctual behaviors. The parrot's capacity to study and learn or copy overrides instinct. Parrots are K-strategists—animals like humans that reproduce infrequently and spend a great deal of time learning successful behavior before actually becoming mature.

While the thought of a parrot living wild is appealing, it's no more

instincts and needs, especially those related to mating. Since reproductive function is usually surgically removed from dogs and cats for behavioral reasons, a parrot's related behaviors are difficult to compare to what would happen if mammalian pets were not spayed or neutered. Whether we're considering life with a female dog that's going to bleed on the furniture a couple of times yearly, a cat that's going to come home cut up from fights, or a male cat or dog that marks territory with urine (sometimes feces), behavioral issues related to their sexual functions can be more unpleasant than a parrot's springtime mate calling, occasional territorialism, or attempts to feed.

Unlike cats, much of a parrot's behavior is socially motivated by such a great desire to fit in that it copies behavior from "flockmates," in the home, which means humans and other pets. Many pet parrots

realistic than the thought of dogs or cats being forced outdoors. Life in the wild is no picnic, and wild parrots have much to learn in order to survive. Not only do they have to compete with other parrots and other animals for habitat, food, and water; they need to know how to find and separate good food from toxic plants, how to defend territory, recognize and avoid predators, find safe water, and communicate with both soft and loud calls. They face the challenges of selecting and keeping a mate; developing role-appropriate behaviors; competing for and defending nesting sites; and creating, nurturing, and teaching their extremely helpless offspring to do the same. They have to be able to evaluate available supplies in order to determine whether nesting should be completed or even attempted, for if food or water is insufficient, eggs or chicks must be abandoned. All these things are done sometimes in blinding rain or oppressive drought.

Wild parrots must adapt to ever-shrinking environments being constantly adapted for human habitation. Whether parrots simply die of thirst, as is happening today in Australia, or are killed for trying to steal a meal from a farm, loss of habitat equals death. The ultimate K-strategists, humans modify the areas they occupy so severely that very few other animals can survive in our cities and suburbs. Wild animals trying to live side by side with humans are summarily removed or simply exterminated. This has, for many generations, been the fate of both parrots hatched wild and those naturalized in new locales almost anyplace on this planet.

Black-headed caique

Birth Control Feed

There is even a new threat to parrots approaching. Soon, probably within the time this book takes to reach you, a new, more humane way to eliminate wild parrots will become available. Those humans "needing" to get rid of, but not actually wishing to kill, wildlife will have access to restricted use of birth control feed that renders wild birds infertile. This could be good news if the product is effective in controlling the Canada goose population and related airline strikes. Naturalized "nonnative" species such as Quaker parrots, which have successfully expanded in range, will be allowed to live out their lives without being able to reproduce. It could be very bad news for other parrot species — some considered rare and treasured in aviculture, but considered agricultural pests in their native habitats now needed by human expansion.

In-house Parrots

The one bright spot on the horizon for parrots is that they have established a protected place for themselves in our homes rather than in our backyards. Parrots are highly adaptable. By easily acquiring a different set of skills, generations of parrots have learned to share life indoors with people rather than compete with them outdoors. Hundreds of thousands of parrots of all shapes and sizes safely and successfully inhabit our homes. Their adaptation as human companions has occurred relatively quickly compared with the thousands of years it took dogs and cats to make their places with us.

Like it or not, companion parrots have greater protection than any other population of parrots in the world. Most of us can do little or nothing to save the lives and habitats of wild parrots, but anyone who lives with a parrot can not only save that bird's life, but, with the help of this book, ensure its quality of life.

Umbrella cockatoo

Expectations and Reality

Dreaming of a "perfect" feathered friend, aspiring parrot owners envision themselves enjoying idyllic evenings with a calm bird snuggled on the shoulder sharing simple conversations as they read or watch television. Some picture a dazzling creature on an immaculate ornamental cage or perch surrounded by lush vegetation, objets d'art, and colorful baskets.

The reality is that some parrots will develop a fascination with removing little moles from human necks, scream when we leave the room, chew through computer cords, "harvest" household plants, and unweave baskets. It doesn't have to be that way.

A premium hand-fed baby parrot may be beautifully feathered, interactive, and talkative, but with inattention or even too much of the wrong kind of attention, it might not stay that way. Some untrained or poorly socialized parrots grow up to be interactive, noninvasive companions. Sometimes the loving rewards provided by human companions establish the bird's most charming, welcome behaviors into habits, but accidental or unintentional rewards can reinforce initially amusing antics into annoying, obnoxious, potentially unhealthy behaviors.

A juvenile parrot is eating independently and has learned to fly by the time it leaves its hatching home. This is the ideal time to begin training; it's

Green-cheeked Amazon

a window of opportunity for teaching cooperation and independence. The wild youngster would be copying behavior from successful flockmates. It is the most important developmental period in the bird's lifetime. If appropriate skills are not acquired at this time, life quality—perhaps even survival—will be challenging for either wild or companion parrots.

Human behavioral development isn't much different. If consideration and manners are neglected during early childhood, the adult will suffer. A maturing parrot might become aggressive, shy, overbonded, excessively loud, or acquire off-putting habits. If the new owner of a medium or larger parrot has not planned the environment and begun appropriate socialization by the time the bird is 18 months old, possibilities for the future can begin to look a little scary. That is, if unwanted behaviors are accidentally reinforced and the bird becomes focused on

African Grey babies

being the center of attention, it might wind up living in the garage or backroom or being sold through the newspaper, emotionally and physically abandoned.

How could a relatively small creature like a bird—a very expensive creature—drive normally reasonable humans to such reprehensible behavior? What kind of "problems" can parrot owners expect?

Most adoption parrots probably lose their homes due to human lifestyle issues: illness, death, graduation, marriage. However, some very well-meaning people might resort to giving up a parrot because of unexpected messiness or because the bird's screaming, biting, or other annoying behaviors have become habitual. These issues must be addressed separately, for only the latter may be truly considered problematic. Chewing and a little messiness must be expected and accommodated.

Cooperation, Confidence, and Trust

No reasonable person would expect to enjoy life with an untrained dog. Although their needs and basic responses differ, parrots also require training to become consistently charming companions. Safety is a significant concern for prey animals that must be forever watchful for danger. Knowing what's going on, who is doing what, and when something is going to happen contributes to a parrot's sense of safety. Routine repetition of successful, enjoyable, interactive behaviors establishes cooperation, confidence, and trust in the relationship between people and their companion parrots. Parrots thrive on routine, ritual, predictability. Any interactive routine you and your bird mutually enjoy will set the tone for all future interactions. Therefore, it's good to be able to immediately access a familiar, well-patterned interaction in order to connect emotionally and behaviorally with the animal.

In dog training, the *sit* command establishes the human as leader and the dog as follower. Likewise, shared rituals performed by birds and humans together establish favored patterns of interaction. Step-ups are the most common of these cooperation routines (see page 103), but almost any enjoyable interplay can also serve this purpose. These daily exercises need be no more than one or two minutes' duration but will enable both bird and human to anticipate the other's reactions. They can be stimulated either by the people or the bird. A juvenile parrot entering its first home directly from being handfed should already confidently step up when prompted and might catch eye contact and lift a foot when it wants to be picked up. Other cooperation exercises might include the towel game (see page 105) and nontactile vocal or eye games (see page 104).

Talking and More

Unless you simply inherited a bird or one jumped on your shoulder and wouldn't get off, the parrot's reputation for speech was probably the first thing to attract your attention. You're not alone. Fascination with talking is the usual catalyst motivating that first parrot acquisition.

When a bird enters the home, many—mostly delightful—surprises await. The first time a new parrot owner walks into the room naked or unkempt and is greeted with a loud wolf whistle, "*wow*," "*hello*," or "*pretty bird*," there's a sense of elation unlike any other. Whether this is "strokes" or ego, it's impossible not to relish the sensation of being welcomed and appreciated (even in the raw). Because our birds hear happy, supportive words, they respond in kind.

We all talk to our animal friends of any kind (even fish and snakes, which aren't really considered pets), but people talk to parrots more than any other type of companion animal. They reward our vocal interactions in a variety of interesting, exciting ways, including our own words in our own voices. Even more, parrots often appear to be communicating *their* thoughts with *our* words.

Their talent for the acquisition and use of words is the parrot's most treasured gift. This ability to turn wild communication skills directly into human language is unique among animals. Even if they don't use words, their natural vocalizations have recognizable meaning to the people with whom they live. Our birds literally sing for their suppers.

In addition to conversation, many parrots prefer hands-off companionship. This is ideal for anybody who doesn't especially like physical contact and yet enjoys the security of an intimate friend who (usually) doesn't share confidences with others. This notion of privacy, however, is just another expectation to be dashed, as a parrot will surely repeat what it hears, sometimes at the right time and sometimes not. Cussing in front of your mother-in-law may be shocking but shouldn't be particularly surprising. A parrot's simulated burp, belch, or other crude eruption will be embarrassing, especially if sounded loudly in polite company, but not totally unexpected.

What Parrots Do for People

All humankind bears great, albeit remote, responsibility for protecting wild parrots. Just as we strive to protect their habitats, their survival also benefits us, for many species are considered indicators of nature's well-being in the locales they inhabit. Like a canary in a coal mine, a parrot species' decline can foreshadow difficulties to come for other animals, including humans.

Likewise, we are often reminded of our obligations to parrots living indoors. We are responsible for pro-

A New Day

Marie had been totally disabled with bipolar disease for more than a decade. After an unexpected relocation, she suddenly wound up with a roommate and a dozen parrots. A dedicated night owl, Marie found this troubling because she hated daytime. Accustomed to pulling a pillow over her head and cursing the sun, she found her roommate's chatty morning feeding routine especially annoying.

"Good morning pretty bird! Heeer's breakfast! What'cha doin?"—combined with backtalk from a few macaws, cockatoos, an Amazon, Jardine's, Quaker, and other assorted birds simply drove her nuts (well, nuttier). In fact, she moved out more than once before settling in permanently.

But the only thing never meant to change is change. Three "short" years later, Marie *was the one* always up first in the mornings, feeding and flirting as she danced from cage to cage. She loved to play "peek-a-boo" with the birds, keep their water sparkling clear, give them showers, clean and rearrange the cages, and share treats in the afternoon.

These fine-feathered friends and the responsibility of caring for them along with modern medications, had transformed her morning disposition from grumbling darkness to shining light.

viding a haven expected to be much safer, healthier, and more comfortable than the chaos of nature. We feed and guide them to a sense of well-being. As with children, providing for feathered dependents can be complicated. Life is real. Sometimes it's easy; sometimes it's hard.

But what do companion parrots do for us? They aren't simply decorations or status symbols. Surely, there's more to life with a parrot than sheer entertainment value. Why else would we choose to tolerate that extra mess, white spots on the sofa, chewed woodwork, and occasional scratched or bruised forearms?

Just as life in close proximity to people changes parrots, the presence of birds changes us. A dedicated new owner intent on providing a healthy diet for an avian companion can easily learn to eat the same fresh, nourishing foods needed for the bird. A parrot owner winds up going out less, watching fewer hours of television, and acquiring playfulness as a part of his or her daily routine. A faithful late-night fan might wind up retiring and getting up earlier as the presence of a parrot can enhance anyone's enjoyment of mornings.

The Unintended Consequences of Joy

Life is teeming with consequences, and most people take it seriously. They go to work, come home and cook, clean, watch a little television, and go to bed. Funny how having that goofy bird in the living room can inspire us to step outside convention and learn to dance and sing nonsensical made-up tunes — with or without actual words.

That parrot in the living room knows when it's time for humans to come home. Commuters often whistle those familiar, shared tunes while negotiating traffic, looking forward to time with their bird. Because we're expected to come home, we have good reason *not* to stop off at the bar or take a frivolous shopping spree. In this way, a parrot is economical, a money-saving device.

Likewise, a parrot owner bears feathered motivation to plan for the future. That may mean calling in July to book boarding or a bird sitter for

Our parrots are ministers of understanding, tolerance, strength. If we learn to accept the broken vase, shredded book cover, and chewed cabinetry, then other annoyances, even tragedies, can seem less troubling. When we find ourselves singing and dancing with the bird rather than watching television, then experience has replaced voyeurism. If we give up smoking or learn to smoke outdoors, then the air in our homes will be cleaner even if floors are not. If we give up Teflon for stainless steel, Tuna Helper for sweet potatoes, and late nights for sunrises, we'll have more assured access to long-term health and well-being.

Comfort and Beyond

A well-accommodated companion parrot is the epitome of happiness, and happiness is contagious—an especially welcome "infection" during times of tragedy. Parrots provide comfort during bereavement as their words may be those of a lost loved one or words spoken with that person. This can be especially beneficial when we've been disappointed, disillusioned, or injured by people around us.

No matter what the loss—home, love, health, or simply a job—we *know* the bird will be there every day, every night. Our constant feathered companions provide emotional structure. The parrot will have the

Christmas. It might mean a will providing long-term survivor's benefits for the parrot after your death, or it might simply mean paying the heating bill and not running out of food. Surely it means driving more carefully when the bird is in the car. Even driving more carefully when you're alone becomes important, for only you know exactly what your parrot needs.

A parrot owner is special—a person willing to love an animal with few or at least minimal expectations—a person open to subtlety and surprise. Happy life with a companion parrot probably involves someone who can enjoy relinquishing or sharing control over the environment rather than over the animal itself.

same needs tomorrow and the next day, no more no less, than it had yesterday; and *needing us* is their greatest gift. Companion parrots inspire us to get up in the morning (maybe even loudly demand it). They give us reason to be. They need us as we need them, and nothing is as crucial to happiness as being needed. Our lives are better when we feel we've made others' lives, especially parrot lives, better. Their presence is an in-your-face daily reminder of the need to do everything possible to protect both indoor and outdoor habitats. What goes around comes around.

Would I? Could I? Should I?

Depending upon the type of bird selected, life with a parrot can be an extremely long-term commitment. If you love a thunderstorm or busy children dismantling toys, if you love watching flowers blossom (and fade), you would probably love a parrot. If you think you could live with something like an occasional indoor tornado and are willing to accommodate some hot air and mess in order to share the company

of sublime feathered joy, then you would probably enjoy a parrot.

The behaviors with which a companion bird pursues its own agenda are well entrenched, but a parrot is also a very social animal with an instinctual need to fit in to the "flock." Since the number of behaviors a parrot can learn outnumber instinctual ones, a well-accommodated bird is more likely to be endearing than annoying. A new parrot owner using techniques from this book and *Guide to a Well-Behaved Parrot* might never see habitual unwanted behaviors.

Green-cheeked conure and Senegal parrot

Chapter Two

Selecting a Companion Parrot

Sure, these critters all have feathers, beaks, and wings; but every parrot should be expected to be its "own bird." Each one can be expected to share traits with like parrots, but also to have at least a few absolutely unique idiosyncrasies

Parrot personalities are not cast in stone. Just because African grey parrots can be said to talk with "association," that doesn't mean every Thom, Doc, and Joco will. Just because cockatoos can be loud and destructive, don't ever think that an Amazon or macaw wouldn't be likewise.

Species and Age

While it's good to have some idea about what a particular species might be like, rigid expectations can destroy the potential in any relationship. The only "perfect" parrot is the one with an absolutely accepting owner, a person who is excited by the little surprises, every nuance, every new sound, syllable, word, or antic. A parrot needs people who are willing to consistently support its most endearing ways and who can ignore and provide alternatives for unwanted ones.

A prospective parrot owner in the United States can choose from dozens of different types of hookbills. However, without a great deal of research or an extremely trustworthy source, there's a chance that the first bird won't be the "right" bird and that it won't last long in its first home.

Consider the possibility that somebody who's attracted to color wanders into a pet store and sees two beautiful blue, orange, and green birds with shining black beaks at a relatively low price. And maybe it seems logical to take both of them home. Two nanday conures can be *very* loud. They might not last 24 hours in the home of an unsuspecting family who didn't realize how overwhelming conure calls can be bouncing off a vaulted ceiling. An experience like this can traumatize both birds and owners.

A similar example of potential failure might go something like this: a glamorous celebrity housewife with a couple of boisterous children is smitten with a lovely baby sun conure and talks her best friend, also a glamorous celebrity, into buying a clutch mate. All goes well for about 48 hours until the young conures find their voices, and they are back in the store before the weekend.

A parrot is an especially unwise impulse purchase, a potentially expensive mistake. Surely it can be difficult to know who to believe about which kind of bird to buy. Every breeder, store employee, veterinarian, and behavior consultant seems to have a different opinion, sometimes strongly different opinions. While it's easy to understand that anyone who specializes in a particular type of bird must surely be partial to that species, a caring, responsible person doesn't sell a Moluccan cockatoo to somebody who came in looking for an African grey or vice versa.

Certain species might be produced in great numbers during a particular season, flooding the market in the area. At least a few of those birds might languish a little long before being adopted. It's only natural for dealers to have a strong desire to place babies in appropriate homes as quickly as possible after weaning. For this reason, caring breeders have a waiting list so that they can produce exactly what is needed and not have to watch beloved chicks grow up without homes.

In addition to choice of species, age may also be considered. Some

of the finest birds I have ever known have been through more than one home. A resale bird can be a tremendously good find since personality may already be well and favorably established. By 2010 any wild-caught parrot in the United States will be at least 18 years old. Even these older wild-caught parrots, which might not have been previously socialized to human touch, may be occasionally available through private or club adoption programs. These birds may require great patience, or might naturally "take to" new people, and may offer wonderful companion potential. In many cases, the only way to identify a resocialized wild-caught bird from a resocialized hand-fed one is by the split USDA steel band placed on its leg at importation.

Selecting the Source

While a notion of preferred species is nice, it's also a good idea to begin shopping with an open mind and heart. Look for a rapport with a breeder or dealer who knows the ins and outs of every feathered charge under his or her supervision. Get to know the people actually providing

The Almost-Pink Bird

Forrest, an antique dealer, loses his canary to old age. Browsing the bird store for a replacement, he happens upon a totally charming off-white bird just the beige/peach color of his fainting couch. Selecting a lovely domed brass cage 24 inches (63 cm) in diameter, he takes a newly weaned Goffin's cockatoo home to his tiny, lavishly furnished loft.

There's a major clash between antiques and beak and between human and parrot needs. A Goffin's cockatoo will scream nonstop or absolutely self-destruct if confined to such a small space. It will destroy anything it can reach and may be adept at escaping from the cage. The bird lasts only three months in its first disastrous home.

hands-on care so that you can ask candid questions about the bird.

Expect a caring breeder, dealer, or adoption resource to ask *you* lots of questions. Those who are most particular about the quality of homes their babies go to are most likely to have done a careful and thoughtful job all around, including crucial early socialization, weaning, and appropriate medical care. Some dealers require applications from potential owners and may have strict requirements to be met. These might include reading this book or *Guide*

Sun conures

to a Well-Behaved Parrot or attending classes before being allowed to take a bird home.

Anyone who lives with birds every day will have favorites. It's easy to share great stories of unbelievable feats, but shoppers need to know both positive and negative aspects of a particular bird's potential. This book was written so that would-be bird buyers could have one place to look to compare expected behavioral characteristics and specialized needs of available parrot species. With this information, a would-be owner should be able to narrow choices down to two or three types of birds. For example, a person who wants a "medium or large and extro-

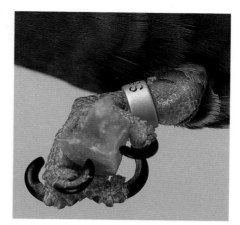

Zygodactyl toes (two opposing two)

verted bird that could be expected to talk" might consider an Amazon or macaw. Of course, a prospective owner should be informed of everything possible about both types of birds. A macaw might require more space and interaction than an Amazon and it might have a louder voice. An Amazon might be very independent and behaviorally stolid, but it might also develop an invasive voice—perhaps even louder than a macaw's—and use it more often. An older bird's personality will be more fixed and will offer fewer surprises than a younger one, so if a bird has a reputation for boisterous behavior, *believe that it is boisterous.*

Convention on Trade in Endangered Species

Since 1992, in accordance with the treaty known as CITES, all young parrots legally available in the United States have been hatched here. That means fewer types of parrots are available. In the 1980s trappers and traders could enter recently leveled or soon-to-be-leveled forests and collect rare species such as the blue-streaked lories that were suddenly available at that time. The capture and importation process was hard on the birds. Many didn't make it, arrived malnourished, or were ill. Today's captive-raised birds are more likely healthy, hearty, and weaned to an appropriate diet.

The Considerate Shopper

Baby parrots don't have fully developed immune systems. A con-

Immature yellow-headed Amazons

siderate shopper visits only one breeder or dealer daily. Bathe, change clothing, and shoes before entering each facility. Expect to be required to wash your hands before handling any birds. Be sure to ask permission before touching someone's bird. Many caring dealers allow babies to be handled only with supervision. This protects the baby (and the interests of future owners) from mishaps involving mishandling at an early age.

Avoid the temptation of an impulse purchase by leaving that checkbook at home (or at least in the car) the first time you go to look at baby birds. Give yourself an opportunity to sleep on such an important decision. Avoid facilities that seem to be pressuring you to conclude a transaction quickly.

A first-time buyer wishing to acquire a parrot locally might ask an experienced person for help. A behavior consultant might refer you to a breeder or dealer with many happy customers, many glowing faces talking about successful feathered companions. A professional with

Mail Order Bird

There is another way to buy a parrot.

If you know an absolutely dependable source in another city or state, you might meet your new bird for the first time at the airport. Zoos and performing bird shows often buy birds this way. You may be able to order one that is already talking or trained to fly to you. This is an excellent option for a novice owner. I have seen very many fine human/avian relationships formed in this way.

years of experience and knowledge of the marketplace is more likely to produce a better match than a novice buying a bird for the first time.

Evaluating a Baby

When selecting a very young parrot, look for an alert, robust chick. Although feathers may not be as neat as an adult bird's, it should be active and curious. Eyes should be shining, interested, and clear. Nostrils should be clean and dry. A little nip or bite can usually be overcome, but babies showing noticeable fear should be avoided.

If talking is important, ask the hand feeder if any chicks are already talking, for some baby parrots learn a few words before weaning. Look for a vocally experimental bird willing to make sounds, even baby sounds, in your presence.

Questions for Baby Bird Buyers

- What's special about this particular bird?
- Has this bird been healthy since hatching?
- Is this bird weaned? When is it expected to wean?
- What has this bird been eating?
- What should I expect to feed it at home?
- Does this bird fly?
- Would you suggest wing feather trimming?
- Would this bird be easy to live with as an adult?
- Do you recommend any particular books or educational resources?
- Will you be available for questions after the sale?
  and, of course,
- Does this chick talk?

Senegal parrot babies

In most species, except cockatiels, gender seems irrelevant to speech capability. Gender may affect disposition, however, with cocks being more commonly territorial and hens being more typically cautious and only occasionally territorial (with notable exceptions in several species). Anyone wishing a more outgoing bird should look for a bolder chick without regard to gender, for although most hens do seem more cautious, we see many very gregarious, outgoing hens, even some who went through a couple of shy phases. We also see territorial hens and shy cocks.

Many parrot breeders and dealers have their babies' DNA sexed before selling them. This process involves the removal of a drop of blood from a toenail, and sending it in a kit to a laboratory for analysis. Now that gender can be safely and easily determined in this way, you may have an opportunity to specify whether you want a male or female parrot.

Weaning and Fledging

Look for a dealer who is sensitive to the bird's needs during the weaning process. During this time, babies rely on each other for support, encouragement, and security. They learn from each other how to play and get around in a cage, how to chew things up, and what to fear.

If you have selected a neonate (an unweaned parrot), visit as often as possible while it is being hand-fed. This allows the chick to get to know new human companions and reduces the stress it can experience when leaving clutch mates for the first time. For reasons involving stress, as well as to ensure the adult bird's sense of security, wait at least a week or two after weaning to take the bird home.

Resist the temptation to suggest that weaning be hurried along. Each bird should be allowed to give up hand-feeding in its own time and not be held to a schedule. Withholding formula to encourage a youngster to turn to solid food might contribute to insecurity related to an obsession with hunger rather than curiosity and independence. The bird might ignore toys and clutchmates as well as solid food while remaining preoccupied with the search for familiar formula.

The young bird should also be allowed to learn to fly. This happens naturally before the chicks can eat independently, as wild parrots must be able to get to food before they can eat it. A bird that has been allowed to fledge before having wing feathers trimmed is more likely to be confident and exploratory and less likely to be shy or fearful.

Older Chicks

Begin an evaluation of a past-weaning age chick by playing eye games (see page 104) and approaching with nonthreatening posture.

Don't be afraid to consider birds over a year old. Many long-time aviculturists who bought chicks before tests were available for Psittacine Beak and Feather Disease advised purchasing chicks after they successfully completed their first molt. Just because a youngster is over a year old doesn't mean it's mature. Most midsized and larger parrots are considered juveniles until they are about two years old. A very large bird such as a macaw is still young at four.

Since a bird's inherent personality is more readily observed when it is older, a past-weaning age parrot chick might be more cautious than a very young bird. It might be reluctant to cuddle. Occasionally the bird will pick a person right away, but usually, a slightly older bird requires more patience and time to bond with unfamiliar people and places.

Bringing Baby Home

Parrots find comfort in familiar things. The fewer changes the bird has to endure when it goes to a new home, the healthier and happier it will be. If the chick has been well acclimated to its cage and toys, and is at least familiar with the new caregiver, the transition to the new home will proceed smoothly.

The Cage

Parrots derive much of their sense of security from their cage.

Resisting a Rescue Purchase

When shopping for a parrot, it's probably best to resist the impulse to "rescue" a parrot in "need." You could wind up spending lots of money on a bird ill suited to your lifestyle. It could also be dangerous for other birds in the home.

Because the "biological clock" is ticking, taking valuable "baby days" from young parrots needing homes, it's only natural that a person with a chick to sell might say whatever is necessary to place the bird. One local store owner in my area was famous for telling prospective buyers, "If nobody buys this bird today, I'm going to have to euthanize it tomorrow."

It's amazing how often that story worked on kind-hearted would-be parrot owners. While "rescuing" a bird that seems to be in danger or in a pitiful situation is surely commendable, giving in to the impulse to be a good Samaritan isn't the same as looking for a suitable new family companion. Unfortunately, buying a bird to save its life may be helping a dealer stay in business and continue the same practices. If a bird really is in trouble, the situation calls for a professional. Contact local animal control or an experienced rescue organization in your city.

Particularly with the more sensitive species, such as cockatoos, *Poicephalus*, and African greys, and a young bird whose self-confidence is

Severe macaw

still developing, this dependence on surroundings should be respected. While it's a good idea for a youngster to spend time in the cage that it will be living in later before moving to the new home, an older bird might relish and enjoy a wonderful larger, new cage.

Before bringing any parrot into the home, check to be sure that the bird's wing feathers are properly trimmed, preferably in the manner suggested in this book (see specific wing-trim charts in this book for each type of bird in Chapters 11, 12, and 13). The first day home is one of the most common times for an accident, especially for an improperly trimmed bird to fly into something and be hurt or blown away.

Whether or not the new baby is trimmed as suggested, *do not* trust that the bird can't fly until you get to know this individual better. Some birds can fly with very little wing

feather, and a newly purchased baby bird has no business outdoors unless it's in a cage or carrier.

- Try to bring the new parrot home as early as possible during the day so that it can become accustomed to its surroundings before dark.
- The bird might feel more secure with a towel over about half of the cage for the first few days.
- Provide a night light, maybe one that plugs into an electrical outlet, especially if there are pets in the home that might move around in the dark.
- Be careful to quarantine any new bird from contact with established birds in the home until the veterinarian says such interaction is not dangerous. Most veterinarians will probably recommend a quarantine period of at least 30 days.

For the first week or so, it's a good idea to keep a newly weaned baby a little warmer (about 5°F) than usual. Try to find out what temperature the bird is used to. If it's cold outside, warm up the car before taking the bird to the car. Transport a parrot in a rigid carrier and use the seatbelt for safety.

The First Trip to the Veterinarian

Most responsible breeders or dealers give a reasonable guarantee of the bird's health, perhaps a week or two or even a few months. Take the bird as soon as possible to an experienced avian veterinarian for any recommended tests. The costs of these tests are not usually included in the guarantee, but if the bird is ill, treatment should be provided by the breeder or dealer who may specify when and where the bird will be treated.

Many veterinarians want to see the bird in its own cage (if it is portable). In this way, the doctor has an opportunity to examine and evaluate droppings, cage setup, and other elements related to husbandry that may indicate or influence health and behavior.

Bands: Be sure to ask the veterinarian whether or not the bird's band fits properly or whether it should be removed. Some parrots are prone to band-related accidents, especially if the band is too large and fits loosely on the bird's leg. In most cases, an experienced avian veterinarian will probably recommend removing a poorly fitting band immediately.

Some bands are so loose that they can be slipped off. Some bands must be cut off, a process usually involving anesthesia in the case of a stainless steel band, or a jeweler's ring cutter in the case of an aluminum band. A band must never be removed with bolt cutters, as the band can quickly twist or flip sideways and break or amputate a leg. An unbanded parrot can be microchipped and registered for identification purposes at a relatively modest cost.

Tests: Expect the veterinarian to recommend laboratory tests. The costs of these tests are not usually part of the bird's health guarantee from the seller, but they could save much expense and heartache down

The Best Time for a Veterinarian Appointment

Dave Flom and Mary Karlquist, well-known aviculturists from Minnesota, go so far as to recommend the time of day to take a baby parrot to the veterinarian for the first time. They suggest making the first appointment of the day so that the youngster won't be exposed to other birds in the waiting room. It's also a good idea to wrap the bottom of the bird's cage or carrier in a plastic garbage bag if it is to be set on the floor of the veterinarian's office.

the road if the baby bird turns out to be harboring unseen illness. If the diagnostic tests determine that the bird has a health problem, a responsible dealer honoring a guarantee will provide treatment. Some dealers will expect the bird to be returned to them for treatment.

Quarantine: If there are other birds in the home, be sure to observe appropriate quarantine procedures as specified by the veterinarian. This period will probably be at least one to three months, during which time the new parrot should also be behaviorally rehabilitated. If training is not begun until after quarantine, you may have already missed the window of opportunity to easily socialize the bird.

Re-homed or "Secondhand" Parrots

Most parrots can be rehabilitated at almost any age; new bonds can be formed, new behaviors (including new words) learned, even new feathers can be grown, but the cuddliness, docility, and trainability found in baby parrots is not usually easily recovered if the bird has achieved breeding age before socialization efforts are begun. A bird that has been merely neglected is a better candidate than a bird that has been either abused or spoiled. Most parrots will probably respond favorably to being moved, and a new home is a new beginning that often brings radically improved behavior almost spontaneously.

Every effort should be made to convince the bird that it has moved to "Paradise." The perceived "drastic" changes caused by coming to a new home usually provide a window of opportunity for reinforcing good behavior during the temporary period of adjustment. This is similar to the developmental period experienced by baby hand-feds coming into the first home, but the window of good behavior may be very, very brief. For more information on adopting and rehabilitating previously owned birds, see *The Secondhand Parrot*, my Barron's book coauthored with Dianalee Deter.

Every effort should be made to help the bird feel safe. If there are no other established birds in the living area, situate the new bird in the living area, but well out of traffic areas. Manipulating cage location or height can help here. Try situating the cage at chest level first, and if the bird still seems nervous, try either raising or lowering the cage until the bird seems most at ease.

If possible, practice patterning routines (see page 103), but don't attempt step-ups from the cage until the bird readily cooperates in neutral or unfamiliar territory. If the bird is not yet socialized to handling, it is better to establish a rapport first with passive games requiring no actual physical contact (see page 104).

Since an adoption or re-homed parrot may not come with a health

guarantee, it could be a "Pandora's box," especially if it will be combined with established birds in the home. If possible, it's best to have a veterinary examination even before you commit to taking the bird.

Naturalized Parrots and Their Offspring

There are occasional opportunities to adopt parrots that have been found living wild, naturalized in the United States. Wild-hatched baby Quakers may be available in Florida and Texas, hybrid Amazons, ringnecks, or conures in California, and lovebirds in Arizona. While it might be argued that naturalized introduced parrots are happy living in their wild state and should be left alone, we must also consider that they might be unwelcome.

No matter where an introduced species originated, free-flying nonnative birds may represent a danger to themselves, to domestic agriculture, and to the local environment. The birds might be living in an area where they would be subjected to extreme or adverse weather. They might con-

Greenwing macaws

sume food and occupy nesting sites needed by native species. They might be in danger of being exterminated to protect farming operations in areas where they might proliferate. As nonnative species, there is no protection for these birds, no reason why a citizen, especially a farmer, couldn't simply kill them. Don't expect naturalized parrots found living wild to be able to reproduce. Soon, very soon, these "pest" parrots will have been provided with Avitrol, a food that renders them infertile, in an effort to control their populations.

Aviary Birds

Just as some birds prefer to live with humans, some prefer to live with other birds. This is more common among wild-caught birds, captured naturalized birds, and parent-raised domestics than in hand-fed domestics. A bird may be so bonded to its wild roles, so intent on its own personal motivations, that it is completely unable to live with humans. Every moment in the company of humans can represent life-threatening stress to such a bird. This is maladaptive only in captivity.

The bird should be provided with as "natural" an environment as possible, with an attempt being made to shield it from contact with humans. A breeding situation might be possible, although some birds of this type are past breeding age, incompatible with available mates, mate abusive, or infertile. Large flights of similar-type birds are best when providing for these birds' well-being.

Chapter Three
Diet and Behavior

For better or worse, diet provides the foundation of all animal behavior. A parrot with too little to eat will have no energy or interest in life. A bird on a highly caloric diet might be noisy and hyperactive and might wind up overweight, malnourished, and sedentary. But even a parrot provided with a well-balanced diet may not consume adequate nutrients. Care must be taken to ensure that the bird actually eats what is offered. Like children, parrots naturally select what they like best rather than eat whatever is in the bowl. When consistently given large amounts of food, many parrots will play with it and eat for recreation rather than develop more healthy ways of entertaining themselves.

I am a professional behavior consultant, not a nutritionist. Generally speaking, I would rather clean bird cages with my tongue than think about diet. I rely on modern manufactured fare to ensure appropriate nutrition for parrots. Now that balanced, dependable, pelleted diets are available, each parrot owner

spends quite a bit less time chopping and worrying about food issues for pet birds. True nutritional emergencies are not as common as they once were, but even I occasionally see the results of dietary disasters.

Although wild parrots from various locales consume different foods, their basic nutritional requirements are probably similar. However, just as

Male eclectus parrot

human dietary needs are affected by age, health, metabolism, and environment, individual parrots and species have slightly different needs. Older, more sedentary parrots should have fewer calories. Macaws need a little more fat. African greys benefit from greater access to calcium and related nutrients, and eclectus appear to prosper on fewer calories than other "typical" parrots. Scientifically formulated commercial diets are available for neonatal parrots, breeding parrots, and simply for pet birds. At least two respected food manufacturers now offer species-specific pelleted or extruded diets.

When the New Bird Won't Eat Independently

Any parrot new to the home, especially a very young bird, should be initially fed what it is accustomed to eating. In spite of care in this regard, a newly weaned youngster might quit eating independently as a result of stress related to the move. Although this is rare, be sure to watch carefully to determine whether or not the bird is eating. The addition of warm foods resembling hand-feeding formula (unsalted oatmeal, grits, rice, or pasta) can provide a familiar sense of security. Offer these warm, comfort foods daily for a while to enhance your bond with the bird as well as to ensure a smooth transition to the

The Cranky Baby

Harriet, a four-month-old Hahn's macaw, was adorable at the bird show where her new family fell in love with her. And she was quiet. As they left the show, she began making something like baby sounds, when she would throw back her head and lift up her wings. It was cute at first, but within a few days, she was doing it constantly except when she was asleep. What was this "Aaack" noise and why was she constantly making it?

Also, she would not sit up very well on her perch or on the hand, but usually rested on her breast bone. Her legs seemed fine, and she frequently climbed all over the cage and even tried to escape; but then she would hunker down whenever they had her out of the cage, and she continuously made that awful noise.

Was she hungry? She seemed to eat well, and the new family had been assured that she was fully weaned. She made the noise when they played music and danced. She made it when they talked to her. She made it when they held her; she made it when they didn't hold her. She made that awful noise constantly.

new home. Eventually, the new bird will probably refuse anything that seems like baby food.

This situation is rare, but occasionally appears in parrots nurtured

Lutino cockatiel

by humans. Some species simply take longer to wean than others, but even thoroughly weaned babies sometimes regress, especially young cockatiels, macaws, greys, and cockatoos. Many breeders mention this possibility in their instructions to new owners. The crying and begging postures may indicate that the bird has regressed to an unweaned state because it no longer sees parents, siblings, and other birds from which to copy behavior. Sometimes it's simply a matter of humans taking the lead and demonstrating what to eat.

A weaned juvenile that suddenly discontinues eating could be demonstrating either a physical or behavioral response. Our first concern is physical health. A bird can succumb to illness quickly. Sudden physical decline, which might take only hours, is called "crashing." If the baby bird has not already seen an avian veterinarian by the time the crying problem appears, it should be taken immediately to the veterinarian.

Sometimes the begging is an attention-demanding device. The bird might be eating sufficiently when humans aren't there. Evaluate this possibility by weighing the bird the first thing every morning before it has a chance to eat. An electronic scale that measures weight in grams is invaluable for this process and useful during the bird's entire life. The youngster is trying to convince humans that it will die if it is not better cared for (occasionally this can

be true). Most of the time, however, the bird's perception that it will die if it isn't fed is merely a misconception based on the bird's own limited experience with life or simply a craving for more attention.

Sometimes the bird must be given hand-feeding formula and then reweaned. Begin by providing what the neonate was eating and mix it fresh every meal. Each incident of crying or fussy begging must be averted before it starts. The bird must be distracted to exciting food or other acceptable activities before begging begins each day. Provide warm food immediately, first thing (after being weighed) every morning.

Be very careful not to offer food too hot (over 104°F [40°C]). Use a thermometer to verify temperature, and don't heat food in a microwave, as hot spots can badly injure your bird. Formula may be supplemented with warm oatmeal, warm nutritious whole grain toast, or chunky warm food such as cooked pasta or sweet potatoes every morning before the "Ack Ack" starts. Even adult parrots prefer warm food to room temperature or cold food any time of day. Many parrots enjoy a warm snack before bedtime.

As with other behavioral issues, improved daily practice of step-up routines (see page 103) can provide the bird with a sense of what is expected and build confidence rather than the emotional dependency provided if snuggling is the primary way humans interact. Continue to demonstrate independent eating by eating and offering to share food. Play with the bird with

food toys when it's hungry. Save those cuddles for the times when the bird is engaging in behaviors you wish to continue or for the evening when even adult birds may naturally snuggle up together. Retained begging can be an enduring issue, so don't be reluctant to seek help from a professional behavior consultant if a parrot other than a macaw refuses to wean by the time it's a year old.

The Maintenance Diet: Pellets vs. Seed

In the past, seed was considered an appropriate basic diet for maintaining captive parrots, and while many aviculturists still prefer seed, it has a few disadvantages for pet parrots. First, it's high in fat in the form of vegetable oil, especially in the larger seeds such as sunflower. Second, seed provides inadequate nutrition that must be carefully supplemented. Most pet parrot owners have neither the time nor the resources to provide adequate nutrition for a parrot on a seed-based diet. In addition, seed is so tasty, even if quality, fresh foods are available, a parrot might prefer seed exclusively, and such a bird can easily become obese.

I suggest a diet of one-half to two-thirds commercial pellets scientifically formulated for companion parrots. Extensive research has gone into developing diets that will

Foods to Avoid

Since parrots are smaller than many other animals, poor nutrition can affect them very quickly. Be especially careful not to allow access to too many "hollow" calories in junk foods. This surely means pizza and French fries, but corn—even fresh corn—must also be considered in this category. While most parrots love corn and can eat any and all corn offered, this can quickly destroy the nutritional balance of the diet. Corn is not a vegetable, but rather a grain. It is high in starch, sugar, and, therefore, calories and contains few nutrients.

- Avocados and chocolate are toxic and can quickly kill your bird.
- Caffeine, alcohol, and junk food (foods with high percentages of fat, sugar, or salt) can kill your bird slowly.
- Stale food, old seed, "honey sticks," moldy produce, and other foods that would be rejected by most humans are also unacceptable for birds. If you wouldn't eat it, don't feed it to your bird.

deliver balanced nutrition in *every bite*. This means that even if you are sick for a week or a month, the bird will still receive appropriate nutrition even if the diet is 100 percent pellets. This is especially comforting when the bird must be boarded or left with a pet sitter.

Evaluate nutrition in the pellet by reading the label. Look for a brand high in actual food sources, such as grains, seed, alfalfa, and kelp. Avoid brands with a long list of chemical additives and little actual food.

While a scientifically formulated commercial diet presumably contains everything needed to physically sustain a bird, you wouldn't want to eat the same food every day. I like to occasionally vary commercial diets and often mix more than one brand together.

In addition, there are emotional and behavioral advantages to supplementing with fresh foods. Vegetables are the best natural sources of vitamins and minerals. They can be served raw, thawed, or lightly cooked. Some vegetables contain many more nutrients than others. Sweet potatoes, carrots, yellow squash, collard or dandelion greens, kale and broccoli (sources of calcium), chard, and peppers (green or hot) are especially good sources of vitamins A, K, and E.

Healthy Habits

Many parrots might spend the whole day sifting through the food dish and rechewing whatever remains there. Most babies start out doing this. A weaning youngster should have many food choices available most of the time, but once the bird is weaned and maintaining its weight with solid foods, it's time to work on healthy eating habits.

Yellow-head Amazon

Eating is a flock activity. Parrots will want to eat whatever, wherever, and whenever companion humans eat. This is a golden opportunity to improve *your* diet, as many people learn to eat healthier as a means of setting a good example for their birds.

Healthy parrots do not need food available at all times. Morning and evening meals are natural and appropriate, with the biggest meal offered in the morning. Vegetables and soft foods such as cooked grains are excellent for breakfast. Pellets and small amounts of table food can be offered in the evening. Many birds finish their morning meal within a few hours. This doesn't mean that the dish must be refilled. If the bird eats everything in the bowl at each meal, then we can be sure of what nutrition was consumed. Leaving food available at all times encourages bad habits such as picky eating and not playing with toys because of playing with food instead. If soft food is left in the cage, it may be spoiled when the bird goes to eat it later.

Searching for food (foraging) can provide physical and mental stimulation during the day. Hide chunks of raw vegetables in toys designed to make a bird "harvest" its own food. If you are away from home all day and will be arriving late, a small amount of dry pellets, which won't spoil, can be left in the bowl or in toys. The bird's vocalizations when you arrive home should be expected and will remind you that it's time to share that evening meal.

Calcium and Other Supplements

A parrot's blood calcium level should be checked during yearly health exams, and an experienced avian veterinarian can advise what, if any, food supplements might be needed. Excess vitamin D-3 can hurt or sometimes kill a parrot, especially mini macaws, brotegeris, and birds with weakened liver or kidneys. Be sure not to supplement vitamins without the supervision of an experienced avian veterinarian with the exception of calcium.

Some parrots, greys, and eclectus, among others, may have low blood calcium, which can lead to seizures and other health issues. Calcium-rich foods such as kale, broccoli, Swiss chard, and almonds are best provided on a regular basis. Additional calcium may be provided with cuttlebone or mineral block in the cage, but many birds chew these up without really swallowing any. Beware of cuttlefish from polluted waters that can accumulate heavy metal toxins; look for brands with specified quality control and references. A human calcium supplement may be ground and sprinkled on fresh foods a couple of times weekly.

Changing an Established Diet

Good habits are most easily established at an early age, as parrots become increasingly resistant to change with age. If a companion parrot refuses to eat anything but seed, is unwilling to try anything new, and stages hunger strikes or temper tantrums until it gets the food it wants, a conscientious owner might find it necessary to change even a mature bird's diet.

Most parrots cannot be simply "starved" into eating something they don't consider food any more than a human could be starved into eating chopsticks. The goal is to stimulate the bird to recognize new foods. Sprouting their seed is often a good start—just barely started (24–48-hour), soaked or sprouted seed still resembles seed, but now has the amino acids and nutrients of vegetables. Cooking seed into "omelets" made up of ½ egg and ½ minced vegetables, or into corn bread that has vegetables in it, can encourage them to experiment. Seed can be gradually reduced and other ingredients increased in size and quantity. Cooked sweet potatoes or squash or vegetable baby food can be mixed with the seed and other ingredients can be added gradually.

You might try replacing the bird's regular food with a new food item for one of the two daily meals every other day. Only one out of four meals is unfamiliar, so the bird will be in no danger of starving. Wild parrots are opportunistic omnivores. They eat what is available when it is available. While some wild parrots may be the picture of health, many suffer nutritional and other environ-

Foraging toys include food

mental disorders in keeping with the ecological health of the area they inhabit. Desert birds, in particular, are literally dying of thirst as global warming intensifies their struggle. Any animal, but particularly birds, can survive on minimal food, but lack of water can be quickly fatal.

Significant changes should be attempted only if the bird is healthy. The bird's weight must be monitored daily as changes are made. It is very dangerous to assume that a bird will give in and eat if it is hungry. Extreme modifications to a mature companion parrot's diet may take a year to become fully established.

Water

Parrots sometimes like to soak their food and lots of debris can quickly foul the water bowl, so it's a good idea to have two sets of bowls so that the bird can begin each day with clean bowls. Water dishes should also be washed whenever the water is dirty. If a particular bird is really bad about quickly fouling the water bowl, provide a drinking tube for access to clean water. Continue to provide a water bowl, however, so that the bird can bathe and play in the bowl.

Water can be better in some places than in others, and a parrot's system becomes accustomed to what it regularly drinks. When traveling, be sure to pack whatever water the bird drinks on a daily basis. For this reason, and because public water can be better at some times of year than others, many caring owners provide their birds with bottled water.

Chapter Four

Parrot Priorities: The Accommodating Home

Every companion parrot needs a cage of its own. It's a castle, a safe retreat, a gymnasium, not a prison. This is where the bird can relax and feel secure. No surprises occur here. Toys and food are there. No threats or demands are made. The cage is a haven. A big part of this is that the bird is not *outside*, but rather, *inside*.

Parrots love to explore. Left unsupervised indoors, they risk being stepped on or shut in doors. They might chew an electrical cord or a toxic plant or take a dive into the toilet. A typical curious parrot can get into a surprising amount of trouble in a typical human environment. In addition to providing a sense of safety, the cage also provides for the bird's needs for exercise and entertainment.

Baby's First Cage

Sometimes a newly weaned parrot can move to its first home and go directly into a large cage appropriate to its lifetime needs. Some baby birds need a cage designed especially for the developmental phases they will go through during that first awkward year or two.

Almost any newly weaned parrot can exhibit poor adjustment to a cage. Especially, shyer species such as greys and *Poicephalus* can react badly to the wrong first cage. A good cage for a shy or clumsy baby should be relatively small with at least two sides of horizontal bars (it can later be used as a roost or travel cage). An inappropriate cage might be too large to provide a sense of security for the baby or be too hard to climb with too many vertical bars. A bird having a bad reaction to a too-large cage might thrash, fall, and engage in attention-demanding behaviors. It might revert back to wanting to be hand fed. It might begin chewing feathers or develop redundant fearful behaviors.

If a large cage has already been purchased and the bird is reacting adversely, manipulate perception by raising the grate, making the cage seem smaller. Use self-locking cable ties to secure the grate or a home-

The Gymnasium

If you don't consider the physics of the matter, it might seem that a bird would have more space and freedom on an open perch than in a cage. But think about it. A typical perch is 2 feet (61 cm) wide. Period. Two *linear feet*. Even a multiple-level perch might be only 4 to 6 *linear* feet (122–183 cm).

A 2 foot by 2 foot by 2 foot (61 × 61 × 61 cm) cage has 4 square feet (122 sq. cm) on each side, and 4 square feet (122 sq. cm) on the top. That's 20 square feet (6 sq. m) on the inside and 20 square feet (6 sq. cm) on the outside. A cage only 2 foot by 2 foot by 2 foot (61 × 61 × 61 cm) is 40 *square feet* (12 sq. m) of climbing space. That's so much more hanging-out space, hanging upside down space, climbing sideways space, holding on and flapping space. Especially if the door is seldom closed, even a very small cage provides a great deal more territory than a perch. Then, of course, there's all that space where toys can be hung, chewables attached, and, of course, perches installed.

For a parrot, a cage is "My Space." It provides multiple opportunities for exercise, entertainment, and safety. A companion parrot with no cage is denied a great deal of freedom of choice to make many decisions about where to sit, how to sit, where to climb, where to flap, ways to play.

made "false grate" to higher horizontal bars. Once the bird begins developing coordination and confidence, it can be lowered. If the grate can't be raised, some birds adjust well to lowering the perches to near the bottom, which are gradually raised as coordination and confidence improve.

Increase the feeling of security by covering the cage top with fabric extending a few inches down the sides. The bird can go up into the top for privacy in much the same way it might go up into a tree. (This cover is best placed on the cage while the baby bird is not inside.)

The Permanent Cage

Once most parrots are 18 to 24 months old, they have usually developed the confidence necessary to move to a spacious permanent cage. A parrot that is frequently out doesn't require a cage as large as one that is frequently left inside the cage for long periods. If the bird is atop the cage or in an open play area most of the day, and the cage is used primarily as a sleeping or roost cage, then there is little need for a huge cage. However, if the bird spends the entire day in the cage while humans work, or if the bird has to stay in the cage for extended periods when humans are on vacation, a larger cage is required.

The bird's emotional needs are also a factor in determining proper cage size. While some parrots do not feel secure in a cage that is too large, some seem almost claustrophobic in a too-small cage. Each particular bird's reaction to its cage is important, for a cage that might seem appropriate to one parrot might contribute to neurotic behaviors in another.

Select the largest cage feasible in the human living space with at least two sections of horizontal bars to facilitate exercise. While parrots can certainly climb up and down vertical bars if they really want to, most must have more motivation to do so. Without horizontal bars, they will climb up and slide down or wind up walking back and forth on perches for exercise. A cage with too few horizontal bars contributes to sedentary behavior and failure of curiosity.

A good cage is safe for the bird and easy for humans to maintain. The easier the cage is to clean and service, the longer most people will enjoy their relationship with the bird. Look for bird-proof door closures and those wonderful wing-like mess catchers that contain both the mess *and* the bird. Some modern cages have tear-off rolls of paper to simplify cage cleaning. Most of them are self-supporting units on wheels for easy access to cleaning, and many of them have three or more bowls for food and water. Avoid round, domed, or cylindrical cages, except in very large cages or flights for very confident species. An arched top rectangular cage is fine for most birds.

Black palm cockatoo

Cage bars should be too thick for the occupant to bend, the welds too strong to snap. There should be no sharp edges and no openings large enough to put a head through or small enough to entrap a toe. Cylindrical or round cages may have bars coming together in a "Y" at the top where legs or toes can be caught. Avoid ornamental cages, especially those with rounded corners, as parrots derive a sense of security from corners or a back to the wall.

The cage should be steel, brass, chrome, or otherwise plated with

Blue-and-gold macaws

non-flaky, durable material. Painted cages are potentially dangerous and impractical for a bird that may live decades. Modern powder-coated cages are safe and usually withstand the beaks of midsized or smaller birds. A wooden cage, no matter what type, will quickly be reduced to toothpicks. Plexiglass cages offer no climbing opportunities—the bird might as well be on a perch—and are difficult to clean and easily scratched. Hardware cloth and shiny welded wire contain zinc, which is toxic to birds. While hardware cloth is always unsafe for chewing birds, welded wire may be made safe by scrubbing with detergent and a wire brush or being left outdoors, exposed to the elements, until it is dull and zinc in the finish is neutralized.

A large door helps to prevent fearful behaviors as a response to going into and out of the cage. The bird should be able to sit comfortably on the hand without having to duck while going through the door. Both entrance and food doors should be easily opened and easily locked. Food and water dishes should be easily removed and replaced from outside. The cage should be easy to clean, with a removable tray and, preferably, a removable grate. Some birds like to roll around on the bottom of the cage. A grate will keep them from rolling in feces and old food that is a disease hazard. The bars of the grate should be as close together as bars in the rest of the cage.

While some birds can merely be removed from one cage and transferred to another, some, especially very young or very old parrots, are best induced to choose to move. This can usually be accomplished easily by placing the new cage in the position of the beloved old cage with the old cage beside it for a day or two. If the bird freely enters the new cage and seeks toys and food there, then food and water can be removed from the old cage during most of the day. By the second or third day, if the bird is eating in the new cage, all toys and perches are moved and the old cage can be set on the floor or laid on its back so that the bird will be more or less required to complete the move.

Feelings of well-being, safety, and security should be associated with the **height and location** of the cage in the home. Most parrots like to be situated where they can experience the most interaction with human flock members and still feel safe. A cage exposed on all sides will not seem secure, so avoid placing the cage in the middle of the room or against a window. A bird located beside a high-traffic doorway could experience fear reactions whenever anyone rushes quickly or unexpectedly through.

An "ideal" location would be against a wall and across the room from entrances and heavy traffic areas. Shelter may be important to some parrots' feelings of safety, and parrots just love peeking out from behind plants and toys

Many birds love to spend time on top of the cage holding on and flapping like crazy. The cage top should be comfortable for this activity. A flat-topped or slightly arched cage is best. If a cage-top perch is used, be sure that the highest point where the bird can sit comfortably is also easily gripped for strenuous flapping. The highest point on the cage should also be easily reached by humans needing cooperative responses for step-ups. Of course, access to height can be denied to birds developing associated territorial aggression. This is common in Amazons, pionus, male cockatoos, and macaws. Cage-top play can be encouraged in birds that exhibit shyness or fearfulness when they are lower.

A Perch Is More than a Place to Sit

Appropriate perches build confidence; maintain beak and nails; provide opportunities for independence; and prevent uneven wear on feet. They are a significant element in the environment, for a companion bird needs a place to sit every minute it isn't hanging, climbing, or socializing with humans.

The most common perches available in stores are made of smooth hardwood dowel, pvc, manzanita, or in some places, madrone. These

DuCorp's cockatoo

Timneh African Grey parrot

woods are hard and difficult or impossible for most birds to chew up. They have no bark or thin bark that is not easily peeled but are more easily cleaned than soft wood. These materials are suitable for durable perches for larger birds such as macaws and cockatoos, but they don't fulfill all the needs of most birds, especially smaller birds.

Cholla wood perches that are hollow cactus with many holes are also available commercially. They are porous, have no chewable bark, and are not easily cleaned; but they are relatively inexpensive and can be thrown away and replaced regularly. They are easy to grip and an excellent medium for preventing falls in baby birds, in birds with a weak grip, or in birds whose toenails are too short.

The most desirable wood occasionally available in stores is citrus. Citrus has the advantage of being a little softer, with bark that can be peeled, even by smaller birds. Some other fruit woods are occasionally available, but avoid apple and other trees bearing fruits with poisonous pits, as these can be toxic during certain times of the year if the birds ingest the wood (this is unusual).

Hardwood perches can be made more comfortable by wrapping them with cotton rope or twine. Additionally, cotton rope perches, stiffened with wire throughout, are now available in most places. Rope perches should be stiff, not flexible, as limp rope used as a perch is difficult to get onto and off of, and contributes to sedentary behavior in parrots that sit on flexible rope exclusively. The option of a vertical climbing rope with knots can accomplish the opposite behavioral result.

Special perches are now available for grooming toenails. Usually made of a coarse stonelike, concrete mate-

Branches and Chewing Behaviors

The most compelling need for branches with bark is to provide birds with an opportunity to learn appropriate chewing behaviors. Chewing is a major behavioral component in the day-to-day life of a normal cavity-breeding bird. It is a necessary part of sexual expression in a wild parrot. The amount of time spent chewing usually increases during the early lifetime of the bird, probably peaking during prime breeding years.

Baby parrots can learn to splinter a smooth hardwood dowel. Some do, but many do not learn it easily or immediately. In addition, if a parrot learns to splinter smooth wood, then any smooth wood—the table, the windowsill, the picture frame—that the bird can reach may be considered fair game. It is observably easier for young birds to first learn to peel bark from branches. Additionally, the provision of identifiably different bird-chewing wood facilitates training away from the culturally unacceptable behavior of destroying furniture and woodwork.

rial, these should not be installed as the highest perch in the cage because the bird spends so much time sleeping there and uncomfortable wear patterns could result on the bottom of the feet. In the wild, most parrots roost or sleep in trees on wooden branches. A more natural placement of these stonelike nail-grooming perches is beside the water source, which is probably the only place a wild parrot sits on rock.

Perch Size

A bird sitting on approximately the same size perches day in and day out will have uneven wear patterns on the bottom surfaces of the feet. The skin may appear red or irritated as the feet wear unevenly. Dianalee Deter taught me that a patch of irritated skin across the middle of the foot indicates that that part of the bird's feet is supporting all the bird's weight on the perch and that the perch is too small. Wear on the outer pads of the toes indicates that the perches may be too large (and, of course, birds on too-large perches might fall and injure themselves or their dispositions).

Perches should be of a variety of sizes (and textures and harnesses) so that some perches may be gripped tightly for flapping exercise and some may be perched upon with extended toenails contacting the bark so that toenails are subjected to abrasive wear. It's probably best to situate the largest perch in the highest place or where the bird customarily sleeps.

It's not uncommon for perches in a new cage to be much too large for the bird that will occupy the cage. This can easily occur when a well-meaning owner selects the largest possible cage for the new bird. As discussed previously, the largest possible cage is not always the most appropriate for a youngster, but it may be tremendously helpful in the successful adjustment of a resale bird. Large-diameter perches must be replaced if the cage is used for smaller birds.

Security

Appropriate perches can prevent the development of anxiety and fearfulness that can so easily progress to feather-destructive behavior and self-mutilation. Appropriate perches provide a grippable, irregular surface enabling the early development of a sure grip. Babies that fall less not only suffer fewer broken feathers, they are also more confident and less likely to fall or thrash about when surprised. This is extremely important, for fearfulness may be at least as significant in the development of feather destructive behavior as failure to develop appropriate chewing and preening skills.

If the baby parrot is falling frequently, the grate should be either removed or padded with towels topped with newspaper. This will help to prevent both damaged feathers and fearfulness related to getting a wing or leg stuck in the grate. I like to supply many interesting, forked, small-diameter branches so that they can be securely gripped, preventing the fall in the first place. Of course, the grate can also be moved up to prevent injury from occasional falls.

If a parrot has only side-to-side perches, it might develop the behavior of pacing from side to side or nervously shifting weight from one foot to another when it wants to approach or retreat from the front of the cage. Therefore, at least two perches, one from side to side and one from front to back, are necessary. Otherwise, you might wind up with poop on the wall behind the cage or on the floor or other things in front of the cage if the bird must cling to the front or back of the cage rather than approach on a perch.

Providing multiple branches, even though the bird may choose to sit on or chew up only a few branches, adds to the development of confidence as it also provides opportunities to make successful decisions. Whether a bird chooses to sit on the highest branch even though it may be almost vertical or the most horizontal branch even though it may be relatively low, allows the bird to develop curiosity, evaluation, and processing skills and related mental, physical, and behavioral patterns that are normal and necessary in the living room environment.

In addition, if the indoor environment remains unchanged for long periods of time, a bird can easily develop fearful responses to any form of change: new people, objects, or situations. The periodic introduction of fresh branches in interesting, stimulating configurations helps to condition the bird to accept changes without fear or aggression, for it is stress caused by a lack of change that is at the heart of many unwanted issues.

Unless a particular bird is suffering from failure of curiosity or is affected by overstimulation, most companion parrots respond favorably to the addition of branches with peelable bark. Older parrots are usually more voracious chewers, as motivation to chew wood develops as the bird matures and is especially apparent during the nest-search phase of breeding cycles.

Appropriate branches with interesting fresh bark can be instrumental in prevention of feather chewing, screaming, and attention-demanding behaviors. Most branches can be presented with or without leaves. Some birds prefer to chew the leaves off branches, and some react fearfully to leaves.

An enterprising bird will methodically eliminate all leaves, twigs, and loose bark, eventually remodeling the indoor "bird tree" to resemble those smooth perches I like to avoid. And then it is time to replace them, for while this beak-modeled shape is not inappropriate, I believe it is the "remodeling" process that helps to save our parrot companions from the mind-numbing boredom that triggers screaming, fearfulness, lethargy, feather chewing, and other unwanted issues.

Selection, Preparation, and Presentation

Provide a variety of textures of wood, preferring those that are neither too soft nor too hard. Apple, apricot, cherry, plum, and some other fruits may be usually or sometimes safe for birds, although they may contain seasonal toxins in bark, leaves, and seed kernels. Apple branches have been reported to cause allergic reactions in some birds (double yellow-headed Amazons) at certain times of year. Also poisonous are boxwood, oak, yew, wisteria, black walnut, and horse chestnut. When I am gathering branches for my own use, I prefer to avoid all fruit woods; when I am buying branches from a dependable supplier I presume their various fruit wood branches are safe.

In addition to naturally occurring toxins, one must guard against offering wood with introduced toxins: insecticides, herbicides, and lead from auto exhaust fumes. Avoid sick-looking trees that grow along freeways as they may be hydrocarbon polluted. Branches should be cleaned with bleach water with a ratio of $\frac{1}{4}$ cup bleach to 1 quart water, then thoroughly rinsed, dried, and examined for insects. (Even purchased perches should be cleaned, unless they are in sealed covers, bags, or containers.)

Branches are ideally presented in treelike positions, with forks occurring at multiple different angles in addition to horizontal. They can be attached in treelike positions to the sides of cages with wire, twine, tape, or plastic self-locking cable ties available in the electrical department at the hardware store. Toys may be hung from higher branches. If the branch is set in a Christmas tree stand, concrete, or situated on the floor, lower branches must be removed to inhibit roaming.

Medium hardness: Woods of medium hardness are best for medium and smaller birds and birds with understimulated chewing interests. Loro Parque in the Canary Islands gives their parrots fresh pine branches weekly. I like all the members of the poplar family, because they are exceptionally peelable. The bark of birch, poplar, and aspen can be removed in a variety of interesting sizes and shapes by almost any artistic and enterprising bird.

Soft woods: These are good for stimulating chewing in birds with a history of attention-demanding behaviors, failure of independence, or failure of curiosity. I prefer the weed tree, Ailanthus (*Ailanthus altissima*), which, although taller, resembles common sumac. Less substantial, but also safe, are the woods from smooth, shiny, or staghorn sumac (*Rhus copallina*, *glabra*, and *typhina*, respectively). These common dry-land weed trees differ significantly from their rarer marsh-dwelling cousin, poison sumac (*Toxicodendron verivix*), the leaves and bark of which has caustic effect on human skin. Both Ailanthus and sumac are too soft to be practical for voracious chewers but are well suited to smaller birds such as budgies, conures, Quakers, *Poicephalus*, and African greys.

Mealy Amazon

Hazards in the Home

Whether the cause is flying into a ceiling fan, toilet, or frying pan, wings and the ability to fly can contribute to fatal accidents indoors. However, even birds with trimmed wing feathers can find surprising hazards in places we might never imagine.

Water: Water is probably the most common cause of death, as a bird that can't breathe dies within seconds. Drowning can happen almost instantly in extremely unlikely ways: head down in a half-full glass on the table, floating in an unattended hot tub, sink, or aquarium.

Dark places: Because of their curious natures and instinct to explore dark places, parrots are vulnerable to being closed into closets and drawers. Behind drowning accidents, being squashed or suffocated is probably the second-most common cause of death in the companion parrot. It's not unusual for a bird to snuggle under an afghan or quilt that might be subsequently sat on with great force. Being squashed or suffocated is an especially common fate among smaller parrots that are allowed to sleep with humans.

Other pets: Another of the greatest threats to indoor birds, because they so frequently flee danger, is the danger from other pets. These birds may be large enough to handle most cats, but they are just tempting enough to be an attractive chase for a dog. A gregarious, exploratory bird in an unfamiliar environment that does not fear dogs must be protected from seeking them out, for many birds, even small ones, are known to tease or goad dogs. A dog that is repeatedly provoked can hardly be punished for fighting back even though the offensive Brotegeris or Quaker may be only a mouthful to the dog.

Play: Parrots can also fall victim to playing accidents. Many are exceptional acrobats who love to dive and spin and swing. They think they're circus performers, but they work without a net, and they occasionally miss their objective. A broken neck during active play is a rare but occasionally reported cause of death for companion parrots, especially *Poicephalus* and lories. This is

another compelling reason for the use of branches with bark rather than smooth or dowel perches.

Other playing accidents are also well reported. Parrots love to stick their heads into things: loops of string, too-large cage bars, and other unusual spaces. Sometimes, if the perch is too close to the food or water bowl, a bird might improvise a way to get its head stuck. Amazons, cockatoos, and macaws are famous for hanging themselves. Be sure that any loops are eliminated from string, fabric, or leather toys. Rigid rings should be large enough that the bird's whole body can pass through. Replace all small clips, split rings, and small quick links with large-gauge quick links at least 1½ inch long (see section on toys).

Parrots also love to play with what humans play with, so they are usually very interested in whatever is in the ashtray. Not only can a curious bird be burned by cigarettes, but also, it can be poisoned by nicotine.

Chewing: Roaming, unsupervised companion parrots are vulnerable to various types of chewing accidents. While they have no saliva and electrocution is rare, these birds can be electrocuted if they chew in just the wrong place at the wrong time. Roaming on the floor, especially, can lead to illness related to unseen microorganisms or unsanitary conditions on the floor.

Toxins: Exposure to toxins such as lead and zinc, especially by ingestion, can be fatal. Common toxins in the home include aerosols, pesticides, insecticides, medications, avocado, chocolate, alcohol, coffee, some incense, strongly scented candles, room deodorants, diffenbachia, philodendron, and some other poisonous house plants. Moldy foods are potentially toxic.

Kitchen fumes: Several types of kitchen fumes, including those generated by oven cleaning, can also be problematic. Be sure to remove a bird from the kitchen and adjoining rooms, preferably remove them from the home, when cleaning the oven. If oven cleaners are used, nonaerosol ones are the least likely to harm birds. Be sure to provide adequate ventilation, fans, and open windows, to prevent the accumulation of gaseous toxins related to oven cleaning.

Cookware: Misuse of polymer-coated and impregnated cookware such as Polytetrafluorethelyene, also known as Teflon, can kill all birds in the home virtually immediately. Fumes from other polymer-impregnated products such as pans, coffee makers, irons, and ironing board covers can also kill a parrot if the product is heated over 530°F (280°C). Even though self-cleaning ovens usually contain no polymer, a coated oven rack, skillet, or drip pan left in during cleaning can emit fumes that can kill birds in minutes.

I have often counseled in homes in which owners were well aware of the danger and owned only one piece of polymer-coated cookware. Not infrequently, however, this is the exact pan chosen by guests (who are unaware of the danger to the bird) in the home. Most of the polymer fume deaths I have documented have involved a person other than the owner and inattention related to alcohol use. The story usually goes something like this: a roommate or guest in the home comes home late after enjoying a few drinks, decides to fix tea or spaghetti, sits down, and falls asleep leaving the coated pan to burn. The pan catches fire, the birds scream, warning humans, then pass away almost immediately.

Alcohol: Inattention caused by alcohol use can lead to a variety of bird accidents in the home. If you've been drinking, leave the cookware in the cabinet and the bird in the cage. If a polymer pan is burned, and the bird is still breathing (rare), get it immediately into fresh air and rush it to the veterinarian before its respiratory system closes down. Something can be done if it's done quickly. Because accidents can happen in the best-meaning homes, just throw all polymer-coated or impregnated cookware away. It isn't worth the risk of losing a treasured bird because somebody burned a pan.

Disaster Preparations: In Case of Emergency

Many companion parrots live a very long time. That means that statistically, if one disaster occurs in a

Budgie Warning System

Callie Rennison wrote an article for *Bird Talk* a few years back describing a harrowing experience involving a variety of birds belonging to her family. On the day before Thanksgiving, in 1997, as her parents prepared to leave for work, they heard something unusual. Michael, the parakeet, who usually rang his bell only in the evenings was vigorously ringing his bell.

When her mom investigated the persistent ringing, she found the bird room in flames. Quickly removing the birds from the room, Callie's parents found that their own panic made very simple tasks difficult. Two budgies, including Michael, were lost in the fire, but the parrots and two humans survived because of the warning provided by the parakeet.

Budgies

typical geographic area every 25 years, then every parrot larger than a cockatiel will be involved in some kind of disaster during its lifetime. Whether threatened by a major natural disaster such as a hurricane, tornado, blizzard, earthquake, or a simple burned skillet, caged birds are completely dependent on humans for rescue.

Whether it's a major natural disaster or a simple household fire, the birds' behavior is often the first clue that something out of the ordinary is going on. It's not unusual for a bird

to lose its life warning humans of fire, even kitchen fires or other localized fires. This can be the best argument for bird homes to be bountifully populated with smoke detectors and easy-to-access carriers. Of course, smoke detectors are only as dependable as the power supply or batteries inside, so they must be checked regularly to ensure operation. Safety experts recommend establishing two regular days yearly to check smoke detectors. That might be Labor Day and Memorial Day or maybe Christmas and the Fourth of July.

No matter what actual process causes an avian emergency, **fumes** represent great danger to birds. Fumes resulting from even an insignificant-seeming event can kill birds while not affecting anyone or anything else. Fires, even small fires, can kill a bird whose sensitive respi-

ratory system can fail in minutes. If you suspect that any synthetic fiber or plastic has been heated sufficiently to release fumes, whether it's polytetrafluoroethylene (Teflon), plastic mini blinds, plastic bottles, carpeting, or chemicals, remove all birds from the home immediately.

Carriers should always be within easy reach for emergency evacuation. Provide one adequately sized carrier (with clean paper already inside) for each bird or other animal. If there is only one dirty carrier and half

a dozen various-sized birds and a puppy, some of the birds might wind up being released from a high-rise fire or other situation where options are limited. It's better than nothing. You can catch them later. If you can't get to the carriers, try containing the birds in pillowcases tied shut.

Don't expect to be able to evacuate a bird usually housed on the second floor in a carrier kept in the back of a closet in the basement. Carriers must be situated adjacent to the area where the bird is kept.

It's a good idea to test the equipment and proposed evacuation plan. Practicing the evacuation process enables humans to know how long they take and maximize efficiency in performing the evacuation. Drills also show the birds what's expected of them and will enable them to more easily cooperate when the chips are down.

Fire extinguishers: While fire extinguishers might help to save the structure, birds succumb so quickly to fumes the best procedure begins with evacuating the birds. Even professional firefighters will probably choose to remove all humans and animals before proceeding to fight a fire. It's helpful, of course, to have some way of advising rescue personnel about the number of animals in the home. Recognizable stickers are available to put on entrances to advise numbers and locations of animals. Additional stickers should advise where to find carriers, and in the case of high-rises, ropes should be easily accessible for lowering carriers.

Weather: In case of a blizzard, a snowstorm, or just an interruption of power during cold weather, don't become overly concerned with immediately generating heat. Most alternative heat sources such as propane or kerosene stoves generate fumes, and birds are much more sensitive to fumes than to cold. A healthy bird with a covered cage should be able to tolerate at least a day of freezing temperature, presuming it is protected from moisture and drafts that would threaten to freeze its feet. Feed occasional warm foods, if possible. If there's electricity, but no heat, as in a gas failure, you can provide a small amount of heat for a bird cage with an electric light bulb situated close to the cage.

Fumes from damaged gas lines will be a danger after tornadoes and earthquakes, but during disasters threatening buildings, seek shelter from falling walls and flying debris. Take birds in rigid carriers into the bathtub and cover your heads with a mattress (be sure to leave a way to breathe).

Hurricanes are especially dangerous since they typically occur in temperate regions where birds may be housed in outdoor aviaries. These birds must be moved indoors when a storm approaches. Especially in large facilities, lack of planned evacuation procedures could prove disastrous.

If you're actually leaving the area such as for a flood or hurricane or suspect that water supplies may be contaminated or interrupted, store a two-week supply of fresh water. Of course, it's a good idea to always keep at least a two-week extra supply of basic diet in the freezer so that if a disaster comes just as the bird's food is depleted, the bird doesn't wind up living on Cheerios for a fortnight, although, in a pinch, you know, Cheerios or other unsweetened human cereal can keep a stranded companion bird alive for a few days or even a few weeks.

Chapter Five

To Fly or Not to Fly: Grooming and Related Complications

There is no argument that a little flying at the beginning of life helps a young parrot to gain coordination and confidence, but once a companion parrot matures, is flight helpful or detrimental to safe and happy adjustment as a companion?

Indoor Flight

While wing trims are unpopular in Europe, where many people keep parrots in large outdoor flights, they have gained great acceptance in the United States. Companion parrots here are more typically involved and included in human home life. Parrots usually share human living spaces rather than outdoor aviaries. A flying indoor bird faces many dangers.

- Ceiling fans—a famous source of injury or death to flying indoor birds—are frequently in evidence.
- Kitchen and living areas often adjoin, leading to many accidents in which free-flying birds are horribly burned.
- Drowning in sinks, toilets, fountains, aquariums, and even glasses of water are among the most common causes of death among flighted indoor parrots in the United States.

In addition, one of the most compelling uses of flight involves the fight-or-flight response, an instinctual reaction in which a frightened bird reacts quickly and instinctively to avoid perceived danger. This is an involuntary reflex. An untrimmed bird cannot help but fly when startled. This is unsafe in contained areas and fraught with dangers in a typical human home.

When fear kicks in, birds fly in a panicked state, and even birds that are well acclimated in a long-time home can suffer accidents that would not have occurred if they did not fly. Allowing a companion parrot to fly indoors increases the possibility of injury or death, the opposite of what a survival mechanism is "supposed" to do.

Those who have not provided veterinary care for parrot injuries may be unfamiliar with the many sometimes grotesque injuries that can occur to flying birds indoors. Avian veterinarians, who see devastating injuries on a daily basis, are extremely vocal in pushing companion parrot caretakers not to allow flight in the home, as even older birds that are very familiar with their indoor habitat can be killed or maimed when startled into flight.

Outdoor Flight

A parrot with untrimmed wing feathers is at risk for being lost outside. This is especially problematic when flighted companion parrots share quarters with families including children. Some people can be trained to be careful about the door; others are easily distracted. Flown-away companions are in danger from wild predators, automobiles, and other free-roaming pets. A newly released animal has only a very short window of opportunity to learn to find food, water, and shelter.

In addition, simply being without a regular food and water source can be fatal to a bird unaccustomed to foraging, as it nearly was to my own scarlet macaw. By the time I was hired by a homeowners' association to capture her, she had been flying free for several weeks. She was severely dehydrated and had "forgotten" how to eat. In spite of being more than five years old (per her band date), I had to hand-feed Scarlet—no easy feat with a mature macaw—for two weeks.

Hyacinth macaw

Of course, it is illegal to introduce nonnative species into the wild in the United States. In California, a special permit is needed to legally free-fly a parrot. While Wildlife Department agents in most states take a hands-off approach to those who allow their birds to fly outdoors temporarily and then return to live indoors, intentionally not recovering a nonnative species is considered an environmental threat. It is also similar to abandoning a dog.

Quaker parrots are especially adept at adjusting to new environments, and have become established (naturalized) in quite a few

parts of the United States. Like pigeons, Quakers prefer living near people and nesting on man-made objects, so they do not appear to endanger either agriculture or native species. They do cause many problems for the power companies in Texas, Florida, New York, and other states as a result of their preference for building nests on electrical towers, stations, and other equipment. Because of their adaptability, ten states now make even possession of a Quaker parrot illegal within their borders.

Many, probably most, companion birds can be recovered from accidental introduction into the outdoors. However, fear of disease is another reason authorities dislike nonnative birds. This is a very real concern, as the dreaded virus, Psittacine Beak and Feather Disease appeared in wild populations of African parrots after the release of infected captive birds. Flown-away companions can also contract diseases from wild birds, especially through mosquitoes, which can transmit West Nile Virus.

Apparently, nonnative species are more commonly tolerated outdoors in Europe and the United Kingdom, but not without tragic consequences. For example, in England only a few years ago one particular cockatoo kept getting out so much and causing so much havoc in the town where it lived that local authorities required the owner to trim its wings. Unfortunately, further measures to contain the bird were unsuccessful. The bird was so accustomed to getting out and so focused on running around town that it was run over by a car!

Trimmed Feathers: Leaving Flight Behind

Whether wild birds retain flight as part of their repertory of behaviors depends upon how and where they live. Like any other unnecessary behavior, flight can become obsolete or extinct in a species. This is one of the lessons we learned by studying birds in New Zealand, an island ecosystem that developed no mammals until it was invaded by humans. As we can read in David Attenborough's *The Life of Birds*, when there were no predators to avoid, many of the birds simply stopped flying. The ancestors of the penguin, ostrich, emu, to name but a few species, found survival easier without flight.

I believe that a properly accommodated wing-trimmed companion bird misses flight no more than a penguin or an ostrich misses it. Some flighted birds pay a gruesome price. Flying is a trade-off, with the bird in grave danger and unable to make an informed decision on its own behalf. Presuming that a companion parrot misses flight is sort of like presuming a teenager missed something by not experiencing sex.

Some things are better missed. The teenager might have missed unwanted pregnancy, hepatitis, and HIV. The companion bird might have missed drowning in the toilet, burned-off feet, a broken neck, or a lifelong deformity from flying into a ceiling fan.

Low-stress Grooming

Even though cutting fully formed feathers is painless, and properly trimmed wings regrow easily twice a year, grooming can be traumatic to an inexperienced or previously trau-matized bird. Some veterinarians occasionally recommend anesthesia for grooming very reactive or unco-operative birds. However, with a little socialization and sensitive grooming techniques, anesthesia should be unnecessary for almost all compan-ion birds. Some forms of low-stress grooming are even possible on poorly socialized or otherwise unconditioned birds.

The following techniques are intended to be minimally invasive, both in the process of the grooming and in the effect of the grooming on the bird's future confidence and on its ability to comfortably regrow feathers. Even low-stress grooming

Trimming Wings Without Toweling

With the bird sitting on a waist-high perch, facing in the same direction as the groomer, looking down from behind the bird, using the left hand, the groomer grasps the bird's left wing by the large bone close to the body, as grasping the end bones could damage the wing.

Carefully spread the wing out and up. First examine wing feathers to ensure that none of them still contain a blood supply (if a feather in the blue-white casing of a blood feather is cut, the bird will bleed). Then, with scissors in the right hand, reaching up from below and behind the bird, and with the scissors pointing away from the bird's body, trim one-half the visible portion of the outer four to seven longest wing feathers extending past the coverts. Trim in a curving shape that roughly mimics the shape of the covering coverts.

Then, again with the left hand, grasp the right wing by the bone closest to the body, extending the wing out and up, and, reaching up from below with scissors in the right hand, trim one-half the visible portion of the outer four to seven longest wing feathers.

Be sure the scissors point up or out and away from the bird's body to avoid accidentally cutting a toe. (If both the bird's feet are comfortably gripping the perch, this can't happen.) Scissors should be nice and sharp so that they leave smooth edges on the trimmed feathers (this prevents potential feather chewing intended to "fix" jagged feather edges).

can be scary the first time, however, and conditioning to tolerate grooming is an important part of being a responsible parrot owner.

The Least Invasive Procedure

Most companion birds I groom, including regular clients and "tame" incidental grooming clients, will endure having their wing feathers trimmed without toweling. This is the least invasive way to accomplish this procedure and is especially appropriate for a parrot's first grooming. A balanced minimal trim allows wings to retain air resistance so that the bird is able to fall, jump, or dive safely. This is an indoor trim for maximum comfort for indoor birds. Birds trimmed as suggested here should be unable to lift off indoors, but not outdoors. NO wing trim should be trusted outdoors where a strong gust of wind can blow even a severely trimmed bird away.

Because it's easy for poor balance, falls, and other effects of improper grooming to contribute to behavioral problems, companion birds should be trimmed absolutely symmetrically for the bird's maximum comfort and confidence. Baby birds, especially heavy-bodied baby birds, need very little trimming to effectively ground them indoors. Trim only four to seven of the outer primary flight (longest) feathers. It's usually best to trim four feathers in younger birds, and up to seven feathers in hearty older birds. Cuts are gauged on how much feather extends out of the shorter covering feathers or coverts. For baby birds, trim about half of the part of the feathers showing beyond the coverts, but older birds and better flyers may require trimming up to two-thirds of the visible part of the primary feathers extending past the coverts (mid-length feathers covering the bases of primaries) when the wing is viewed from above or behind.

If the wing is gripped far enough out on the bone and is carefully extended up and away from the body, the bird can't reach the groomer's fingers with its beak. It might take a little practice, conditioning, and loving reinforcement to acclimate the bird to allow its wings to be extended. Be sure not to hold or extend the wing only by the feathers, as this can be painful to the bird.

This balanced minimal wing trim also works well for most mature African greys. The remaining feather length provides good support for new feather growth and adequate balance for the bird to enjoy holding onto the top of the cage for energetic flapping.

Recoverable Results

The bird's safety is the primary goal of wing feather trimming. Comfort is the secondary goal. That's why we no longer use trims developed for the poultry industry, such as uneven trimming (cutting all primaries on one wing close or under the coverts and leaving the other wing full) for companion birds. This leaves the bird uncomfortably unbalanced. Even something as simple as holding onto the top of the cage and flapping is complicated by the huge amount of lift and wind resistance provided by the one full wing as opposed to virtually no wind resistance to flapping the cut wing. This leaves the bird's tail held radically to one side, with the spine curved to that side. This can't be comfortable, and, indeed, young birds, especially, trimmed in this manner tend to fall more than symmetrically trimmed birds. Older birds who have been trimmed in this manner for a long time tend to be inactive, a condition that can contribute to all sorts of other physical and behavioral problems.

Safety is also why we don't leave those two or three outside primary feathers long, as it's not unusual for those long unprotected feathers

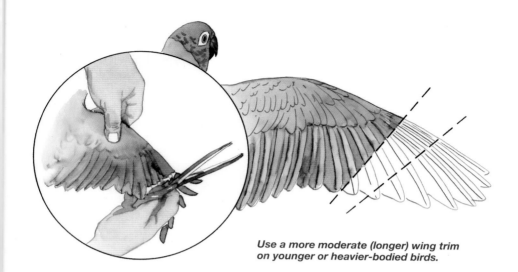

Use a more moderate (longer) wing trim on younger or heavier-bodied birds.

sticking out to get caught in cage bars or accessories. In addition, if there are only two feathers sticking out there, and one is molted, then the other mature feather is more vulnerable to being knocked out, leaving a new blood feather coming in completely unprotected. Cockatiels, especially, respond better to having half to two-thirds of the extending primary flight feathers trimmed rather than leaving the end flights long, because the exposed long feathers can be easily knocked out during their famous "night frights." Leaving the end feathers long can also contribute to special problems in phobic, extremely shy, or untame parrots.

Low-stress grooming also includes protecting the bird's ability to regrow feathers easily. While some birds seem to tolerate and recover from short trims, other birds encounter disastrous results. Wing feathers that are trimmed up to or under the coverts are especially vulnerable to being knocked out as they molt and regrow one at a time. Each individual blood feather is exposed as it grows past the coverts. Without the protection and support of (partial) feathers on each side, each primary blood feather can be repeatedly broken or knocked out when it grows past the coverts. This can be painful for the bird and can result not only in feather cysts and the inability to regrow these feathers, but also can produce a sedentary bird that prefers not to use its wings, a bird that chews feathers, or a bird with a phobic or aggressive personality. Inappropriate cage, perches, and over-groomed nails can also contribute to this condition.

Maintaining Low-stress Trims

Wing feathers should fall out (molt) in a symmetrical pattern along the feather trails (paths of circulation), regrowing two feathers at a time, in mirror image, one on each side. That's the way it's supposed to work, so that the feathers molt and regrow symmetrically and the bird retains maximum flight ability.

Of course, with a minimally invasive wing trim like this, some birds can regain flight with only one feather regrown on each wing, and, therefore, this noninvasive trim must be maintained more meticulously

Under-the-Covert Trims

The most unfortunate error I see in wing feather trims involves cutting the feathers too short. If flight feathers are cut under the coverts (feathers that protect the bases of flight feathers), emerging new feathers are vulnerable to breakage because they have little or no support from remnants of feathers trimmed earlier. Unfortunately, as I travel around the country for educational events, I often see young birds, especially African greys and cockatoos, enduring painful situations including an acquired tendency to wing feather cysts and a breast that is repeatedly split open by falls because flight feathers were trimmed up to or under the coverts.

An effective wing trim doesn't have to be short; it just has to be kept up to date.

than some more severe trims. This can be accomplished in the home during towel play or other socialization processes. That is, once the new feather regrows completely, it can be trimmed along the same line as the adjacent feathers. We must wait for the protective cuticle encasing the feather (when it contains blood supply) to flake away, revealing the completely formed new feather. If we trim the feather before

Potentially harmful trim leaves no support for blood feathers (top). The least invasive trim offers protection for regrowing blood feathers (bottom).

Toweling a Bird for Examination or Grooming

Begin as you would for the towel game (see page 105). Place the bird approximately in the center of the long side of the towel. Grasp around the neck with one hand, carefully joining the thumb and opposing finger (outside the towel) just under the jawbone. Hold the bird's feet with the other hand, being careful not to restrict the in-and-out movement of the breast (a bird has no diaphragm and cannot breathe if the chest cannot expand). Even if there's a little space in the circle formed by the fingers, a bird restrained in this way cannot bite.

Once the bird is safely held in the towel, a second person can examine the bird, groom it, or perform whatever other procedure is necessary.

it is completely regrown, we risk cutting the blood supply (then the feather would have to be pulled) or having the cut end of the feather continue growing outside the line of the trim (this can be easily remedied by trimming again once the feather has reached full length).

While most companion parrots will tolerate having the wing-feathers groomed without toweling, it may become necessary to wrap the bird in a towel for medical examination or for grooming toenails or the beak. If a companion bird has been well conditioned to playing peek-a-boo

in the towel, then necessary toweling is tremendously easy. In this way, the towel game can actually save a sensitive bird's life.

Toenails

Sharp toenails are important for clumsy young baby parrots (so they won't fall often and develop related problems), but they can interfere with handling adult parrots. Nails are usually too long (and can entrap the bird) if the ball under the end of the toe is displaced off a flat surface by the tip. Although some birds may be socialized to allow a favorite person to file the tips off the toenails with an emery board, most birds will probably have to be toweled to have toenails groomed even by a professional groomer or avian veterinarian.

Groom toenails of birds smaller than a cockatiel with tiny little human nail clippers. For birds the size of a

Quaker or larger, I prefer to grind toenails with a cordless Dremmel. The cordless tool minimizes the risk that a large bird could chomp through the power supply cord during grooming.

The heat produced by the spinning of the grinding stone can cauterize the blood supply in the toenail as the nail is being groomed, thereby minimizing the risk of bleeding. Occasionally, however, a little blood is encountered, and care must be taken to ensure that the bleeding is stopped with coagulating powder rather than a styptic pencil because it is less painful.

The Beak

Grooming the beak is the most stressful part of grooming for most birds. An active, interested parrot with sufficient wood of appropriate hardnesses seldom actually requires beak grooming.

Birds that are well acclimated to the towel game often enjoy having their beaks filed by favorite humans. The beaks of unsocialized or uncooperative birds may require professional grooming.

However, if our cavity-breeding companions have sufficient wood of diverse appropriate hardnesses to chew, their beaks seldom need grinding. A few species, red-lored Amazons, for one, have occasional tendencies to beaks that become malformed with growth. Often a beak malformation of this type involves a maxilla (upper beak) growing to one side and a mandible (lower beak) growing to the other side rather than maxilla and mandible being centered over each other. This condition would require beak reshaping, which must be done gradually and by a professional.

A professional groomer or veterinarian should know that a Dremmel should not be used on the beaks of birds smaller than the Timneh African grey, because the vibration of the tool could injure or kill the bird. The beaks of small birds such as Quakers, brotegeris, cockatiels, and budgies can usually be maintained easily with an emery board. Done sensitively, lightly filing the tip of the beak with a fine emery board can seem like mutual bird-to-bird preening (allopreening) to a well-socialized bird.

When Grooming Fails: What to Do when Your Bird Flies Away

Accidental escape is one of the most common calamities suffered by companion parrots. In the past, escaped parrots were considered potential agricultural pests because wild-caught birds could survive easily in the wild. However, an escaped hand-fed parrot's chances of long-term survival are not particularly good, especially in areas where food or water is scarce or where there is raptor activity or extended periods of very cold (below freezing) weather.

Fortunately, today's hand-fed parrots know where "their bread is buttered." In my twenty-something years of experience recapturing parrots in urban settings, I see that hand-fed parrots often find accommodating humans to take care of them, usually within the first 24 hours of escape. For this reason, I expect a hand-fed parrot recapture to be primarily a public relations project.

Advertise

If you don't know where the bird is, you must advertise to find it. This is a simple "numbers game." When more people hear that your bird is missing, it's more likely that the person who has your bird will be able to find you. Typically, the bird is returned by humans who have been caring for it as soon as they see an ad for the lost bird.

Call local newspapers, humane societies, animal control, local bird dealers, avian veterinarians, groomers, and recapture services. Be sure to report this lost "property" to the police. If the bird is found and the people holding the bird won't relinquish it, the police may intervene. You must be able to prove ownership, possibly with a recorded band number, registered DNA configuration, microchipping, with photos, or by records of unique physical or behavioral properties in the bird.

Place ads in local newspapers, on church and grocery store bulletin boards. Make a flier with a photo or reasonable likeness of the bird. Prepare an 8½ × 11-inch (21 × 27.5 cm)

white original so that it can be easily copied onto brightly colored paper. The flier should contain a contact phone number; an alternate contact number; and the street corner or local landmark nearest to where the bird flew away. The flier should mention small rewards available for information leading to the location of the bird and a more sizable reward for the bird's return. It's a good idea to minimize the value of the bird, possibly mentioning that the bird is not in good health, noisy, or of less-than-perfect disposition. Identifying characteristics may be mentioned, such as missing toe or banding on a particular leg. If the bird has a band,

Marty's Choice

He was the tax man in my life—kindly and sensitively auditing my income taxes. Years later, when he no longer worked for the Internal Revenue Service, he became my friend and client. Marty was vital, active, and wheelchair-bound. He was the long-time owner of an African grey parrot.

One summer morning, as he emerged from the shower, Marty discovered that his wife had left the back door wide open when she went to work. On that particular morning, Marty had taken Ben, the grey parrot, into the shower with him. Turning the corner to the kitchen with Ben perched on his lap, they both saw the open back door, and at that exact moment, the door behind them blew closed with a loud "Bang!"

Startled, Ben (who was scheduled for a wing trim that very day) flew out the back door. Marty, wet, dripping, and "dressed" only in a towel draped over his lap, followed out onto the patio in his rolling chair. There was Ben, perched in the fork of a young crabapple tree beside the picnic table. He was only inches out of reach, clicking and

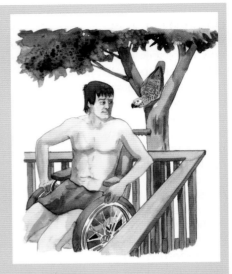

pinpointing his eyes, obviously enjoying his sunny freedom.

Marty took no time making his decision. Hoping that his neighbors weren't watching, he chose his bird over modesty. Pulling himself almost upright, Marty flipped the towel over his errant gray friend, pulled him from the fork of the tree, and wheeled, naked, back to the house with an angry gray parrot wrapped in the towel.

Ben would be on time for his wing-trimming appointment, and Marty would be avoiding his neighbors for a few days.

don't reveal the band number, so that the information can be used to differentiate between a person who really has your bird and an unscrupulous person who might be pretending to have your bird.

Most people will be honest and helpful. Talk with everyone you see, and make lots of fliers to post around the neighborhood and to hand to people. Use a different bright color each time the flier is reprinted. If the recapture process lasts a while, the signs may have to be occasionally reposted after bad weather, and a new color will help people to understand that the search is still "fresh," and they should call if they see the bird. Don't forget to take your fliers down immediately upon recovering the bird. It's only polite, and in some places you may be fined if you do not take them down.

Don't give up. Keep looking. A bird doesn't usually just disappear. Somebody has it or somebody has seen it, or they will see it eventually. A friend told me that he lost a pair of Quakers in northern Colorado on the 4th of July in the 1980s. Exactly one year later, also on July 4th, he was contacted by a neighbor who reported that he had captured the birds in his hen house. There had been no reported sightings of the birds in this rural setting for that entire year.

Luring the Bird

When you know where the bird is, a well-bonded, hand-fed parrot can usually be enticed to come willingly to the beloved owner or other friendly folk. A really good flyer might fly down, but a less confident bird or a poor flyer will climb down. It's easier to lure a parrot down with jealousy than with food. Have the bird's very favorite person stand hugging the most hated person or bird or giving the bird's very favorite food to the most hated person. If you're using a live bird as a lure, be sure to leave it protected in a cage (see "Saving Bernadette" on page 213).

Usually, if the very favorite person can reach the bird, then the bird will step up. That means, sometimes ladders and sometimes more elaborate equipment must be used. Fiberglass or wooden ladders reduce the possibility of electrocution, the most common cause of injury or death in bird recapture.

When climbing to retrieve a bird, be sure to take a pillowcase so that you won't have to climb down with an angry, resistive creature. Just put the bird into the pillowcase, tie a knot in it, and the pillowcase can be dropped to someone on the ground. Be sure to take a favorite food to entice the bird closer, and be sure to get a good grip on the bird's foot, preferably both feet, as you may have only one chance to do so. Don't worry about being bitten; a parrot can't usually do much damage. Just be brave and grit your teeth, hold on, and get that bird into the pillowcase.

When trying to persuade a bird to fly down to you, be sure to stand with the wind at your back. If you are looking up at the bird and the wind is blowing into the back of your head, it is blowing into the parrot's face. In order to fly, the bird must jump into the wind where wings are provided with lift. It is very difficult, if not impossible, for a bird to take off with the wind at its back.

A device called a "cherry picker" is probably the safest way to "climb," especially because it comes with an experienced operator. While a cherry picker (which comes attached to a large truck) carries a pretty hefty rate (usually at least $60–120 per hour), it doesn't usually take long to get a well-bonded bird if the bird's favorite person is allowed to actually go up in the bucket to the bird.

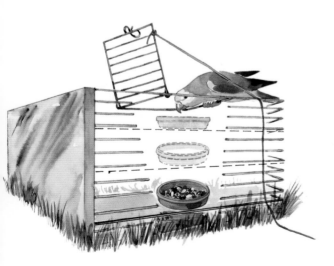

Avoid the use of water hoses in bird recapture as they are not effective either at grounding the bird (a wet bird can fly) or at "herding" the bird to lower branches (because most hoses have such a short, limited range). Those enormous "Supersoaker" water guns that can shoot up to 50 feet (15 m) are much more effective at coaxing a bird from one branch to another. While it may not be possible to coax a bird all the way to the ground in this way, a bird can sometimes be moved from tree to tree until it is in a tree that can be climbed or accessed with a cherry picker.

Outdoor Parrots

A parrot that has lived outdoors for more than a few weeks might have to be trapped. This is also typical of small, good-flying birds. Especially during late summer or early fall, there may be sufficient ripe fruits to sustain the wild bird for quite some time. If there is food readily available in the area, a parrot will probably be more difficult to recover.

Begin the process of trapping a bird by establishing a food dependency. If the bird is spending the same block of time every day in the same place, such as in a fruit tree in your yard, take the time to construct a feeding station. Do this when the bird is away from the area so that it will not become overly wary of humans and things touched

The food dish is lowered on a movable shelf until the bird must enter the cage to get the food and a human waiting out of sight pulls the door closed with a wire.

by humans. Put food on a white surface, maybe a sheet, towel, or board painted white. This helps the bird to see the food.

If the bird is spending time in a fruit tree, then it will be looking for additional "fruits" as the tree's fruit ripens and then disappears. Save some of the good fruit in the refrigerator so that as the tree's fruit wanes, the same fruit can appear on the feeding station with the "new" foods you are using to entice the bird. You may put fruits from the tree on the feeding station, but more appealing foods might be necessary. Try corn, pomegranates, grapes, and nuts (both in and out of the shell). Some birds will come to seed, as many feral exotics survive through the winter from bird feeders intended for native species.

Once the bird comes readily to the feeding station, set up a trap there, either a manufactured one (sometimes available from local humane societies or animal control) or a homemade one (made from a bird cage). A cage trap (see illustration) involves providing a moveable shelf for the food, then gradually moving the shelf down so that the bird has to enter the cage to get to the food. Then a person waiting just out of sight can pull the door closed with a long thin wire (a curious parrot-type bird being trapped will probably chew through a string before it goes into the trap). While it may take weeks to establish a food dependency, it might take only minutes to trap a bird that is already food dependent.

Whether it's your bird or somebody else's bird in your backyard, there are several ethical reasons to persist in recapturing the bird. First, most parrots will probably be sorely pressed to survive cold winters. While it is certainly possible and has been done many times before, it's difficult and represents discomfort and possible death for the bird. Additionally, while an escaped exotic bird represents a threat to native species, consuming food meant for them and taking their space, the native raptors, coyotes, and all manner of humans represent an ever-present threat to the bird. In most cases, it's probably best to recapture any solitary feral exotic bird. Just keep trying. It's easier than fishing; it's only a matter of time until you figure out how to be smarter than the bird.

It is usually considered more "humane" to allow older established ferals that have found flocks to live life wild. This seems reasonable in the case of Quaker parrots, nanday and cherry-headed conures, Senegals, and other small escaped exotics that have become established. While the low numbers of these birds mean that they, themselves, do not represent a threat to the habitat, their ability to reproduce forms a potential threat. The promise of soon-to-be-released birth control-laced food will allow these birds to live out their lives without causing irreversible damage to native ecosystems.

Chapter Six

Behavioral Development

A parrot learns more and more quickly during the period between fledging and sexual maturity than at any other period in its life. As physical coordination increases, a healthy youngster exhibits a compulsive desire to explore every aspect of the physical, social, and behavioral environment.

When a sweet, perfect, newly weaned hand-fed baby parrot moves to its first home, a predictable cycle usually follows. There is a *"Honeymoon" Period*. The bird is cautious, social, eager to fit into the new "flock." During this time the bird will seem like a little angel. However, this phase is usually followed—sometimes very quickly—by a *Developmental Period* in which the rapidly learning creature explores everything, including the limits of the social environment. If everything is in the right place at the right time, appropriate behavior is easily reinforced. After all, how could a well-meaning human start with a perfect baby bird and wind up with a biting, screaming, or feather-chewing bundle of neuroses?

Making the Most of the First Days in the Home

A juvenile parrot watches anyone and everyone, trying to copy their "successful" behavior. (Well, if they do it and they're still here and alive, it must be successful.) The bird will be improvising behaviors it can't exactly copy. Behaviors that are reinforced, even if the bird rewards itself, will become habitual. Effective socialization is, therefore, a matter of reinforcing only wanted behavior.

The first form of reinforcement a parrot encounters is comfort. The mother parrot—sometimes both parents—sit on the egg, providing warmth and protection for the developing embryo. If they don't hear a baby inside the egg, they might choose not to take care of it, and the egg won't hatch. Upon hatching, the nestling is given food in response to vocalizing and actively competing to be fed. This new reward is reinforced by the familiar feelings of comfort.

Food remains a significant reinforcer throughout a parrot's lifetime. A neonatal parrot learning to eat is taking the first step toward the development of independence or self-reward, that is, learning to do what feels good because it feels good. In an adult human, this would be like spending money, assembling a jigsaw puzzle, or playing golf.

Because they are highly social, interaction with other creatures also stimulates feelings of well-being in a parrot. Almost any kind of interplay, vocal or physical, is a reward. This can be problematic, however, as many baby birds love interaction so much that *any* attention—for better or worse—might be interpreted by the bird as a reward for the previous behavior.

While consistent rewards may be required to establish a new behavior, intermittent rewards are even more effective in establishing randomly occurring behaviors into habits. For this reason, once a bird has been rewarded even once for an unwanted random act, the one-time innovated behavior will probably be repeated.

Since any attention can easily be interpreted by the bird as a "reward" for the previous behavior, careful attention should be paid to what people do. Every effort should be made to reinforce only positive behaviors in the baby bird. Intermittent rewards for quietly playing alone are important. It is especially important not to reinforce unwanted behaviors—screaming for attention, jumping on the dinner table and

The ABCs

It's all about payoff. Anything anyone or any animal does will be repeated if it is rewarded. No matter what stimulated the *antecedent* (stimulus), once the *behavior* is performed, a favorable *consequence* (reward) will help to ensure that it will be repeated and repetition creates habits. This "ABC" formula is used in all types of animal training, but companion parrot training can be just as frequently accidental as purposeful, so care must be taken to avoid unintentional reinforcement of unwanted behaviors.

The youngster is studying just how much pressure to exert on any given object to obtain the desired result. Much interest and dedication is given to this educational process. When too much pressure is exerted on skin, care must be taken that the response is neither enjoyable nor provocative to the young bird. If the response to the bite is fun for the bird, biting may become habitual. Even if the response excites or annoys the bird, it could provoke increased or continued beak use.

The best response to baby nibbles is to divert the beak to a different object such as a hand-held toy. If nothing is available to immediately place in the bird's beak, then just put the bird down if it gets nippy. When attention is withheld as a consequence of unwanted behavior, the bird will try an alternative in order to gain that treasured social interaction.

Bonding and Territory

Toward the end of the Honeymoon Period we see the beginnings of the development of a protective attitude toward territory, both actual and human. It is important at this time to move the bird's cage occasionally, to rearrange and change toys periodically, and to require the bird to maintain balanced relationships with at least two people.

Maintaining cooperation patterning such as step-ups (see page 103)

walking through plates, or stealing food—no matter how cute they seem the first time we see them.

A healthy young parrot becomes increasingly confident, experimental, exploratory, and territorial. This is readily apparent as juvenile beaks grow both stronger and harder. Most youngsters are delighted with the process and results of using the beak, which can be troubling if the bird figures out that it's really fun to watch people scream and jump and other people laugh when beak is applied to flesh.

Most early beak–on–skin activity is experimental behavior in which the young bird tries jaw muscles in combination with the beak for effect. Remember, it's all about that payoff.

Accidental Reinforcement

The laughter of the favorite human is probably the most powerful reinforcer of companion parrot behavior. The one companion bird behavior principle that is, in my opinion, "cast in stone" is "Never, never laugh when your bird bites your spouse or partner." This would be the ultimate cruelty. Reinforcing a spontaneous natural behavior (routing a rival), quickly reinforces it into a habit, thereby abusing both your partner and your bird (by creating a habit that might wind up causing it to be banished to the back room or lose its home).

also helps the bird to overcome territorialism through the process of being carried from place to place. The bird should have at least two regular areas in which to spend time: a "roost" (cage) in which to sleep, and one or more "foraging" area(s). If the bird's wing feathers are trimmed, it will depend on humans to get from one place to another by stepping onto the hand to get from the cage to the perch or shower every day. This "transportation dependence" helps the bird to understand that successful interactions with humans are rewarded with interesting, exciting things to do.

Although the bird will often, but not always, demonstrate an obvious preference for one person over another, this should be discouraged lest it progress to territorial aggression against everyone else. A youngster that is showing aggression against a less-favored person during the Honeymoon Period might "change loyalties" during the Terrible Twos and begin attacking the previously favored person. I have seen periodically changing loyalties frequently in African greys, cockatoos, Amazons, and conures, but I believe there is probably potential for this behavior in any parrot-type bird that is allowed to attack all but the favorite person.

The bird should interact with numerous "regulars" and "strangers." A social young parrot will enjoy attending as many human gatherings as possible in a safe and structured way. If the bird expresses "dislike" of one person and it can be determined that the bird's responses are not related to the signals or body language of that person, then efforts must be made to improve the relationship with that person. Anyone

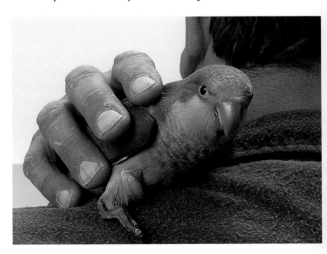

being picked can improve the relationship with the bird by providing transportation to foraging areas. The person and the bird should share showers and outings. Other household members should use the two creatures' names in tandem "Barney's Paco" and "Paco's Barney."

Problematic issues can develop if the bird is allowed to establish territory of the human shoulder. It might threaten or bite anyone who comes near. It might chew ears, earrings, or moles on the neck. It might preen or pull hair. A parrot needs to know that you are a loving guide, not a "place" to be defended.

An unweaned or under six-month-old bird that is already threatening and biting people and/or inanimate objects must be given sound behavioral backup immediately as this can be a sign of serious problems developing. Redundant fearfulness or aggression in an unweaned or newly weaned bird can be easily reinforced during this phase. These can escalate and become a routine, habitual part of the bird's personality. Don't be shy about accessing professional assistance. The sooner unwanted activities are addressed, the less likely they are to become permanent.

The Developmental Period

Just as teenagers and healthy, developing baby parrots go through phases of requiring large amounts of food—devouring everything within reach and demanding more—young children and birds go through periods of extreme "intellectual gluttony" (compulsive curiosity). Any youngster being frustrated in the quest to see all, hear all, do all, and know all can exhibit behavior that can, in turn, frustrate their elders.

While establishing limits and cooperation may have seemed unnecessary during the Honeymoon Period, these daily exercises are preparation for the months and years to come, for this phase can end abruptly and confusingly when the bird begins to realize its own agenda. Although this doesn't happen at the same age in all parrots, the appearance of self-motivated new behaviors can seem a little like the Terrible Twos or adolescence in humans.

If the bird has not already learned some behavioral and environmental limits, then the Developmental Period may be very difficult. There may be an enormous clash between the owner's wish to teach the bird to "be good" and the bird's desire to "be everything." A human baby that has been encouraged to touch and examine everything within its grasp may be frustrated when, upon learning to walk, it is suddenly punished for touching and examining everything it can reach.

The Developmental Period can be especially conspicuous in juvenile Amazons (particularly in some yellow-napes), conures, Quakers, cockatoos, and macaws (particularly in some severes and in some scar-

lets), but it can become prominent in any companion parrot's behavior. It is not unusual for me to receive a call from a tearful owner reporting that his or her nine-month-old bird has "turned on" them, biting everyone (often including the previously most-favored person). Attempts at modifying these behaviors at this time may have been met with aggressive and hostile resistance. The owner, whose "heart" and ego have suffered damage, may be considering giving away a bird that was the light of his or her life just a few months earlier.

With both parrots and children, the desire to investigate everything isn't limited to a desire to investigate every physical thing. During the Terri-

ble Twos, youngsters also study the social environment by examining their position or status in the family "flock." Healthy, intelligent parrots go through several such periods in which they "test" their social rank like an athlete challenging the next player up on the tournament ladder. If a cooperative interactive relationship has not been previously established or is not established at this time, the bird might never be confident about its place and role in the family social group (flock) and may seem to be going through painfully intense "status struggles" for the rest of its life. If cooperation has been effectively established as routine in the bird's personality, these contests are transitional and pass quickly.

Approaching Maturity

As in other creatures, reproduction is the parrot's strongest instinct. Unlike companion dogs and cats that are spayed or neutered for behavioral reasons, companion parrots are allowed the full influence of their reproductive urges. A parrot expressing the influence of this very real natural instinct might chew Grandpa's rocker to toothpicks; decide to allow no one near the end cabinet near the cappuccino machine, sing lengthy, lusty, LOUD parrot songs at sunrise, regurgitate in strangers' hair, or masturbate on the dog.

As with humans, instead of surgically altering the animal, we must learn to alter its behavior. The techniques described here are intended to enhance favorable behaviors in companion parrots and to suppress or minimize most behaviors related to breeding.

Make an effort to continue to handle the maturing companion parrot daily. Some birds will be easily kept tame; some will be difficult. Expect every bird to be a little different, with vast differences between species and between successfully socialized birds and unsocialized birds of the same species. The more consistent we are in all interactions, the more predictable the bird will be.

As the time to breed approaches, we will see heightened exploration and physical and emotional experimentation. The bird might even change emotional and/or territorial loyalties, becoming aggressive around a newly selected territory or a new favorite human (mate substitute). If a parrot has been allowed to overbond to one human in the past, at this time, the formerly favorite human might be dumped for a more easily dominated companion. We must be ever vigilant at this time to ensure that the bird is not excessively defensive of the territory around any human so that previous and predictable loyalties will not be abandoned. It might be necessary to take an arrogant young bird out of its familiar territory for at least a few days each year in order to repattern the bird and to enjoy interactions with unfamiliar humans. Vacations and indoor "outings" (visits to unfamiliar territory) are very helpful at this time. Even a simple car ride with the bird in a carrier can make a wonderful difference in a parrot's disposition. Careful transporting and meticulous wing feather trims will ensure safety on these outings.

At home the maturing parrot will become increasingly concerned with control issues, especially immediate environmental control. The bird might start attacking tissues, or people sneezing or blowing into tissues. A maturing parrot might also attack someone cleaning with quick motions with paper towels. The bird might suddenly decide it loves (or hates) a particular dog or cat or stuffed animal.

A maturing parrot allowed a great deal of liberty in the home might become hyper vigilant or aggressive around a suddenly and mysteriously selected territory. The bird will be seeking both companions and interlopers in its reflections. Expect heightened reactions to mirrors, shiny objects, and small appliances. The bird might attack the vacuum cleaner or hair dryer. At this time the bird might fixate strongly on an inanimate object, treating it either as a potential mate or an enemy to be attacked.

Environmental Support

Raising or lowering the bird's usual relative height, combined with increasing access to "rainfall," destructible chewables, and exercise will help to compensate for pent-up energy that might otherwise be expressed as aggression. A bird that suddenly becomes excessively territorial must have its territory manipulated either by moving the cage or redesigning the cage interior.

Enemies

Mature companion parrots occasionally decide that a particular chrome appliance is either a mate or a rival, leading to many courtships with toasters and wars with hair dryers. A sexually mature parrot might decide that no one is allowed in the kitchen. A bird that has fixated on a human-owned object or territory must be denied access to it. An attacking bird might be picked up using a handheld perch, a towel, or "Good Hand/ Bad Hand" (see page 121) and placed with the approved "surrogate enemy" toy. Again, we must encourage the bird to express hostility against an "approved enemy" toy. This is usually a self-rewarding behavior. Hostile energy will be expressed somehow; it is best expressed against a toy.

There must be at least one enemy to be regularly thwarted or beaten up. To a very real extent, the bird must "select" or "identify" this enemy independently. Most parrots will do this. Of course, it's very important for this enemy to not be a living creature or a treasured human possession, so

Brown-headed parrot

terned to cooperate with the use of praise, rewards, and patterning. The more successful behavioral experiences we have at this time, the more the bird is patterned and reinforced to cooperate, the more likely the bird is to cooperate when it becomes fully mature.

Chewing and Other Predictable Phases

By two to three years of age, most parrots will be exhibiting chewing behaviors. We will see a transition from a time when toys were hardly scratched, through a time when they are dismantled into parts, to a time when they are completely demolished into splinters. As these behaviors develop, it's necessary to increase the number and frequency of chewables in the restricted environments of either the cage or the play area.

As with human children, new behaviors will seem to appear out of nowhere. For months, the bird will leave the picture frame behind the cage alone. Then one day, the picture frame is splintered on two sides. For years, the bird might put nothing into the water, then one day it will begin filling the water bowl with debris. A maturing parrot might suddenly begin pulling newspaper up through the bottom grate. These behaviors are probably part of the parrot's instinctive need to attract a mate. An industrious mate is highly prized in the

several potential approved "surrogate enemies" must be provided. Safe, unbreakable toys such as the "Little Birdy Man" or loud, safe bells are excellent candidates for this parrot-selected "enemy." If a companion parrot has no opportunity to release natural aggressive energy against an approved surrogate enemy at this time, the bird is likely to begin to express that "excess" energy against whatever or whoever is closest.

If the bird is enjoying attacking a toy, leave them both alone. There will continue to be many times when the bird will solicit human attention. Those are the times when even a mature bird can be successfully pat-

wild. The bird is doing what it was programmed to do. We must provide other appropriate things to chew and reinforce the bird for chewing appropriately until it can learn to self-reward for chewing appropriately.

As parrots mature, they will become increasingly obsessed with control of their immediate environment. Different birds will react differently to these phases—some will go through nippy phases and some will go through fearful stages. Consistent handling is the key to bringing a maturing bird through any suddenly appearing episodes of unwanted behavior. To ensure that these phases are transitional, to ensure that they will pass, avoid reinforcing unwanted behaviors. That means, especially, don't laugh when the bird does something you don't want to see again. A good disposition can be detrimental here. It's hard not to laugh when the bird decides that no one is allowed to touch the chrome sculpture on the coffee table, but reinforcing repeated battles over just such turf can lead to blood letting.

Fearfulness

Some parrots, especially some cockatoos and African parrots, that are repeatedly confronted in ways that stimulate and reinforce panic, will become increasingly shy. At this point, shy, cautious, or fearful birds must be permitted to hide whenever they choose. We must carefully discontinue eye contact and do everything we can to avoid stimulating the bird's instinct to fight or flee.

If we see a trend of developing fearfulness, we must take action to improve the bird's confidence, perhaps allowing it to live higher (or lower depending, upon the bird), allowing it to choose whether to leave the cage on its own, or providing a place to hide. A little fabric tent, or just a towel over one end of the cage can provide a sense of security for a cautious companion parrot. While we might see an increase in territorial aggression, in such a case this is exactly what we want to see in this bird. We can seldom treat fearfulness without seeing at least a small increase in aggression, at least temporarily.

Nipping

A companion parrot overcoming shyness will go through at least one nippy period. These phases will appear and disappear, sometimes with great regularity throughout the bird's lifetime as breeding seasons come and go and pressure to breed asserts itself. Enhanced cooperation routines and use of hand-held perches can easily compensate for these transitional behaviors. Remember not to completely discontinue interactions during these periods, as many unwanted behaviors can be reinforced by neglect.

Maturity and Sexual Expression

A time will come when threats might be accompanied by aggression; a bite might actually break the skin. A sexually mature companion parrot is usually more difficult to handle than a strutting little adolescent whose challenges might be mere practice for the future. At this time, new programs, people, and changes might be met with strong resistance. If, however, the bird is accustomed to accepting change, its behavior might be maintained merely by manipulating the environment.

If a parrot has not been appropriately patterned to cooperate until this time, attempts to socialize or resocialize might be met with resistance from the bird. During this time it is not unusual for both predictable and unpredictable bites to occur, especially in the bird's perceived territory. Usually there will be plenty of warning: flashing eyes, looking at what it wants to bite, leaning toward the bite with beak open, spreading feet apart, extending wings, flaring tail, charging, or any other body language that you should recognize to avoid being bitten.

The best way to deal with aggression at this time is to give the bird space to be a brat. That is not to say, reinforce obnoxious behavior. Never allow the bird to chase or harass. Merely remind the bird to be a "good bird," then return it to the cage in the calmest possible way. A bird nipping during a step-up might be sensitively wobbled by the hand it is sitting on. A bird being prompted to step-up might be distracted with a toy or other inanimate object when being given the prompt

for step-up. We call this distraction technique "Good Hand/Bad Hand." The distraction object must be neither too large (which might scare the bird off the perch), too small (which might be ineffective), nor toxic (soap or a piece of lead or solder).

We might also choose to handle an otherwise well-adapted bird either with the towel or with handheld perches during nippy stages. We don't want to discontinue handling now because the bird's interactive behavior might be lost. It's more difficult to regain lost interactive behavior in some parrots than others, but it's usually easier to keep a bird tame than to retame it later. We also don't want to reinforce biting. Careful techniques can help to maintain tameness here, for if the bird has no chance to bite, biting can't be reinforced.

Parrots are very sexual creatures. Expect to see masturbation in almost all healthy, solitary male birds and in a high percentage of females. Although many companion parrots will limit "sexual" behaviors to courtship behaviors, including chewing, eating, and feeding, many birds will more overtly seek to gratify their natural instincts. A companion parrot might solicit copulation from a favorite human or engage in masturbation, a masturbation display, or anxiety behaviors that sometimes include sexual gestures.

Actually, masturbation behaviors are an occasionally dependable way to determine gender, as male and female birds tend to masturbate in

Saucey's Choice

When Lolita the blue-crowned Amazon came to live with us, it was obvious that she had been through something awful, something like a prison camp where some individuals were injured and died. She had survived, like some humans have survived such nightmarish settings, by finding the only kind of pleasure she could access, self-gratification. When Lolita arrived in my home, she was habitually masturbating several times per hour in the noisy Amazon way called "winking."

You could hear her from anyplace in the house, and within a few months, Saucey, my male bird, was doing the same. The sounds they each made during their amazing displays were not typical of any other sounds they customarily made. These characteristic Amazon sounds inspired some of my online Amazon friends to call this behavior the "cluck dance." Sometimes the birds would do the "cluck dance" at the same time. Sometimes they would do it at different times.

One afternoon, hearing much honking and clucking from the other room, my friend Vera and I peeked around the corner to see what was going on. There was Saucey, noisily flaring eyes and tail in full masturbation display. Lolita was situated directly in front of him with her tail straight up in the air in front of his face. Looking over her left shoulder,

she repeatedly said, "Step-up! Step-up! Step-up!"

Saucey, alas, was more interested in his own silly dance than in mating with Lolita. We saw this same interaction about twice after that and never saw it again. Like any other unreinforced behavior, it simply disappeared.

Each different bird's masturbation process is usually accompanied by that species' characteristic sexual sounds. An astute owner can tell what's going on by hearing that particular sound, which is made only at that time. My own hen cockatiel Pearl, who neither talks nor whistles at other times, whistles a typical male cockatiel song as she backs into the corner of her cage.

It's probably not a good idea to encourage these behaviors as they can be accompanied by aggression or feather picking. In addition, a companion bird that habitually engages in masturbation behaviors may later choose those self-gratification behaviors over mating, even if a mate is offered. Just ignore masturbation; don't reinforce it. If the behaviors don't get attention, they're less likely to appear frequently. However, since self-gratification is the very definition of self-rewarding behavior, it may continue regardless of whether it is reinforced by humans or not.

Exaggerated chewing, allofeeding, or regurgitation are also commonly seen sexual behaviors. If the bird is regurgitating on humans, just put it down. This is neither to be rewarded nor discouraged, with this exception: If the bird has a problem with excessive vocalization. Reinforcement or provision for occasional sexual-related behaviors such as chewing and beating up toys can replace some unnecessary vocalizing if other distraction techniques and frequent drenching showers prove ineffective.

positions approximating mating postures. In most species, the male bird stands on the female bird's back; she elevates her tail and everts her cloaca. The male bird lowers his tail and after rubbing his cloaca against hers deposits semen onto her everted cloaca. The semen is then retrieved when the hen's cloaca pulls back into her body. A male bird, therefore, often masturbates with tail down on perch or toy or human hand. A female bird does so with tail straight up in the air behind her by backing into something like the corner of the cage or a favorite person's ear.

Chapter Seven
The Talking Parrot

We all talk to our pets. We talk to companion parrots even more than to any other type of pet. They reward our vocal interactions by responding with our own words in our own voices. Even more, parrots communicate *their* own feelings with *our* own words.

The undeniable ability to learn and use human language is their most-treasured gift. This adaptation of wild communication skills directly from the jungle to the living room is unique to all animals. Even if they don't use words, their natural vocalizations have recognizable meaning. Our birds literally sing for their suppers.

Fascination with talking is usually the catalyst bringing that first bird into a human home. Even people who cannot tolerate other pets sometimes are drawn to parrots.

Talking Species

While most types of domestic hand-fed parrots can learn a few words, my intent here is to guide new bird owners to individuals that can be expected to learn many words and to use at least some of them appropriately. Getting the right bird is more than half the battle, for most baby domestic parrots of the species mentioned below will learn to talk with very little extra effort on the part of humans. That is, a healthy, well-socialized young parrot of a species with a reputation for

*"Nothing that does not speak will come into this house,' he said.
...he never imagined that this hasty generalization was to cost him his life."*

And so it was that Dr. Juvenal Urbino's distaste for animals opened his home to a parrot and no other pet in Gabriel Garcia Marquez' *Love in the Time of Cholera*. This foreshadows the tale of love of a talking bird that literally brings death to the prominent (fictional) physician.

Parrot stories throughout Garcia Marquez' Nobel Prize-winning work are a testament to the popularity and prominence of talking birds in Iberian culture.

Two yellow-nape Amazons

vocal ability will usually learn speech if people merely talk to it, interact with it, and talk to each other in the bird's presence.

In three decades of observing parrot behavior, I find that budgies, Quakers, African greys, certain Amazons (yellow-heads, napes, blue-fronts, and blue-crowned farinosas), and macaws demonstrate the most dependable, easily accessible language ability. I hear incredible stories about talking ringnecks, Jardines, and lories. I've seen some exceptionally good-talking macaws, especially blue-and-golds and militaries. I have also seen incredible talking ability in individual ringnecks, lories, conures, eclectus, cockatoos, and male cockatiels; but I consider the first group listed to be most likely to consistently produce individuals with large vocabularies used with association.

While Dr. Irene Pepperberg has observed that budgies probably use words in a manner consistent with song; many Quakers, grey parrots, Amazons, and macaws will probably use at least some words with association to their meaning. That is, these words will be spoken at appropriate times in appropriate ways.

Gender plays an occasional role in talking ability. I sometimes get the notion that hen African grey parrots, especially hen Timneh grey parrots, talk more than males of their kind. Both genders of grey parrots talk well, however, often acquiring large, constantly growing vocabularies. They're smart, but there's a downside to the grey parrot: They're so smart that they sometimes encounter developmental difficulties during the first year. In the case of the African grey parrot, it might be a good idea to purchase a well-socialized bird that is over one year old or has already completed its first molt.

Except for budgies, cockatiels, grass parakeets, and cockatoos, I believe both male and female birds have approximately equal ability to acquire speech. Although I occasionally encounter talking hen budgies and, sometimes even talking hen cockatoos, I don't expect hen cockatiels or grass parakeets to talk at all. In most species with good reputations as talkers, a more demonstrative, experimental, exuberant bird of either gender is more likely to be motivated to communicate than a shy, withdrawn bird.

The Talking Youngster

Younger birds are more likely to learn human speech than older ones, but "young" is a matter of definition. Some birds, especially smarter species like the African grey parrot don't acquire words until past a year of age. According to a *Bird Talk* survey a few years back, readers reported that the average time it took for an African grey parrot to say its first word is about 14 months in the home. That means, of course, that probably about half the birds took longer than 14 months to acquire their first word. Additionally, birds are not dogs. You can teach an old bird new tricks, and older birds, even teenagers and beyond, moving into a new home with people excited about their presence, are often so stimulated by the new environment that they begin acquiring words.

Much of the research into local availability of good-talking species can be done at home. Check newspapers, Yellow Pages, and favorite bird magazines for breeders or dealers in your area. Call ahead to inquire about chicks the age and type you desire. Some aviaries require an appointment to see birds.

Look for an interactive youngster exhibiting interest and attention by leaning forward, puffing out its head and neck feathers, stretching its wings (singly with a leg out or both shoulders stretched straight up), bobbing its head up and down solicitously, or quickly wagging its tail from side to side. These easily observable behaviors are indications that the bird is excited about what's going on. Look for a bird that responds to your voice, especially if it is so young that feathers aren't completely opened. If the bird is old enough and has light enough eyes, look for one that frequently demonstrates excitement by narrowing the

pupil. This is called "pinpointing" or "flashing." I believe it is an important indicator that this particular bird is motivated to talk. Although you may select an unweaned bird and speech training can begin before the bird is weaned, be sure to wait until after fledging and weaning to take it home.

Language Education

In the past, it was believed that repetition was the best way to teach parrots to "talk." Many birds throughout the ages have acquired human words this way, but I believe that birds trained in this way are more likely to merely mimic the sounds of the words rather than use them appropriately. Modern parrot fanciers are more excited about the prospect of talking rather than mimicking parrots, and so our ways have changed.

A baby parrot needs a tremendously stimulating environment. For the first two years, the juvenile environment should look a little like a nursery school, with lots of toys and interesting things the bird can use to learn to entertain itself. Repetition is important, but speak to the baby parrot just as you would speak to a human infant, expecting it to learn the words it hears most. Use words in context, just as you would use them with a human baby. The bird doesn't have to be held during speech training, for much of the

Competition/Rivalry

The work of Dr. Irene Pepperberg, a Harvard-educated cognitive ethologist (one who studies the evolution of thought), astounded the world and the aviculture community by opening our eyes to possibilities that were often previously ignored or disbelieved. Noting that there were scientific studies underway to demonstrate talking abilities in apes and dolphins, Dr. Pepperberg began her research in 1976 with a presumed-to-be-average, resale African grey parrot purchased from a pet store.

Amazingly, Dr. Pepperberg's research dealt specifically with avian speech capacity. It also evaluated techniques for training. Among other things, she learned that attempts to teach grey parrots with audio and video tapes were useless. The birds learned only the sounds of human staff coming in to start the tapes, and not what was on the tapes themselves.

Dr. Pepperberg's most famous bird, Alex, learned to identify and describe objects, even demonstrating the ability to use some nouns as adjectives, hence "rock corn" for dry hard corn kernels and "cork nut" for almonds. Alex developed his abilities to use words with appropriate meaning through use of the model/rival method wherein one bird interacts with two humans demonstrating the behaviors (words and identification) that are being trained. One "trainer" questions the other human about colors, shapes, and objects. This person is the model for the parrot's behavior and the parrot's rival for the attention of the trainer. The model answers the question, receives a reward, then roles of model, rival, and trainer are reversed.

This technique probably resembles the way young parrots learn to communicate with the flock by listening to older birds "duet" or talk back and forth. Although it is best to include humans or other talking birds in this process, if the parrot is young and not too distracted or if it is properly conditioned, the "rival" might even be one of those stuffed, talking parrot plush toys.

baby parrot's first communication efforts will probably be used to induce you to pick it up. Holding the bird might actually interfere with the process in some instances.

Try talking a little "baby (parrot) talk"; your first step to success might be in baby parrot language. If you can make a sound the bird is known to make, and the bird repeats the sound, the bird can then be rewarded with praise and affection, and you will have established the pattern by which the bird will acquire

words. Use soothing, cooing sounds if the bird is a little shy. Avoid hissing or "shhh" sounds as these are made by the bird's natural enemies, and they might make the baby nervous.

Use lots of single-syllable words at first like "*what*," "*hi*," "*ciao*," "*bye*," and "*night, night*." Use the words in context, just as you would use them with a human infant. While the youngster will not usually be immediately able to repeat a word, early signs of progress include the bird sitting around "muttering" or "babbling" in incoherent sounds, as it picks up the cadence of human language first, with understandable words and phrases following after much practice.

Easily acquired phrases include "*What 'cha doin?*'" and anything with "*itty*" sounds such as "*pretty bird*" and "*here, kitty, kitty, kitty*." Once you start combining words into phrases, mix them up, like "*pretty kitty*" and "*What's kitty doin?*"

Many baby parrots, especially Amazons, learn to talk in high-pitched "feminine" voices. It is not unusual for African greys to acquire deeper "male" voices. The voice the bird mimics can tell us which human the bird is most bonded to, for I believe the greys, especially, tend to mimic the voice of the perceived human rival for the affections of their favorite person.

Singing loudly, almost directly into the bird's head, is an excellent way to get its undivided attention. Many birds will stop dead still and sit there with flashing eyes as long as

Unintended Associations

Whether it's accidentally expressed expletives or unexcused burps, our parrots report our own actions to us just as children do. I was not surprised when Kenya Sue, my Jardine's parrot, learned to mimic the smoke detector whenever she saw me cooking. It took me a while, however, to figure out why Scarlet, my macaw, sometimes would say, out of nowhere, "Ouch!" One day, I looked down and realized that it happened whenever I picked up a hammer. She had, apparently, noticed how frequently and consistently my hammer use resulted in a smashed finger and my resulting cry of pain.

you will sing to them, perhaps joining in or practicing later what they have heard.

Modeling whistling is probably not a good idea for most good-talking types of parrots. Since birds have no vocal cords, the mechanism by which they "speak" more accurately resembles whistling. Therefore, whistling is probably easier to accomplish than "speech," and the bird might choose to whistle *only* rather than use words. Whistling might be a good transition for teaching a type of bird not known for talking ability. Cockatiels and conures, for example, that might not acquire more than a few words, can often become accomplished whistlers. Try

"Colonel Bogie March" or the theme from "Mayberry."

Be sure to include the baby in daily activities: eating, sleeping, showering, and expressing affection to other humans and animals. These activities replicate the feeling of being part of the flock and should stimulate the baby parrot's natural instinct to communicate with other members of the "flock." If there is no problem with aggression, it might be helpful to allow the baby parrot to sit higher than anybody else during speech training.

A baby of a good-talking type of bird will learn the "most exciting" words it hears—words spoken with the most gusto and enthusiasm. Therefore, profanity and angry words might be learned with only one repetition if the bird is really "tuned in" to humans in the household.

The Older Talking Parrot

Sometimes, even though the species is known to talk and the owners have done everything possible to encourage the bird to talk, it doesn't. Every bird is an individual, and not every individual wants to communicate with language.

The only way to be absolutely guaranteed a talking parrot is to acquire a bird that is already talking. Sometimes this means looking for a young bird; sometimes it means acquiring a parrot that is already mature. Because teaching human speech to a parrot is an inexact science and because it is inherently time-consuming, many trick bird shows prefer to acquire older birds that are already talking.

When moving an older bird into the home, be sure to see the veterinarian and observe appropriate quarantine protocol. Try to make the bird feel as though it has just moved to a much more exciting place. Keep a few familiar toys, but don't be afraid to make improvements in housing and activities. A wonderful new environment often inspires new words and happy new behaviors.

Foul Language and Other Nuisance Sounds

An old Mexican teacher I used to spend time with loved to say:

"Live so that you could sell the family parrot."

This means, of course, to be careful what you say in front of the bird, because it will repeat in its next home what it heard in this one.

Of course, caring, modern parrot owners know better than to intentionally teach their birds profanity. Sometimes, however, in spite of the best intentions and carefully edited adult language, even the best-meaning parrot owners wind up with a bird that screams profanities at battered toys, whistles shrill electronic signals at ear-splitting decibels, or turns belching into avian opera.

While the screaming parrot may present a problem for neighbors, frequent or untimely nuisance sounds or profanity can adversely affect the quality of a bird's life by annoying humans in its own home. A foul-mouthed bird may be increasingly

Gift from the Past

When my own baby Jardine's parrot, Kenya Sue, started exuberantly screaming "*F. U.*" (and I don't mean Felix Unger), at her favorite toy, I was shocked and certain that my mouth was not the source of such words. Calling the store where Kenya Sue was raised, I asked the owner if my baby bird could have heard those words there.

"Well," Dianalee reluctantly admitted, "she wouldn't hear that here from a human, but I took in a couple of macaws that say it. They get really 'wound up' in the evenings, using lots of profanity after the store closes."

I can only imagine what reminded Kenya to repeat these words, but thankfully, they disappeared almost as suddenly as they appeared. This "occasional" behavior was not reinforced and, therefore, did not become an established part of the bird's habitual vocabulary.

---

isolated and left to gradually lose interest in interactions with humans. Especially, foul-mouthed birds are often banned from exciting, mind-expanding outings as well as social interactions with honored guests.

Prevention

Probably the most common nuisance word or phrase for a companion parrot to acquire is an occasional obscenity, "hot damn" or "darn" or more colorful expressions that most of us would not repeat in front of parents, children, or favorite teachers. A parrot doesn't exactly spontaneously "invent" words (although it can happen); the bird is usually copying some sound it relates to and repeating it at related times. It's amazing how many humans seem truly unaware that they are, obviously, saying the words their birds repeat.

But something else has to happen in order for the new words to become a part of the bird's behavior. There are three components to the establishment of habitual behavior: modeling (being shown what to do), enactment (doing the behavior), and reinforcement (being rewarded for enacting the behavior). Even if a bird has learned to speak a human word, the word will not be repeated frequently if the bird is not rewarded, usually with attention, for saying it.

The easiest way to get a bird to discontinue saying something is by getting it to say or do something else. This usually involves an initial inventory or evaluation of the problem followed by diverting the bird to different words or behavior before the unwanted words or sounds are made. This may or may not be necessary in dealing with a new word that has appeared only recently, for often, simply ignoring a newly appeared behavior will eliminate it.

Remodeling

Something I call "remodeling" is another valuable device that can be easily used to vanquish new nui-

part of the bird's routine behavior. A bird that has been habitually repeating a nuisance phrase or sound for a few months or a few years will be a more difficult challenge than a bird that has only recently started repeating a noxious expletive. Actually, the bird will never forget how to say a word that has become an established part of its vocabulary. Just as you can remember how to say a word that you may not have spoken in many years, and just as you can remember how to play Monopoly and ride a bicycle (although you haven't done those things for quite some time), a parrot will remember things it said years ago. However, if there is sufficient reason not to say or do those old things from the past, humans and birds alike simply will not do them. How does this happen?

Behaviors that no longer serve a purpose become obsolete and are replaced by behaviors that have a purpose in the current environment. Superfluous old behaviors are replaced by useful new ones. But changing any habitual behavior isn't usually easy, and the first of the unwanted behaviors to be eliminated is always the most difficult (for example, for a habitual beer drinker, the next, first beer is the hardest one *not* to drink).

In helping a bird to discontinue an established, habitual use of profanity, we begin by evaluating when the profanity appears. Is it during play or during the regular practice of the bird's vocabulary? Does it occur at a particular time of day or when

sance words. If the bird is saying, for example, "*damn it!,*" we can often "divert" the pronunciation of the newly acquired word to something like "*can it!*" This can be done either as a spontaneous response to the word or as a planned distraction used before use of the offensive word.

"Remodeling" can be combined with use of the model/rival method studied by Dr. Pepperberg. This process involves setting up a competitive situation in which a human or other bird "rival" is rewarded for saying a more desirable word or pronunciation. If the bird says "damn it!" and is not rewarded, and the rival bird or human assistant says "can it" and is rewarded, then the bird, seeking to be rewarded, will learn to say "can it."

I believe that if a behavior has been repeated and reinforced for about 21 days, there is a good chance that it has become habitual. That is, it has become an established

events in the home stimulate it as a response? If we know when a sound is usually made, we are well on our way to replacing that sound with a different one.

Human Body Sounds

Although most parrots will probably manage to avoid the accidental acquisition of profanity in the vocabulary, many of them will acquire other nuisance sounds. African greys are especially fond of burps and belches and other gastronomic body expressions. Quakers and caiques apparently love to mimic human coughing and sneezing.

Guiding a companion bird away from crude body rumbles and eruptions is usually more difficult than guiding it away from profanity, as few spoken words resemble these sounds. The bird must be distracted to sounds that are both more acceptable to humans and that are just as fun for the bird to make. Laughter is such a self-rewarding activity. It's usually easy to distract an interested, well-motivated bird to laughter before the farts begin. Be sure not to laugh after they begin.

Whistles and Beeps

Both greys and their cousins, *Poicephalus*, as well as caiques, pionus, Amazons, and lories seem especially attracted to ear-piercing parrot versions of electronic devices: the alarm clock, telephone, microwave, or smoke detector. These sounds may resemble some of the more-or-less "natural" alarm calls these birds use in the wild. Shrill whistles and ersatz electronic beeps have the potential to be the most annoying of all nuisance sounds. They might be delivered at greater volume than annoying words and can be used more insistently as attention-demanding behavior as well as true expressions of alarm.

While the actual volume of these sounds might not carry even from one room to another, they can be outrageously painful to the sensitive human hearing mechanism (a bird's eardrum can handle it). An agitated or excited bird might parrot the smoke alarm at outrageous volume for enough time to cause humans in the room to want to rip their own eardrums out. And while time-outs or briefly covering the cage are ineffective at changing this behavior, if the bird is very "wound up," briefly covering the bird or removing it to the roost cage for a nap might calm it enough to be subsequently

Meyer's parrot

distracted to different behavior. Showers may also be helpful. A bird recovering from being wet is not usually motivated to attract attention with vocalizations.

Other Bird and Animal Sounds

Some of the most annoying, and often treatment-resistant sounds acquired by parrots are the sounds made by other birds or animals. A few years ago, I worked with a Mulluccan cockatoo that had somehow managed to acquire a lion's roar (at *cockatoo volume*!!), and some of the most nervous grey parrot owners I have ever seen live with grey parrots that learned the monotonous call of the hen cockatiel (with grey parrot precision of tone and volume). While it's sometimes amusing to hear a lovebird's version of umbrella cockatoo screams, the Amazon version of "hen cockatiel" or the African grey version of "crow" can be exceptionally annoying.

Acquired animal sounds, like human body sounds and electronic sounds, are usually more difficult to modify than human words. They are, however, also sometimes more predictably enacted at a particular time of day. A companion grey parrot might do "hen cockatiel" at sunrise or a Jardine's parrot might do "blue-crowned Amazon" when it's time to eat. To divert from these behaviors, the daily routine must be changed in some substantial way so that enactment of the behavior is avoided. The grey parrot that does hen cockatiel

at sunrise might have to have a more lightproof cover so that it doesn't know when the sun rises. Then breakfast routine can be changed in some way to create an entirely different interactive ritual, maybe by removing the bird to a perch to eat breakfast rather than providing the morning meal in the cage.

Addiction and Diverse Experiences

As in humans, a bird that finds joy in only a few things is likely to become obsessed with (or addicted to) those few things. This is just one more example of how lack of stimulation creates unwanted behavior in companion birds. That famous old source of almost all bird behavior problems, boredom, also contributes to habitually redundant behaviors including the repeating of nuisance words and sounds. Here we can expand the bird's experiences so that it learns new ways to enjoy life. If the bird is encouraged to do many different, diverse behaviors, then statistically, the relative amount of time allocated to repeating nuisance sounds will naturally become smaller. The offensive words and sounds will gradually disappear.

Stimulating the Reluctant Talker

Gina and Mark B. Dazzle dreamed of their own talking parrot. With books and magazines in hand, they carefully researched their choice to add a baby Congo African grey to their small family. Parrot fancy held great allure for the young couple.

Things being what they are, once it became known that Mark and Gina had a parrot, more parrots, almost immediately, seemed to come their way. They were given a pair of cockatiels that began blissfully laying eggs. They adopted Maizie, a Goffin's cockatoo, that would let no one near and turned her into a snuggle bunny virtually over night. They inherited Zipper, a wild-caught Quaker, when a neighbor moved to a state where Quakers are forbidden.

Two years down the road, they shared their home with five birds, none of whom spoke more than one or two human words. Although they had tried audio tapes, video tapes, food, and toy rewards, their dream of a good-talking parrot had eluded them. They were very discouraged and also were depressed because their house was a mess. They were considering "getting rid of" all their birds. I was asked to help them decide what to do.

Evaluation and Planning

First we considered the reasons why a companion parrot vocalizes: to have its physical needs (food, housing, environment) and emotional needs (society, independence, confidence, reproductive urges) met. If any of these elements is missing, inadequate, or otherwise ill-suited to a particular bird's temperament, the bird may lack motivation to vocalize.

Moluccan cockatoo

A parrot is a social creature. Parrots in a group communicate by using the same language. If a bird identifies with other birds, it is most likely to acquire the other birds' vocabulary; and it will be less likely to acquire human speech. A bird that identifies and relates to people is more likely to want to communicate with them. A bird that is already using human words can stimulate a new bird to use human speech as a means of competing to attract attention. So the timing of the addition of subsequent birds is very important: *When* a second bird is added can determine whether or not the group (flock) acquires human speech.

Mark and Gina added their second through fifth birds, all non-talkers, before Johnny, the baby African grey, started talking. Maizie, the cockatoo, was extremely needy, so they handled her more than the baby grey. Apparently seeking to attract the attention given the cockatoo, Johnny picked up something resembling Goffin's cockatoo sounds, but not human speech.

Mark and Gina began playing more games like "Peek-a-bird" around the corner, games that involved calling out to a hidden friend. They tried to entice Johnny to vocalize by mimicking the sounds he sometimes made. They were careful to handle the grey parrot at least as much as they handled any other bird in the house.

The adopted cockatoo had come with a larger and taller cage than the grey's. The grey parrot's status as only bird was thwarted, and the baby parrot had to reevaluate its social posiiton. Under many circumstances, birds in lower situations make no noise at all, possibly because of concerns about safety. Gina and Mark agreed to purchase a cage like the cockatoo's for Johnny, situating his perches so that he was, if he wished to be, always looking down on the other birds.

Of course, raising a bird's height can contribute to increased aggression. In cases like this, that is exactly what we are hoping to accomplish. When a good-talking type of bird doesn't talk, we must examine other aspects of behavioral development. Did the bird exhibit the development of "normal" nippiness during the post-weaning stage? If the bird never expressed nippiness, it may not have achieved true emotional independence. In that case, the bird might not feel safe enough to vocalize. The development of a little aggression in a previously shy bird can signal the coming of confidence that can precede vocalization. When Johnny began nipping a little, apparently, to get his way, we knew that his behavioral development was again following an expected path, and that vocalizations would follow. Meticulous step-up practice easily managed the temporary nippiness.

Grooming and Exercise

Most baby red-tailed grey parrots spend a great deal of time holding onto something and flapping.

Johnny wasn't doing that. Again, he just didn't seem to feel safe. Since failure to vocalize can be statistically linked to shyness, anything to increase confidence can help to overcome the problem. We considered the possibility that Johnny needed more wing and sharper claws to improve confidence.

Mark and Gina decided to let Johnny's wings grow out so that he could enjoy more physical activity. Gina began including Johnny in her morning showers. We knew that increased bathing and flapping would stimulate Johnny's metabolism and hoped it would improve his motivation to vocalize.

Perches

I noticed that Johnny didn't grip the hand he was sitting on and also observed that his only two perches were too large for his feet to grip. The Dazzles' removed his nail-grooming perch and replaced his large iron-hard perch with smaller, softer poplar branches. Johnny was encouraged to hold on and flap. The new branches had smooth, peelable bark that gave him true control over the shape and feel of his perches. Johnny first peeled the bark off the branch where he slept, then he went to work on other sites requiring "remodeling." Within a very few days, Johnny's grip had improved and he was more active in the cage. Johnny was also spending more time on top of the cage, where he enjoyed many exciting moments in fantasy flight.

Goffin cockatoo

Lighting

The Dazzles and all their birds lived in fashionable, indirect lighting. It was obvious that they all needed more light. Gina and Mark added full-spectrum fluorescent light fixtures beside each bird cage and to their own dining room. All the birds were immediately, noticeably, more active and vocal.

Diet

A bird on a boring or otherwise inadequate diet may not be motivated to talk. Mark and Gina were meticulous and organized and fed their birds exactly the same thing at the same time every day. We decided to play a little "peek-a-bird" along with feeding and tried to stimulate interest by offering different foods in different ways.

Mark learned that he could generate differing reactions by feeding the birds in a different sequence. Gina found that she could stimulate vocalizations by putting one piece of yummy fresh food in the cages, then waiting a little while to serve the rest of the meal. Of course, these techniques can generate screaming, but Gina and Mark combined this "wait-a-minute" feeding schedule with increased modeling (calling or talking softly to the birds and back and forth to each other) when out of sight.

Rituals, Modeling, and Delivery

A parrot must be excited by or attracted to the sound of a word or phrase, attracted to its meaning, or attracted to the emotions occurring with the sounds. For example, it is probably unusual for an Amazon or Quaker to sit in a room where it can hear the sounds of people laughing and not pick up something resembling laughter. They also love ritual; in particular, many Amazons love to deliver a painful bite, scream with pain, then laugh. Some of them wait for the humans to fill in the painful scream, then they laugh. They are attracted to the drama associated with the sounds and the predictable sequence of the sounds.

Interest in speech can be stimulated by manipulating the timing, presentation, and delivery of words.

While an "average" parrot might never learn one word from a tape recording, it might pick up something from a tense television drama, especially something repeated often. An Amazon might be unwilling to mimic a male voice, but it might go nuts for a female or falsetto voice. A grey parrot might not like a high-pitched voice; it might even attack or run from a falsetto voice. Such a bird might pick up the first words a male human utters upon returning home.

Many parrots respond very favorably to the use of questions and answers or series that involve a response such as the Amazon biting sequence described above. I suggested that Gina and Mark begin a program involving ritual response. Each time they returned home, they would walk from cage to cage, starting and finishing with Johnny's cage and say,

"Pretty bird" (pause)
"Who's a pretty bird?" (pause)
"Oh, Maizie's a pretty bird" (pause)
"And Zipper's a pretty bird." (pause)
"And who else is a pretty
    bird?" (pause)
"Is Johnny a pretty bird?" (pause)
"Johnny IS a pretty bird!"

The Dazzles were using the exciting moment of homecoming, coupled with the exciting sounds of "pretty bird," combined with the enjoyable element of ritual, and a little rivalry to stimulate the motivation to talk. They also added "thank-you" rituals at mealtime and "night, night" rituals at bedtime.

Self-rewarding Behavior

It is especially helpful if the words modeled are fun to say so that the bird learns them merely for the joy of saying them. Words that fall into this category include all the "itty" sounds, but the very most exciting thing for most companion parrots to learn to say is probably "*pretty bird.*"

Most companion parrots know and love what "pretty bird" means: owner attention, love, and admiration. A bird that understands the meaning of these words will not only use them to get attention, but also will use them as a self-rewarding behavior. A parrot loves to be told that it's a "pretty bird," and since a

healthy, happy parrot also loves hearing the sound of its own voice, most companion birds love to say "pretty bird." A healthy, happy companion parrot will incorporate these words into the courtship display. That means that the bird will *look* its prettiest when it is strutting around saying "pretty bird!"

Mark and Gina noticed that all the birds loved the new "pretty bird" ritual greeting. Especially, they could see more happiness behaviors: increased preening, puffing out, tail wags, soliciting, and foot lifting during the rituals. Within a very few days, they were hearing increased muttering in the mornings before the cage covers were removed.

Occasionally Obstructed View

Birds that cannot always see people are more likely to acquire human speech. If they are covered too often or isolated too severely, this can stimulate screaming and attention-demanding calls. On the other hand, if the bird never spends time in the cage or out of sight of humans, it may never develop necessary independence, and other, also serious, problems can result.

Manipulating this element can be considered an artificial stimulation of barrier frustration, for it has long been observed that caged birds appear to talk more than birds housed on open perches. This is also a possible consequence of the feeling of safety that a cage provides. Manipulate barrier frustration very sensitively and in concert with other behavioral and environmental manipulations, for simply erecting barriers, can lead to numerous complications.

Mark and Gina decided to cover their birds at night so that they could manipulate the visual barrier in connection with enticing feeding practices. Each morning they slipped a little grated low-fat cheese into each cage, then spent 15 or 20 minutes calling to the birds, asking if they were ready for the rest of their breakfast. Soon the birds were peeking out from under the covers and vocalizing for attention.

Health and Urges

Vocalization is an important indicator of a bird's interest in breeding and a bird's interest in breeding can be an indication of the bird's good health. Any program to stimulate talking in a nontalking individual of a good-talking species should include a veterinary evaluation. There are many, many major and minor physical conditions that can sap a parrot's motivation to attract a companion, and therefore, to vocalize. A very minor health problem can easily affect motivation. Even a human can tell you that a sinus infection can be very uncomfortable; can a sinus infection be any less uncomfortable for a bird? The Dazzles had already eliminated health issues as a concern in this case.

Signs of Well-being

When monitoring a failure-to-talk program, we know we are making progress when we see an increase in the number of expressions of happiness: preening, puff-outs, and tail wags. To stimulate these behaviors, always provide an interesting and diverse assortment of destructible and indestructible toys. Allow the bird to occasionally spend time in a very high place. Include a parrot on safe outings both inside and outside the home. (Parrots love to ride in the car and in elevators.) Include music and singing more often, especially in the car and in the elevator. Exciting music can work wonders in stimulating motivation to vocalize. Many companion parrots love Rossini's "Thieving Magpie" and The Artist's "When Doves Cry."

Gina and Mark, devoted videophiles, were amazed at their birds' response to music. They were surprised at how often Johnny and Zipper were wagging their tails. They could easily see that our program was working long before the birds actually learned new human words.

Attitude, Depression, and Family Planning

The number of birds in the home can easily affect the amount of attention each bird gets, the attitude of humans, and, therefore, the quality of life, connection with humans, and the motivation to use human words. Humans can easily become depressed by the demands of maintaining the birds' environment. Improved equipment and accessories can make quite a difference in the amount of time and energy necessary to keep a parrot environment tidy, adding to the time available to provide for the birds' happiness.

The Dazzles repainted with waterproof paint, added mess catchers to all cages, and (disposable) Astroturf under each cage. After much soul searching, they decided that flock size was an important part of "family planning," and that they were not cut out to be breeders. They learned to say "No" when they were offered "free" birds. They donated their cockatiel pair to a local bird club's Aviculture for Youth program and focused on the education of their grey parrot, Goffin's cockatoo, and Quaker.

Expectations and Appreciation

Even a parrot that develops no human speech can wind up being the household favorite. Once an appreciation of their ways is developed after years of living with parrots, sometimes the bird that doesn't talk is easier to live with than ones that do. Some of the most beloved companion parrots use *no human words* — zero, zip, nada. Regardless of its reputation, talking is only one of many, many reasons humans enjoy the companionship of birds.

It's not unusual for a bird to start talking after humans have discontinued their expectation of talking behavior. Maybe we all perform better when there's no pressure to perform. Sometimes lowered expectations bring surprising results. Gina and Mark reassessed their expectations and decided they loved their birds whether they ever said one human word or not. Within six months, Johnny had added a dozen words and phrases, including "*Step-up*" and "*Johnny's a pretty bird*" in Mark's voice and gave kisses and called the dog in Gina's voice. Zipper, the Quaker, had learned to say "*thank you*" for treats; and the Goffin's cockatoo, Maizie, would often say "*night-night*" repeatedly, emotionally, at sundown and in the car on the way to the veterinarian.

Chapter Eight

Socialization and the Supportive Environment

The goal in socializing a baby parrot is to produce an adult bird that is neither fearful nor aggressive, noisy nor quiet. An enjoyable parrot is eager for attention when the time is right, but can readily entertain itself when human companions have other things to do. For this reason, self-reward or self-motivated (play) behaviors and related independence are the first and foremost things a young parrot must learn.

I occasionally encounter advice to "take time off to hold the new baby bird a great deal during its first few weeks in the new home." While this is appropriate for an older, wild-caught, or imported parrot, it can be detrimental to a hand-fed domestic youngster. Of course, a good relationship begins with love, and cuddling may be first on both your and the young parrot's mind. However, too much cuddling during the first few days or weeks in the home can be counterproductive, monopolizing time in which the bird should learn self-reward or independent play. Cuddling can become something like an addiction if the bird prefers it above all else.

Early interactions form patterns that become habits seeming like expectations in a parrot. If an already tame bird is cuddled 8–10 hours today and 8–10 hours tomorrow and 8–10 hours the day after, etc., then the parrot's cuddle buddy suddenly has to go back to work, the bird may feel abandoned. Several potentially harmful behaviors can result.

The Development of Independence

A parrot in the wild is never at a loss for what to do. Activities essential to continued existence, including social interactions, allow for little spare time. Apparently frivolity—play—is crucial to juveniles in many, if not most, species including humans.

The wild predecessors of today's puppies developed social roles and the ability to communicate dominance, submission, and everything in between as a means of surviving in cohesive groups called packs. Kittens can be easily observed watching, stalking, evaluating, pouncing, and marking in ways that enabled wild ancestors to bag dinner and defend important territory. Obviously, some of these "skills" are unnecessary and, indeed, unwanted in our homes, especially in adult companion animals.

Patagonian conure

Play

Play may be even more necessary for young parrots than to puppies or kittens. Unlike animals that survive by reproducing quickly and in great numbers, parrots undergo a long, intensive learning process between fledging and sexual maturity. Wild juveniles stay in groups and with their parents, playfully, often amusingly, trying to copy the behavior of others. Youngsters learn to groom, climb, fly, open things, chew, communicate, and make lifesaving decisions about what to eat and when to fight or flee. Without a sound and thorough "education" a wild parrot will not survive. Much of this learning process involves play—hiding, chasing, trying to groom or steal from clutch mates as they also practice animated responses, vocalizations, and displays.

The need for play extends well after maturity in companion parrots and bears components that would be unnecessary in nature. While their wild counterparts actively pursue the business of surviving in a hostile environment, the greatest stress in the living room may actually be *lack* of stress. A companion parrot must learn or develop appropriate activities in order to function in a stress-free environment. Such a bird doesn't need to decide which foods to eat and which to avoid (although many do actively select and reject certain items); there is no need to avoid predators at the water bowl.

So what's a parrot to do? What happens in those long hours when humans are away from home fighting for survival in their own "jungles?" Unless a companion parrot learns independent play, time alone may be used for problematic, coun-

terproductive, or outright destructive activities.

"An idle mind is the devil's workshop." Consider what happened when electronic games became increasingly available to teenagers. By the late 1990s personal computers began making their way into many, if not most, socioeconomic strata in the United States. Involved parents complained that their youngsters played video games rather than studying, volunteering, or exercising. Surely one can find no fault in this, but some unexpected consequences appeared. In Brooklyn, Queens, and other New York City boroughs, law enforcement statistics documented declines in juvenile crime. Anecdotal evidence suggested that teenagers were breaking fewer windshields, snatching fewer purses, and stealing fewer cars because they were busy playing video games!

Adult play—recreation—functions in human culture by replacing competition, interpersonal drama, and violence—even self-directed violence. Likewise, play behaviors in companion parrots can replace socially and physically inappropriate actions. A bird banging a bell is not screaming for attention. A bird untying knots in leather strips is not making holes in the curtains. A parrot demolishing a wooden block or perch is not damaging furniture. All of this parrot "recreation" has a somewhat "unnatural" component—it's autonomous, solitary—unusual for these very socially motivated animals. If a companion parrot doesn't learn to play alone, it won't go out breaking car windows, but it may find something equally obnoxious to do. If a young bird is accustomed to face-to-face interactions with humans and doesn't learn side-by-side and independent play, it will almost certainly become increasingly vocal in its demands for attention. A frustrated parrot can be *loud*.

A parrot can become habituated to face-to-face interaction just as easily as a teenager can become addicted to "Grand Theft Auto" (a video game). As a single habit becomes increasingly entrenched, the urge for it is so great that it's difficult to do anything else. This is behavioral addiction. Just as teenagers are advised to pursue many activities to avoid the formation of obsessive patterns, newly weaned parrots must be guided to exploration and diverse adventures. That doesn't mean expensive toys, but it does mean lots and lots of opportunities do make *appropriate* decisions.

Freedom of Choice

Humans are as confined—by jobs, home, family, and other responsibilities—as companion parrots or any animal surviving in a limited niche. A freshwater fish can't suddenly decide to move to the ocean. Few wild animals can deviate from the time-tested paths of their parents. Likewise, very few people can simply walk away and continue to live as they have lived before. The process of choosing between alternatives is the closest thing most of us have to freedom. When we go to buy a garment or car, we want to see many before making a decision. When we go on vacation or take a holiday, we want to go where *we* want to go.

The process of selection provides a similar sense of well-being for a companion bird. A well-accommodated parrot has appropriate options regarding how and where it spends its time and numerous toys with which to play. Even if it chooses not to access a small second perch joined to its main play area by a rope or if it decides not to play with a particular toy, the presence of the second toy or play area has provided an opportunity for "successful" decision making. This builds confidence and stimulates exploration and experimentation (risk taking.)

A busy, well-adjusted companion bird might choose to talk into an empty cup (sound out a hollow), chew up a perch (carve or display nesting skill), aggressively bang a toy against the cage (vanquish a rival,) or throw out only the green pellets (avoid "toxic" food). It might decide to chew through wads of paper looking for treats (forage).

Without access to appropriate activities, the bird might wind up regurgitating on cage bars or masturbating on the water bowl. The more opportunities it has for *appropriate* activities, the less time it has to consider and improvise *inappropriate* ones.

A Sense of Passing Time

A bird inhabiting a controlled environment never sees the shadows grow long, then short, then long, or hears the frogs start croaking exactly 30 minutes before sundown. An indoor bird never knows the heat of the noonday sun followed by cooling afternoon rain showers. During my in-home evaluations, I am often entertained with stories of birds that stare at the clock for 10 or 20 minutes before Mom/Dad gets home from work or start screaming half a minute before the approaching car is in sight. I believe a bird with an opportunity to easily perceive passing time is not as likely to damage feathers or to demand attention because it has experience with understanding that there is a time for all things—time to play, eat, and shower with the flock, and time to play, eat, sleep, and bathe alone. A juvenile parrot has to learn this. Environmental elements can demonstrate the passage of time: a chiming or cookoo clock, a full-spectrum light that comes on and goes off every day at the same time, or a television on a timer that comes on at the same time with the same program a few hours before Mom/Dad gets home from work. My own birds love the clock that features a different song bird every hour. They can easily gauge how much of the day is left by which bird sings.

"Rainfall"

A sedentary bird stores up energy and might wind up with a powerful urge to release that energy by first attracting, then biting human companions. This bird might first be distracted from the biting behavior and helped to release unused energy with exercise provided by frequent drenching showers. Both enjoying the bath and recovering from being

Cinnamon pearl cockatoo

wet can lessen aggression, roaming, screaming, or other inappropriate activities.

This is a preventive activity differing from squirting as punishment as it is administered carefully in a manner resembling rainfall and provided *before* unwanted behaviors rather than after (which might be perceived as a reward). The water source, usually a spray bottle, is held lower than the bird's head and far enough away that the bird is not focused on the tool. A fine mist is sprayed over the bird's head so that it falls down like rainfall rather than being directed at any part of the bird's anatomy.

Good Ideas Rather than Bad Suggestions

Negative terms or reprimands such as "bad bird" can be confusing and counterproductive, especially when prompting a bird to step-up. If a trainer is saying both *"Step-up"* and *"No"* or *"Bad bird"* at the same time, the bird either freezes or reacts negatively.

Saying what *not to do* is easy. It seems to come naturally. It feels so much more spontaneous to say *"No, don't bite,"* but saying the word *"bite"* can stimulate, suggest, or reinforce the behavior.

Saying *what to do* is harder. Positive suggestions are actually counterintuitive, but they are much more effective. Naming something introduces it into thought, and does, for better or worse, stimulate the desire for it. A "No Smoking" sign can initiate a craving to smoke; a "No Run-

Sweet Talk

A tall, shy man brought his baby cockatiel to my office for "taming." The bird was a parent-raised pearl hen of exceptionally charming demeanor. The owner was unsuccessfully trying to teach her to enjoy interactions with his hands. She would not step-up or allow petting. Seeking to scratch the little bird's neck, the tall man would quietly, stiffly reach out to touch her; and she would hiss and nibble threateningly at his fingertips.

I said, "Talk to her the way you talk to your wife. Tell her that she's pretty and you love her and want her to be happy."

The man looked up with surprise on his face. Then he turned back to the bird and began whispering sweet, affectionate words. The little cockatiel just seemed to melt in his hands, learning not only to step-up, but also to be petted in somewhat less than half an hour.

A few weeks later, they returned for a "grooming lesson." The little bird was sweet, tame, and affectionate. The man looked even taller than before. When I commented on the changes—the well-reinforced step-up-response, etc.—the happy cockatiel owner grinned and said, "If you think that's something, you should see the change in my wife!"

ning" sign reminds a happy child that it's fun to run. Modern behavior managers now advocate using words describing preferred rather than unwanted behavior. Lifeguards are advised to say, "*Slow down* or get in the pool!" rather than "No running on the sidewalk."

Parrots seem to naturally appreciate and understand the words "good bird" and "pretty bird," especially when delivered with a cooing intonation. The bird may pinpoint or display in response to this type of verbal caress. These expressions of affection can function as rewards that can be used any time the bird is engaging in appropriate activities or any time it is not engaging in inappropriate ones. Later, these words can be used to remind the bird to engage in behaviors associated with those words. A normal, creative parrot thus becomes willing to seek new, innovative ways to be rewarded with those kind words. The bird also gradually abandons activities that do not bring at least occasional reinforcement.

Kind words supplied in response to or anticipation of good behavior (cooperation) are among the strongest tools available in the shaping of behavior in any creature. Although this technique sounds subtle, the results can be spectacular, and it doesn't require the use of hands, whistles, props, or food. This is absolutely the easiest way to train a bird. It is often successfully employed even though humans may be unaware of what they are doing. A "verbal praise" style of training

Be Careful!

The words, "*Be Careful*" can be useful to distract from unwanted intended behavior. Here's how it works: Whenever you see that the bird is going to fall or about to drop something, or some other unwanted occurrence is about to take place, say "*Be Careful.*" The words "*Be Careful*" naturally become a termination stimulus. When the words are followed by a fall or dropping something, the bird eventually learns to stop, evaluate the situation, then continue or change tasks. Later, when you see that a bird is about to fly, bite, or do anything you don't want, the words, "*Be Careful*" can inspire the bird to take a different path. The words "*Be Careful*" work effectively in tandem with any command such as "*Step-up,*" because they plant the appropriate behavioral course in the bird's mind.

might be more commonly used naturally or as a matter of conditioning by females and may contribute to the large number of companion parrots that favor females.

While spouses, lovers, and baby hen cockatiels obviously respond well to sweet talk, even the wickedest, wildest parrot (or human) can respond to conscientious use of kind words—if it likes the person offering the rewards. Be careful not to overdo verbal praise, for too much adoration can come to seem like a courtship song to a sex-starved companion parrot. If strutting, pinpointing, tail-fanning sexual displays are frequently reinforced, we might wind up with a beautiful little "fire-breathing dragon" that bites, regurgitates, and masturbates on your head, shoulder, or foot.

Food Rewards

Food rewards can be used by multiple trainers, whether or not the bird likes the trainer. However, food is more important to some birds than to others. Some birds will do anything for food rewards and respond to them like they read a book on the subject. Cockatoos have a frequent tendency to this play-rather-than-eat behavior. Many cockatoos would rather have face-to-face interaction such as being held or talked to than side-by-side interaction such as eating together. Many birds don't appear to be motivated by food at all. Some stubborn individuals might have to be half-starved before they will take food from the human hand and eat it. While a few of these birds are demonstrating alienation, the overwhelming majority, especially cockatoos and many domestic hand-feds are simply so crazy about people that they would rather play or cuddle than eat when humans are present.

Also, food rewards might not be in the bird's best interest. Several popular types of parrots have a tendency to become overweight and develop related health problems if food, especially high-fat human junk food, is given often. Food rewards must be carefully monitored to ensure that they contribute to good physical, as well as emotional, well-being.

Step-Ups

While any successful, peaceful interaction can be used to establish a cooperative rapport, step-ups are quite easily accessed and serve the dual purpose of picking up the bird. These routines need be no more than one or two minutes' duration and may initially have to take place outside the bird's established territory in the home. A laundry room or hallway is usually perfect, as the bird will probably never spend much time in these types of areas, and therefore should not develop territorial behavior in them. The pattern works

Bronze-wing pionus

No-Touch Play

Some companion birds enjoy touching and being touched, but some simply prefer to interact passively, with eye games and body language, and with no physical contact. Especially in the case of shy birds, it's a real advantage to know how to connect emotionally without actual touching the bird. However, don't take it personally or decide that a bird doesn't like people just because it doesn't like being touched. Some people are the same way, and we simply learn to interact with them differently.

1) *I'm too scared to look at you.* Any eye contact may be threatening to a shy bird, so don't maintain eye contact; look away if you catch the bird looking at you. Close your eyes, turn them away, or otherwise break eye contact until the bird is comfortable looking at you and letting you look back.

2) *I'm like you.* Some birds react fearfully to two eyes the same size. This might appear to the bird to be the gaze of a predator, an animal with both eyes in the front of its face. Look at a cautious or unfamiliar bird in the nonthreatening manner, with only one eye at a time in the manner of a prey animal, a creature with its eyes on the sides of its head.

3) *I'm too scared to move.* Try to be absolutely motionless when you first see the bird. Many birds freeze when they see a stranger. If you freeze when you see the bird, you are saying, "I'm not sure about you. Are you going to eat me?"

4) *I'm shorter than you.* Try crouching over so that your entire head is lower than the bird's body. Many parrots find this absolutely baffling and will climb down to see what on earth you are doing.

5) *Blink.* A frightened animal will not close its eyes while maintaining eye contact with a potential predator. Demonstrate that you are neither fearful nor dangerous by blinking while maintaining eye contact from a distance. An interested, interactive parrot will close its eyes or blink back to show that it is not afraid. When the bird blinks back, you can move closer.

6) *Peek-a-boo.* Peek cautiously around any available corner, reading materials, towels, or clothing. Try combining this with the blinking game and I'm-shorter-than-you.

7) *I can do what you do.* Copy the bird's body language. When you see the bird stretch a greeting by extending one or both wings, demonstrate that you feel the same way by extending arms.

8) *I can say what you say.* Mimic simple sounds from across the room or around a corner including tapping or knocking when you hear the bird tap or knock. If your bird plays with a bell and rings the bell, try ringing a bell in response. Try to entice the bird to respond to your response.

9) *Keep away.* If the bird is cautious and has never taken food or toys from you before, offer something, then pretend to share with another person or bird. Wait a minute or two, then offer it again and take it away before the bird can reach it. By the time you play this game the third time, the bird will probably take whatever you offer.

10) *Fetch.* Offer a toy, drop it before the bird can reach it, then give it to the bird and see if it copies your behavior. Many birds will immediately drop or throw the toy. You retrieve the toy and give it to the bird. Look for the bird to initiate this game. It might look at you then drop the toy or spoon or grape, then look at the item on the floor, then look back at you, then back at the floor, etc. Many birds will play this as long as they can find anyone willing to play.

best when it includes stepping the bird from
- a hand to and from an unfamiliar perch
- hand to hand
- a hand-held perch to and from an unfamiliar perch
- a hand-held perch to a hand-held perch, and
- a familiar perch to and from both hands and to and from hand-held perches.

Although step-up practice might work with a cooperative young parrot in familiar territory, unless it is cooperative enough and well patterned enough to step-up from an unfamiliar perch in unfamiliar territory, it may refuse to step-up from the cage or other familiar perch.

There is no substitute for affection or warm, genuine human enthusiasm as a reward for the bird's success in stepping-up. This is crucial to good patterning. Especially with shy or cautious birds, the most important part of this exercise is the *bird's* enjoyment of the process. If the bird is not eagerly, or at least willingly, cooperating with step-ups and step-up practice, something is going wrong. Seek professional help immediately rather than risk reinforcing unsuccessful behavior.

Step-up practice is the most significant tool for maintaining cooperative behavior throughout the companion bird's lifetime. Any parrot will exhibit mood changes. They can be little feathered dragons, and sometimes they must be allowed to breathe a little "fire." Daily step-up practiced combined with occasional towel games can quickly return peaceful, cooperative behavior in well-socialized birds.

The Towel Game

This might also be called "peeking out" patterning. It's an easy way to access a sense of safety for both birds and humans (towel-covered hands are more difficult to bite). The towel game really isn't like restraining a bird in a towel for physical examination; it's more like playing peek-a-boo under the covers, only you use a towel instead of a blanket (the bigger the towel the better, so that, at first one or more humans can get under there, too). Just try to make the bird feel happy and secure and let it peek out (cavity breeders spend a lot of time in small spaces peeking out) and sometimes hide the bird's head or eyes and then expose them and say, "peek-a-bird."

Many parrots naturally enjoy towel cuddling even before they learn to step-up. If they have missed this, however, they must be initiated carefully to this delightful experience. Begin by playing the towel game with another human or pet. Sit low, across the room from the bird and hide your face with the towel, then lower the towel, peek around it, and blink, giggle, or say "peek-a-bird."

If this interaction is fun for everybody, including the bird, in a very short time it will be useful for gaining the bird's attention. Soon, you'll be able to put the bird on its regular step-up practice perch, maybe a chair back, in unfamiliar territory, and, approaching with the towel draped over both hands from below, gently surround the bird with the towel. At first, you don't even have to pick up the bird, but the approach from below is extremely important. If the bird is approached from above, the towel can stimulate a feeling of being attacked by a predator. Later, you can step the bird up onto a towel-covered hand or scoop up the

bird enfolded in the towel and snuggle it like an infant.

Eventually, you will be able to cover only the bird's head with the towel, and the bird will perceive that it's inside the towel. Then you can pet any known-to-be-enjoyable place on the bird. (The neck is a good place to start, of course.)

Another way to start is with the towel laid over your lap with the long ends hanging down on each side. Put the bird on your lap and put one hand under each end of the towel. Lift the ends of the towel up to the sides of your face, making a sort of canyon or cavern with the bird and your face inside. At first you don't have to put your hands together; but you can eventually, and you can drape each end of the towel over the bird and then start looking for the bird and playing "peek-a-bird."

Another fun type of towel play is with two humans and one bird under the towel together. Put one end of the towel over each person's head, and sit facing each other (knee to knee) or stand a foot or so apart, and bring the bird up into the "cave" formed between your faces and the towel, then "flirt," pet, and play with the bird. Actually, there's no "wrong" way to play peek-a-bird; any form of towel play is probably beneficial if the bird is interacting and enjoying the process! It's just peeking around "flexible corners."

Younger birds usually take to these games more readily, but older birds, which naturally "enjoy" spending time in restricting enclosures

Even the Worst of the Worst?

Even male cockatoos that have been removed from breeding programs because of mate aggression, may be turned into total "pussycats" with the towel game. It may take only a few weeks, days, or minutes to transform a devoted slasher and bringer of blood into a creature that will dive breast first into a snuggly towel and commence cuddling at any opportunity.

such as a nest box, also benefit. It is not unusual for a retired breeding bird to learn readily to absolutely adore towel play.

If a particular bird resists or fears a towel, try using something that looks less towel-like such as a nice, puffy down jacket or large comforter. Using a towel about the color of the bird's body or under wings can be beneficial.

Towel stress: Extreme towel stress appearing at the wrong time can harm a bird physically or emotionally. Towel stress, as any experienced groomer or veterinarian can tell you, can kill a bird. A good professional avian behavioral evaluation should include an evaluation of the bird's responses to toweling. A bird that is extremely afraid of towels is existing in a life-threatening state and should receive behavioral intervention, possibly professional behavioral intervention, as quickly as possible.

Blue-throated macaw

Of course, every parrot is different. One bird might need more careful patterning. Another might need more stimulating activities, while still another bird might absolutely have to have a bath every day. Be ever alert to averting unwanted behavioral issues by anticipating your bird's physical and emotional needs, for negative behaviors appearing early can be enduring and life- (or life-quality) threatening.

Punishment, the "Evil Eye," and Unintended Consequences

Punishments for unwanted behavior are not only inappropriate for feathered prey species; they are ineffective and potentially harmful. A bird that is subjected to painful or frightening techniques is not learning peaceful, cooperative behavior. It may, in fact, be learning the exact *opposite*. A bird punished with punitive methods is more likely to respond either with like behavior or with unintended consequences such as fear, mistrust, or aversion. Therefore, effective socialization involves guiding a parrot to replace unwanted actions, including biting, with appropriate, acceptable ones.

Parrots that are dropped or thumped on the beak are in danger of physical injuries as well as adverse reactions. A bird punished with a squirt of water is in danger of developing behavioral complications such as fearfulness, loss of trust, feather-destructive behavior, and/or aversion to bathing. These issues may be observed as direct responses or they may contribute to more subtle reactions that don't appear immediately.

A stern look—sometimes called the "Evil Eye"—can suggest that a bird end one behavior and begin another (a termination stimulus). In more sensitive parrots, this can inspire fear just as punishment might. This is an instinctual prey response stimulated by straight-on eye contact in which human eyes resemble the eyes of a predator. The eyes of parrots and other prey species are located on the sides of their heads. This eye placement enables them to see danger approaching from beside or behind, and therefore, to avoid being eaten. Human eyes can be used in ways to more resemble prey species' eyes when contact is made with one eye closer, nose pointed to one side then the other. Although the "Evil Eye" may not be perceived as predatory by all and may be used as a termination stimulus with some parrots, it might also be totally ineffective.

Chapter Nine
Behavioral Issues

Extreme screaming, biting, fearfulness, and feather-destructive behavior can be both obvious and troubling to caring humans. Although each may be behavioral, we first consider the possibility of contributing medical issues. Begin any conscientious program to modify unwanted behavior with a trip to the avian veterinarian. Today's veterinarians are trained to provide the "gold standard" in health and medical care, and although they don't usually practice behavior modification, they are the first to note that the most common questions from parrot owners relate to behavior. An experienced avian veterinarian can also often distinguish between a behavioral and medical issue with a simple physical examination, although some conditions may require laboratory tests.

A veterinary consultation for a behavioral issue is an extremely good way to establish a rapport with your avian veterinarian. A true medical emergency may not be. Years later, when my Amazon had an apparent stroke on New Year's Day morning, Dr. Welch met me at his office immediately to help my bird.

I'm sure an unfamiliar veterinarian would have been reluctant or resistant to the notion of meeting a distressed client on a day when his clinic was obviously not open.

Extreme Screaming

Excessive screaming is the most common complaint from people who live with parrots, but a solution is usually easily found. A well-executed program can reduce loud vocalizations from the very first day. With a little extra attention and energy directed appropriately, caring owners can recapture peace in the home within a very short time.

While screaming behaviors can't exactly be "erased," we can replace most of them with quieter activities. We can also establish locations where the bird does not scream. Having seen and heard many stories of surprisingly stealthful behavior, I know that wild parrots encounter situations and visit sites in the wild where they simply do not scream. This is probably a matter of safety. It is also, obviously, a behavior that is learned from

Scarlet's Anorexia

My dishwasher broke down Friday morning, the day before Marie Digitano, speaker for my local bird club meeting, was to stay as a guest in my home. A repairman arrived within the hour, and the use of the word "repair*man*" is no accident. Single and fiftysomething, I seldom had men in my home; and Scarlet, my macaw (I didn't name her) is bonkers for men. Yielding to her preference, I always wind up paying a little more when workers come so that they have time to flirt with the big red bird.

That day, the unfamiliar dishwasher repairman was especially well prepared, being the proud owner of an African grey. He actually wound up spending more time playing peek-a-boo with the macaw than examining my defunct appliance (I replaced the dishwasher that evening). Scarlet pinned repeatedly, leaned toward the man, stepped up, climbed to his shoulder, and tried to feed his ear. He knew just how to manage, simply returning her to his hand, and holding a typical "parrot/human conversation" including, "Of course, you're a pretty bird and a good bird, but I don't want to get married, etc." Eventually, he put her down, gave her an almond, and me the tiniest possible bill.

Marie arrived from Minnesota the next day, and although she preferred my Amazons, she spent a respectable amount of time interacting with the macaw. Marie noted that Scarlet had not eaten her morning meal. I didn't think much of it, but was stunned when Scarlet ignored the offer of an almond, merely dancing and doing her best Stevie Wonder imitation.

The next day, Sunday, when we returned from the club meeting, Marie noted again that Scarlet had not eaten. I emptied the pellets and stinky sprouts and plunked a couple of almonds (her favorite treat) into Scarlet's bowl. Again the bird preferred dancing to eating. I was dumbfounded, not just surprised, realizing that this was her second day without food! I worried for my bird's well-being.

Marie and I rushed to the health food store where she guided me in selecting organic cactus and pecans. I purchased only a small amount of each of the very expensive foods. We spent Sunday evening and what we had of Monday morning trying to coax Scarlet to eat. We fed each other the exotic produce, repeatedly saying, "Uhmmmmmm!" (Scarlet's favorite vocalization when enjoying treats). I telephoned for an emergency veterinarian appointment the next day.

After dropping Marie at the airport, I rushed Scarlet immediately to Dr. Paul Welch. I was practically in tears as we waited in the examination room. When Dr. Welch entered, my macaw's behavior was as it always was with him. Scarlet is totally smitten with Dr. Welch, apparently considering him the finest specimen of manhood on this planet. She leaned as close to him as possible, pinned her eyes so tightly they appeared to be solid platinum/gold, jerked her head back into her neck a couple of times and regurgitated into his hand. He stood there with steaming bird vomit in his hand as I frantically recounted the story of her sudden-onset anorexia.

Then he laughed. "What did you say happened on Friday?"

I told him about the dishwasher repairman.

He laughed again. "I'm guessing she decided that he was a potential mate, and went on a hunger strike pining for him to come back." Dr. Welch held his cupped hand under my nose. "What does this smell like?"

The warm contents of Scarlet's crop—organic pecans—smelled delicious, like a fresh caramel praline from my favorite Mexican restaurant.

"She's obviously eating now," Dr. Welch said, "and she's molting. Sick birds don't molt."

The good doctor proceeded to relate many stories of coughing, limping, goofy parrots who scared their owners into visiting his office with behavioral issues. He sent me home with a very small bill.

other birds, for a wild baby parrot attracting too much attention of the wrong kind will, by experience, soon be a dead baby parrot.

Learned Behaviors

Mature parrots develop calls for mates and to celebrate eating and evening companionship, but these aren't usually extreme or excessive. Superfluous screaming can develop like any other habit in companion parrots: It is improvised or copied from another source; it is reinforced and becomes habitual. Most screaming in human-identified parrots probably starts as a demand for attention; that is, vocalizations are used to obtain interactions with humans or the favorite human. Responding to talking, but not screaming, can prevent the formation of this habit.

Screaming has another component in parrots: It appears to be fun just for the doing. That is, some birds scream simply because it feels good. A behavior that is fun to do just for the doing, like playing video games and spending money, is a self-rewarding behavior. These activities are most easily replaced with other self-rewarding behaviors, but external reinforcement can also play a part. Like other nuisance behaviors, screaming is best modified sooner rather than later.

While it is probably unwise and unhealthy to completely train a par-

Two Jenday conures

rot not to scream, it is probably more possible than most people think. That is, if humans can be trained to function as well as wild parrots who teach screaming or non-screaming behaviors to their young, then we can teach parrots to be quiet at certain times and in certain places.

Most companion parrots respond almost immediately to this simple four-step program. To correct excessive screaming:

1. Evaluate the bird, its environment, and habits. Knowing the elements of a habit is crucial to ending it. Carefully evaluate all elements of the bird's environment. Usually either related times or situations can be identified: *Mom is on the phone, Dad is reading the paper; isn't someone supposed to be holding me?*

Examine when, where, why, and how the bird is screaming. Is the bird's cage size appropriate and favorably located? Is the foraging (play) area exciting? Does the bird have ready access to interesting things to do—multiple branches to climb and peel, a variety of textures of destructible chewables, a selection of interactive or foraging toys? Does the bird have good-quality lighting and at least 12 hours of sleep daily? Can it constantly access fresh water? Is the bird's eating schedule regular? Is the diet interesting, nutritious, and diverse? Does the bird have adequate social time, with some face-to-face (talking, step-ups, towel games, petting, etc.) and some side-by-side interactions (eating, showering, watching TV, etc.) with humans? Does the bird enjoy adequate exercise, access to bathing, and occasional excursions outside familiar territory? Does the bird have a way to gauge the passage of time if left alone during the day?

If a parrot's basic, reasonable needs aren't being met, then it has cause to scream. Sometimes, something as simple as more sleep, frequently changing a fouled water bowl, or providing new, bark-covered branches can create contentment and fulfillment in a bird that has been both vocal and truculent. The bird might be inspired to be quieter merely by being lowered (or raised) or confined to the cage a little more often. It might be quieter if it is allowed more time out of the cage. The bird that doesn't get enough sleep at night might benefit from access to a dark, quiet place to nap midday.

Keep a log or journal to document:

—*time, duration, and volume of screaming*
—McPaco screams at 5:25 P.M. for 20 minutes at a volume of about "5" or until he is picked up *and*
—*apparent stimuli for screaming*
—McPaco screams when the baby cries, when people leave the room, or when the baby or puppy plays with a rattle or squeaky toy.

If the bird, especially a cockatoo, macaw, or Amazon, is screaming with great volume, it might be wise to begin this program with ear protection for humans in the home. Hearing damage can result from a constant barrage of loud screaming.

If the screaming behaviors are a response to a new infant in the home, we might have to send the bird away temporarily for behavior modification. This is probably unnecessary in most cases, especially if the home is large enough to offer shelter from the sound.

Soundproofing or white noise—a fan, air conditioner, television, or radio—may help to prevent the bird from yelling in response to a baby or bird sounds from another part of the home. An acoustical consultant (listed in the Yellow Pages) can determine the decibel level of bird screams in various locations and advise whether these are dangerous or damaging levels. An acoustical consultant might also advise decorating elements or architectural modifications to improve sound absorption properties in the home.

2. Identify potential screaming incidents. The journal is the most important tool in addressing any screaming problem. If there is no record of exactly how much the bird is screaming, how long, and how loud, then it's difficult to evaluate whether or not progress is being made. It is a list of clues. Sometimes only one clue provides enough information to "break the case." Some clues may be relevant; some may not. We probably won't be able to tell the difference between the relevant clues and irrelevant ones without investigating all of them.

3. Provide distractions before screaming incidents occur. Once we know when problem screaming occurs and what it is a response to, it can be averted by removing the stimulus, if possible, or by offering compelling distractions before the behaviors occur. Diet can often be manipulated to distract from morning and evening screaming. Give McPaco a new toy or inspire him to ring his bell by shaking it loudly in his face to stimulate a different behavior (attacking the bell) before you leave the room.

A regular feeding schedule can do much to minimize screaming. An improperly planned or poorly executed schedule might exacerbate a screaming problem. If the bird screams at a particular time, we might arrange to offer an interesting assortment of food a few minutes before the usual onset of screaming. If a behavior can be prevented even once and the replacement behavior can be immediately reinforced, we have a good chance to modify the original behavior. This "quick fix" might be the turning point to a long-term solution. If each potential screaming incident can be prevented for 21 days, then we can presume that our program to replace unwanted behavior has been successful.

4. Supply external and self-provided rewards for acceptable behavior. Positive reinforcement including verbal and food rewards lets the bird know that it is meeting your expectations. This is a very powerful tool. If the bird knows what "good bird" means or merely responds emotionally to melodious words, then any behavior except screaming can be easily reinforced with loving words. If McPaco figures out that he is receiving favorable attention for particular behaviors, he will repeat those behaviors. He will also gradually discontinue behaviors that do not bring at least occasional rewards. Avoid reinforcing inappropriate behavior.

Extreme screaming is best resolved when the bird can self-reward its own good behavior. Therefore, built-in, environmental distractions (rewards McPaco can give himself) are the stuff that true emotional independence is made of. Intermittent reinforcement for spontaneous acceptable independent behavior may generate increasingly independent behavior. When the bird learns that it will be rewarded for playing alone, it will repeat the behaviors that generate rewards. The bird will also be more experimental in seeking new opportunities for rewards, frequently including innovating both active and passive forms of self-rewards. That is, not only do birds frequently successfully learn to play alone, they often learn to provide their own rewards for doing so. I have seen and heard many stories of birds that often congratulate themselves on being "very good" or "very pretty" or "very smart"!

Behavioral "First Aid"

Screaming can be a true behavioral emergency wherein loss of home or living space is threatened. Sometimes, the only thing to do is

The Rainy Season

Never underestimate the value of bathing on appropriate, well-measured behavior in companion parrots. Most of these creatures' ancestors evolved in rain forests and developed metabolisms capable of flying around, foraging for food, finding water and minerals, finding and defending nests sites, courtship and raising of offspring, and they must be capable of doing so, sometimes in pouring rain, for more than 300 days a year. A bird that is not adequately showered may be nervous and high-strung. A bird that is neither flying around, foraging for food, etc. (see above), nor experiencing frequent drenching showers might have an abundance of unused energy. A bird with too much energy is a bundle of behavior problems waiting to happen, and screaming is only the first. A bird going through a "screaming phase" during warm weather might be treated to several showers of different intensities during the day. This is not to say, squirt the bird in a "There! Take That!!" kind of way, but rather, provide nonthreatening misted "rainfall" falling from above in a "Where did those beautiful clouds come from?" kind of way. Recovering from being wet is often enough of a "self-rewarding" behavior.

first to find a way to immediately quiet the bird. Unless quiet behavior can be accessed, there is no acceptable behavior to reinforce.

If McPaco is screaming out of control, begin by finding a way to calm him without actually reinforcing his poor behavior. That might mean providing a spray bath (cold shower) or ringing a bell until he attacks the bell. Probably, the only thing that will work more-or-less immediately is covering the entire cage with light-proof fabric or otherwise removing enough light from the room so that the bird dozes off. Obviously, this is a quick fix, and long-term application of this technique without adequate controls and reinforcement can worsen the problem. It could even injure the bird's health.

The Termination Stimulus

Covering or removing all sensory input by placing the bird in the dark is probably the fastest way to quiet a screaming bird. This will not usually change behavior, however, with some very intelligent birds, we can use an intermediate technique known as a "termination stimulus" to give the bird a chance to "switch gears" by giving clues that something unwanted is going to happen if something isn't changed.

We all know that something unwanted will happen if we don't take action when an alarm goes off: if we don't get out of bed, we'll lose our job or miss an appointment; if we don't take the cake out of the oven, it will burn. The alarm clock is not a punishment. It's a warning that an unwanted consequence will occur unless behavioral change occurs.

For screaming parrots, you might try a termination stimulus I call "flagging." Provide a signal that if he doesn't stop screaming, McPaco will be isolated, required to take a nap, or will be covered. Begin the flagging or signaling process by placing the bird in the cage with one towel draped over the side of the cage from which the most distraction is visible. Sternly advise McPaco that he must be a "good bird" or more measures will follow. If he stops screaming, reward and remove the towel. If he continues screaming, a second reminder to be a "good bird" and a towel applied to the second most distracting side of the cage will further advise the bird that no screaming is allowed at this time. If the bird continues to scream,

a light-proof cover is applied to the entire cage; and we set an alarm clock or timer for about 10 minutes after screaming subsides. This gives the bird time to "cool off" emotionally and, hopefully, to forget what was happening before the required "nap." Following the "cooling-off" period, direct social or indirect environmental distractions are provided, and the bird is reinforced for quiet behavior. Be sure to use a timer as a reminder to uncover the cage. It can be very hard on McPaco if he is forgotten and remains covered all day!

As the modification program proceeds, the first "flag" (or warning flag) may be all that is needed to quiet McPaco. If the bird stops screaming with only one towel in place, we have made real progress. The first time or two this happens, reinforce immediately. As the program progresses, wait a minute or two to ensure that the bird has, in fact, stopped screaming, then reinforce the behavior. Wait a few more minutes, then remove the towel; and if the bird remains quiet, reinforce.

Note: "Flagging" contributes to the actual modification of screaming behaviors only if all the bird's needs are being met. If the bird has a legitimate gripe, if important elements are missing from the bird's environment, this kind of treatment may aggravate the situation. Influencing the bird to stop screaming is only a "quick fix." True success in "curing" screaming issues doesn't come when the bird

Blue-fronted Amazon

stops screaming; it comes when the behavior has been truly replaced with (acceptable) self-rewarding behavior.

The Self-rewarding Environment

Fresh branches with peelable bark and a stimulating, ever-changing environment to be indispensable parts of the "quiet" parrot's habitat. A busy bird is not screaming, and branches are the easiest, least expensive way to quickly alter the environment and keep a parrot busy. If the bird has indirect distractions such as interesting branches and textures to chew; if interesting direct activities are provided before screaming occurs; and if all appropriate, independent, and inoffensive behaviors are intermittently reinforced, non-screaming behaviors will become a fixture in the bird's behavior. That is, we will have successfully replaced screaming with golden silence.

Of course, "quiet" is in the eye of the beholder. Anyone who can't embrace (or at least tolerate) parrot vocalizations would be better off with a cat or a bunny (but not a canary).

Beyond Biting

The parrot's beak functions as a hand, a nut cracker, a grooming device, and a courtship tool, among other things, but it can be sharp and painful if used against skin. This is especially true of cockatoos that may have three points (two on the

bottom and one on the top) that can pierce skin.

The beak might be used in an aggressive way to encourage a too-aggressive human to leave it alone or to let you know that a particular interaction is unacceptable to the bird, but it might also be used in friendly interactions. Parrots love to groom or preen beards or the hair on favorite humans. Unfortunately, they also want to remove anything "foreign" on skin, and this might include moles. This is merely "grooming" with no intent to cause pain. A parrot that wants to be picked up might grab at a human walking by or will gently pull a hand closer in order to step-up. A

able way, biting will *never* occur and will *never* become habitual. This is easier than it sounds, as observant humans should be only too willing to prevent pain.

Peaceful Use of the Beak

Most early "beak on skin" activity is experimental behavior in which the youngster tries jaw muscles in combination with the beak for effect. The bird must learn just how much pressure to exert on any given object to

parrot might want to feed favored people or to groom their teeth. This must not be allowed, of course, for human saliva contains organisms harmful to birds.

Knowing how to respond to beak use can prevent damage to skin. Humans must learn to use their hands appropriately to stimulate and reinforce only peaceful interactions. When petting the beak, tongue (parrots love this!), or skin around the beak, always position the thumb and index finger on opposite sides of the beak so that if the bird opens and closes its beak the digits are pushed apart, rather than winding up in the beak.

Hostile use of the beak must be prevented. As with other behaviors, if it has been rewarded even once, especially by laughter of a favored human, a random bite may become habitual. If the bird never gets a chance to use its beak in a disagree-

How to Tell if a Parrot Is Going to Bite

A parrot's intention to bite is demonstrated in the following ways:

- The bird will look at what it intends to bite, perhaps with flashing eyes.
- The bird may extend wings slightly or ruffle neck or head feathers.
- When on a perch, the bird will spread feet apart and grip soundly.
- It will lean or charge toward what it intends to bite.
- The bird's beak will be open in anticipation of the bite.

Anyone seeing any combination of two or more of these signals is best advised to avoid contact with the bird. This is not a demonstration of fear, but rather a show of respect, as it has been said, "Discretion is the better part of valor."

Why Parrots Bite and What to Do About It

1) Fear or anxiety biting is generated by the instinct to fight or fly, especially when complicated by containment, trimmed wings, or the perception of no choice. This might occur when a bird is first confronted by polished nails, a new hat, hair color, balloon, light fixture or other environmental element.

Don't force a beloved companion parrot to do anything unnecessary. Address fear biting by being less confrontational and improving access to safety. Improve cooperation patterning using towel games, eye games, step-ups, or other nonthreatening strategies. Demonstrate cooperative behavior. Learn to stimulate and reinforce alternative behaviors.

2) Territorial biting defends mate, nest site, height, toys, food, or water. This may be seasonal and includes displaced aggression, which is biting something or someone the bird can reach when it cannot reach what it wants to bite.

Watch for signs of territorial biting, maintain eye contact, and put the bird down or use hand-held perches. Improve cooperation patterning and bonding with increased handling and outings, or if you know this is seasonal, simply don't handle the bird until it passes. Look for ways to stimulate and reinforce other behavior. Don't let a parrot on your shoulder.

3) Manipulation biting is learned behavior intended by the bird to get its way, such as biting when the owner looks away, is on the phone, or when returning the bird to the cage. This includes "test" biting taught by unsteady humans who offer a hand, then pull away. This includes "drama-reward" biting where birds bite because they enjoy seeing humans scream and jump.

Make the behavior obsolete by denying opportunities for enactment. Behaviors that are not done cannot be reinforced into habits. Anticipate and avoid biting situations. Improve cooperation patterning, techniques, or methods. Don't quit eye contact when holding or returning the bird to the cage. Put the bird down before answering the phone.

4) The "wound-up" bird bites. Healthy parrots, especially Amazons and cockatoos, can be overstimulated in a manner similar to hyperactive children at a family picnic.

Look for signs of escalation and ways to calm the bird. Train to a termination stimulus. Be sure the bird is getting enough sleep. It might be time for a nap when Peaches is slashing for the apparent joy of it. Consider adding a roost cage. Don't try to handle a bird that is overstimulated or aggressively playing with a toy. Use environment to distract from the behavior. Provide more opportunities for exercise and bathing. Don't try to interact with a strutting little horny parrot exhibiting a sexual display.

held easily learns different behavior if different behavior is provided.

Environment

Environment can also be used to address biting issues. Raising or lowering a bird's usual relative height, combined with increasing access to "rainfall," destructible chewables, and exercise will help to compensate for pent-up energy that might otherwise be expressed as aggression. A bird that suddenly becomes excessively territorial must have its territory manipulated either by moving the cage or redesigning the cage interior.

Prevent a parrot from developing chasing behaviors by removing it to service the cage. That is, whenever feeding, cleaning, or changing accessories, first remove the bird to a chair back or play perch.

Mature companion parrots occasionally identify a particular chrome appliance as either a mate or a rival, leading to many courtships with toasters and wars with hair dryers. A sexually mature companion parrot might decide that no one is allowed in the kitchen. A bird that has fixated on a human-owned object or territory must be denied access to it. An attacking bird might be picked up using a hand-held perch, a towel, or "Good Hand/Bad Hand" (see page 121) and placed with the approved "surrogate enemy" toy. Again, encourage the bird to express hostility against an "approved enemy" toy lest it self-identify a beloved family member as an "enemy." This is usu-

obtain the desired result. Much interest and devotion is given to this learning process. When the youngster exerts too much pressure on skin, take care that the response is neither enjoyable nor provocative to the young bird. If the response is fun for the bird, then biting may become habitual. If the response excites the bird, it could provoke increased or continued aggression.

The best response to baby nibbles is to divert the beak to a different object such as a hand-held toy. If there is nothing to immediately replace in the bird's beak, then just put the bird down. A social young bird that knows attention will be with-

The Wobble Distraction

This distraction device may be used when the nipping or biting bird is sitting on a hand or on a hand-held perch. It is best employed just before the nip or bite; it may also be used just as it occurs, but never after it occurs, which would be analogous to punishment.

The hand or perch that the bird is sitting on (not necessarily the one being nipped) is gently and quickly wobbled so that the bird must momentarily pay attention in order to regain balance. This is usually best accomplished by quickly tipping the outside end of the hand or hand-held perch, first down and then back up. The bird will have to discontinue whatever it was doing to retain grip and balance. Be sure to maintain eye contact and remind the bird either to *"Be a good bird"* or to *"Be careful."*

This correction must be done quickly, gently, and sensitively so that the bird is not affected either physically or emotionally. It is not used with very shy, fearful, or phobic birds.

mon time for a nip or bite of a hand offered for step-ups is when the bird is being removed from a familiar perch, the inside, or top of the cage. This behavior can usually be defeated with improved technique and more frequent step-up practice in unfamiliar territory.

Maintain eye contact and offer the hand to be stepped on, approaching from below, as usual. Just as the prompt hand begins its approach to the bird, present an unfamiliar object just out of reach of the bird's beak (with one hand) and give the "step-up" command (with the other hand) followed by *"Be a good bird."*

If a bird demonstrates a threat to bite the approaching hand, pick up a small object (a spoon or a telephone or piece of junk mail) and hold it about an inch below and in front of the bird's beak, give the step-up

ally a self-rewarding behavior. Hostile energy will be expressed somehow; it is best expressed against a toy.

Good Hand/Bad Hand

A bird might begin to bite even a well-placed hand prompt for the step-up command. The most com-

command, and suggest good behavior. Usually the surprised bird, responding to the familiar behavioral pattern, and knowing what "good bird" means, responds also by being what it is expected to be (a good bird).

Eye contact is especially important here. A bird will often maintain eye contact rather than bite. If the bird's eye is distracted by the introduced object, it will seek to regain eye contact immediately rather than take the time to bite after being distracted.

Even if the bird bites, that unfamiliar object, rather than the hand being offered, will probably be bitten. Care must be taken to ensure that the distraction device is not frightening to a shy parrot. The distraction object must be neither too large (which might scare the bird off the perch), too small (which might be ineffective), nor toxic (a lead or painted object).

The most *appropriate response* to a bird testing beak on flesh is no response at all. A behavior that is not reinforced is less likely to become habitual, and very interactive birds might perceive almost any response to be reinforcement. While humans not reacting to a nip might seem counterintuitive or unlike the way humans would "naturally" react, this strategy eliminates the possibility of accidental reinforcement, for sometimes any reaction may be perceived by the bird as a reward.

Carefully reinforce any appropriate use of beak on flesh. If a bird

What to Do if the Beak Is Around Your Flesh

Of course, the best way to deal with biting is to prevent it, but if all efforts have failed and you are looking down at a tiny cockatoo lacerating your flesh and unwilling to quit, what do you do?

Moving what is being bitten toward the bird is one effective option. This interferes with the bird's grip and balance—it must release the bite. Anyone who pulls away runs the risk of ripping flesh, injuring the bird, or actually teaching the bird to bite by a response that will reinforce the behavior.

In addition to the wobble correction, some relief may be seen by putting the bird quickly, gently, and unceremoniously on the floor. Some birds will release if light-blocking fabric is placed over their heads. If the bird is hanging on and grinding, you might try stuffing something else into the beak, deflecting the bird to bite down on a magazine or a handy pair of glasses.

Eye contact is really important, here, for often, if you can catch the bird's eye, it will usually release the bite. A manufactured distraction may be necessary to change the bird's focus on the bite. That could mean slapping a magazine loudly against a table with the other hand, popping a balloon, or suddenly turning the television volume way up with the remote.

learns that it will get all the attention it needs with sweet kisses, it will most likely use that beak sweetly and sensitively each time it touches human skin.

Recovering Confidence in a Fearful Parrot

Wild parrots are prey species surviving with their unique ability to take flight when danger threatens. This hard-wired response is called the "fight-or-flight" response.

While the instinct to flee danger serves the bird well in the wild, the same reaction can be difficult, even dangerous, indoors. First, there is always the danger that a panicked bird could fly into danger: a mirror, window, ceiling fan, or pot of boiling water, if wing trims have not been maintained. Additionally, fear reactions are stressful to the bird, and prolonged stress can affect its immune system and the ability to fight off disease, ultimately weakening the bird physically. Prolonged or habitual fearfulness can result in painful isolation, as fearfulness is an undesirable social trait, that can make both humans and birds uncomfortable in each other's company.

Some parrot species have a stronger tendency to flee fearful situations than others. Among the common companion parrots, African greys, *Poicephalus*, cockatoos, grass parakeets, and cockatiels are generally reported to more often develop fearfulness as a part of the personality than their New World cousins. However, any type of common companion parrot, including large macaws, can develop fearful

The Sexual Display

A parrot is never more beautiful than when it extends its shoulders and fans its tail feathers in "display." This beautiful exhibition is part of both courtship and defense. The display is used to attract mates or intimidate rivals. Colors and markings are vividly revealed. All feathers might be spread, with body and head feathers sticking straight out, making the bird look much larger. In conflicts over mates and territory, this demonstration usually takes the place of actual battle as one parrot drives the other away merely by showing how large and fierce it can look with all feathers fanned and beak open in threatened attack. A parrot in this pose may be considering mating or biting. In indoor settings where the bird does not have the option to stay or fly away, fanned feathers and an open beak could be more than a threat. Again, discretion is the better part of valor. If you don't intend to fight or mate with the bird, simply don't handle it, or use a hand-held perch. A T-shaped perch is safer than a simple stick.

Leadbeater's cockatoo

behaviors in response to pain, abuse, neglect, or other perceived threats occurring in its environment.

Many birds are innately cautious, but when cautiousness turns to thrashing or falling off perches when humans enter the room, the behavior has crossed the line to fearfulness. If it endures, it might even be called "phobic." Heightened cautiousness appearing in a young parrot between four and 24 months, could be a developmental phase that passes as the bird gains confidence and independence. Sudden-appearing fearfulness can be a response to an inappropriate environment or to a shocking experience. If fearful responses are repeatedly stimulated, reenacted, and reinforced, they can become habitual.

Early cooperation patterning is especially helpful in the prevention and treatment of fearfulness. Preventive practice of the step-up command and early conditioning to the towel game provide alternatives to panic behavior. Even a bird that has no shyness to its personality might someday experience a tremendously fearful situation, and a sense of security can be returned to the bird with alternative routines. If step-ups have been well reinforced, then usually, at least one person in the family can continue step-up drills even during a fearful phase.

Early conditioning to enjoy towel play is extremely beneficial in the treatment and prevention of fearful behaviors. These are usually even more helpful in treating fearfulness

Step-up/Step-down: Keep It Simple

Some trainers advise training every bird to respond to both a "step-up" and a "step-down" command. Some humans and birds are perfectly capable of training and maintaining both commands. However, some birds experience difficulty retaining dependable response to even one command. Of course, only one pattern is more easily maintained than two.

Since response to either the step-up or step-down command virtually identical—stepping from one place to another—I feel that the same stimulus should always be used. That is, instead of prompting for the same behavior with two commands, a more reliable response is retained by using only "Step-up." Good technique during daily training involves holding the hand the bird is sitting on lower than the perch it is being prompted to step on (if possible).

than step-ups. Many terrified birds can recover more dependably with appropriate use and maintenance of this activity, which involves no perceived interaction with hands.

If heightened fearfulness appears suddenly, begin to reestablish emotional connections with the use of the eyes, voice, and body language (see No-touch Games on page 104).

The Safe Environment

In addition to evaluating and adjusting the bird's responses to passive human interactions, examine the environment for contributing factors. Especially, if a young bird is falling frequently in the cage, review the sizes, types, and textures of perches.

In some cases, nail-grooming perches overgroom when situated where the bird sleeps (usually the highest perch). Instead, try placing the nail-grooming perch—if one is needed at all—in front of the water bowl. Here, nails will be groomed, but not overgroomed. Younger, clumsy birds should be allowed a little more toenail for gripping confidence and should be provided with smaller branches of softer wood in order to prevent falls.

Larger birds and more voracious chewers probably need very hard woods such as manzanita, because they're so durable and easy to clean. Smaller birds need branches such as poplar, citrus, or ailanthus that can be more easily gripped and destroyed. An assortment of various sizes installed at diverse angles can provide interesting climbing opportunities that build confidence in a bird that has previously fallen or had difficulty with smooth, too-large, or hard-to-grip perches.

If falls continue, try raising the grate so the bird can't fall far if it falls. Some cages are designed to allow the grate to be moved up and down. Some cages may require that a special temporary grate be fashioned from welded wire or other material appropriate to the size of the bird.

Height manipulations: These can be extremely helpful in addressing fearfulness. Some birds become more confident, territorial, and aggressive when they are higher. This is a good thing in the case of a timid bird. Some benefit from being able to climb a branch or ladder to play on a little wooden shelf near the ceiling (as high as possible). Some birds, such as Patagonian conures and *Poicephalus*, dive down when frightened and might be calmed from fear reactions by being housed lower, perhaps with a little visual shelter, such as behind a plant.

Location: This also can contribute to fearfulness by making the bird feel vulnerable to predators. A cage near a high-traffic location can increase fearfulness if the bird is repeatedly startled by noisy dogs rushing by or by quiet humans that seem to appear from nowhere as they rush through a doorway. Enhance a parrot's sense of security with the addition of hiding opportunities that might include a little tent (a hide box), a towel over one-third of the cage, restricted sight of other birds, or moving the cage to a more sheltered location, perhaps across the room from traffic areas.

Choices: Provide the bird with access to choices, such as deciding between multiple toys, perchs, and foods. Each time a bird makes a successful decision, it is more willing to make other choices rather than simply reverting to instinctual fear. Especially, don't force an unwilling, timid bird to come out of the cage on a hand or perch. If necessary, the bird can be removed by turning the cage on its back or side with the door up and allowing the bird to climb out.

A fearful and panicky bird might be tired. Be sure the bird has adequate opportunity for 10 to 12 hours of **undisturbed sleep** daily. Don't go in and out of the room at night, as some birds are absolutely terrified of disturbances in the dark. Most shy or cautious birds probably benefit from having at least half of the cage

If a Parrot Fears New Toys

It's not unusual for a poorly socialized bird to fear new toys. A simple trick can often be employed to overcome this.

Start by rolling a clean, unscented paper towel from one corner diagonally as one might roll a bandanna handkerchief to go around a skier's neck. Tie the rolled paper towel around the bird's favorite toy. Most birds will immediately remove the paper towel "bow" by chewing it off. If the bird is reluctant, or if it takes more than a few hours to chew the paper towel bow off, try starting with tissue rather than a paper towel.

Once the bird has learned to remove the paper bow from the favorite toy, begin introducing new toys with the bow already in place. If every toy is introduced with a paper bow around it and the bird has to remove the paper bow to get to the toy, then every toy will seem like an old familiar friend (or maybe surrogate enemy), and the bird will no longer fear new toys.

covered at night, and may also appreciate a night light.

Loud sounds: These can easily destroy a bird's sense of security. Large, noisy species such as full-sized cockatoos or macaws may upset shyer birds that may perceive that the vocalizations indicate danger. Likewise, parrots must be protected from loud construction noise and the sounds of gunfire and fireworks. Obviously, a sense of constant danger can harm a bird's disposition as well as its health.

Grooming. A shy parrot's sensitive temperament is best served with very noninvasive wing and nail grooming configuration and technique (see Low-stress Grooming, page 52). Consider the possibility that a bird overcoming fearfulness might regain self-assurance exactly as those old, cut wing feathers are replaced with full new ones. Consider the possibility that an overly cautious bird might need full wings or only slightly trimmed wing feathers to regain confidence. Consult a professional, or carefully match the bird's responses to the amount of trimmed feather. A brave bird that's a great flyer might require a much shorter wing trim than a shy, pudgy bird that likes to walk and climb instead of fly.

Provocation and Unintended Messages

Sometimes, the stimulus for a panic response comes from human caregivers. Of course, we must never allow people or other pets to tease any bird, especially a shy or fearful one, although some humans might be provoking the bird's fear unintentionally. If a bird has developed a fear of fast-moving hands or if hands it knows well change in appearance (read here, brightly manicured nails), the bird might benefit from not being exposed to the sight of hands at all (keep them in pockets or behind back) until calm behavior can be stimulated, patterned, and reinforced. Also expect reactions to changes in hair color, cut, or hats.

A parrot that has been previously panicked by even an unintentional "Evil Eye" might thrash, bite, or flee any eye contact. This can be distressing when feeding or cleaning the cage. Don't look at the bird if you must service the cage with the bird inside. Remove it to a play area if this can be done without eliciting, and therefore, reinforcing fearfulness. Take another look at those No-touch Games on page 104.

The Power of Preference

Sometimes a bird experiencing a fearful phase meets someone to whom it is naturally, inexorably drawn. This can come like a thunderbolt, like love at first sight. Curiously, in some birds, this is not always a situation of "overbonding" wherein, after falling for a particular person, the bird remains fearful or aggressive with others. Previously panicked parrots may learn to accept contact, interest, or interaction with other humans after meeting only one trustworthy person.

If fear behaviors are *specific to one person*, use his or her name in tandem with the bird's: "Paco's Uncle Charlie" or "Uncle Charlie's Paco," working to convince the bird to include that person as an accepted associate.

Outings. Sometimes new and better bonds can be forged by outings into unfamiliar territory, especially outings with less-favored humans. This might take the form of attitude changes generated by feelings of a particular person being the only familiar thing in a scary, unfamiliar place. Improved bonding can result, especially if the bird feels that it has been "rescued."

Sometimes just taking the bird for a ride in the car generates noticeable improvement. Many very shy birds cannot be easily taken out of the carrier, so simply don't remove them. Experiencing new territory from the safety of a carrier can help to increase the bird's sense of security.

Nervous energy. Wild parrots are amazingly active. Conversely, most companion parrots don't have flying opportunities, foraging opportunities, aren't allowed to "defend nest sites," and don't court or raise young. This can contribute to skittishness. Showers may be the most easily provided opportunities for exercise for these birds, as the energy expended when feathers go from wet to dry will not be expressed as panic. Other opportunities for exercise for a shy bird might include round rope swings; long, hanging, swinging ropes; and provision of accessible places where the bird can hang on tight and flap its wings hard and fast in simulation of flying. Opportunities for flapping exercise absolutely require symmetrical wings, for birds with only one full wing can learn to avoid this exercise and will ultimately suffer behav-

ioral consequences, possibly including fearfulness and feather-destructive behavior.

Feather Chewing, Snapping, and Plucking

Few issues are more troubling to
owners of companion birds than
feather-destructive behavior (FDB).
And while limited self-induced damage may be neither harmful nor
enduring, its development may be
an indication of something gone
awry. FDB can appear suddenly
over a period of minutes or hours, or
can develop gradually, taking
months or even years to be noticeable. It might resolve apparently
spontaneously or endure and
progress with passing years.

Because FDB is generally considered to be a stress reaction, the first
place to look when it appears is for
illness or medical issues. Make an
immediate appointment with the
avian veterinarian at the first sign
of unexplainable feather damage.
Don't wait; go quickly, before the
behavior becomes habitual. It's all
right to ask about potential illness,
zinc and calcium levels, yeast, and
giardia. New challenges appear in
this rapidly changing field every day,
so be prepared to hear your local
veterinarian's experience with
potential medical issues in your geographic area. If the veterinarian finds
no health-related issues, diet or

habitat manipulation and/or behavioral counseling will be suggested.

When necessary, sometimes
merely treating the health issue will
resolve a feather-damaging incident
immediately. Sometimes, however,
even though the primary factor stimulating the initial stress reaction is
identified and eliminated, ongoing

feather destruction can remain. Here, FDB has become a behavioral issue, for habits can remain even after an initial physical cause is removed.

Some conditions must be treated with drugs such as Valium, Haldoperidol, or Prozac. While these treatments are a temporary, last resort sort of thing, they can save the bird's life until a more permanent solution is found.

Molting and Other Explainable Feather Loss

A surprising number of novice parrot owners become convinced that their new birds are "secretly plucking" because feathers are found on the bottom of the cage. I am usually unconcerned if these are full individual feathers or feathers in pairs and if this occurs during warm weather, for this is part of molting. During this annual process, the bird will lose and regrow all feathers in a symmetrical configuration along the lines of circulation known as feather tracts. This is the facility by which wing feathers are molted and regrown in mirror image pairs, a "system" that would not, in the wild, inhibit flight ability. If wing feathers are not regrowing symmetrically, this could be an indication of damage to the follicles on one wing or an indication of feather cysts. This is another good time for the veterinarian to examine those wings.

Consider, too, that some other forms of feather loss or removal are explainable or appropriate and not usually ongoing. These include feather loss or damage caused by other birds or by occasional seasonal or other transitional behavior. New owners are sometimes concerned when parent-raised youngsters have noticeable bare spots, chewed, or irregular feathers on the back of the head or neck. This is not uncommon and is evidence of the vigor with which parents sometimes seek to quickly wean and fledge chicks. The appearance of feather chewing on the cheeks, head, or nape of one bird housed with another is a clarion call to separate them.

Exuberant juveniles may also damage feathers during active play. Baby African parrots, macaws, and cockatoos commonly have bent, dirty, or completely broken tail feathers. This situation usually resolves by age two, when a clean whole tail emerges. If the situation persists after the age of two, again, it's time to talk with the veterinarian (nutritional deficiency?) or a behavior consultant (suspect a housing problem). Youngsters that have not experienced their first molt may chew dirty or damaged feathers. This is probably temporary and not usually cause for concern.

If all of a companion bird's wing or tail feathers suddenly wind up on the floor, consider the possibility of a traumatic incident. Although tail feathers can be extremely loose, especially in hot weather, wing feathers are connected to the bone and are intended to stay in place

and function even under the most arduous circumstances. Night frights in cockatiels and some grass parakeets, not uncommonly, result in the loss of all tail feathers, and occasionally in lost wing feathers. This is uncommon in anything except cockatiels, and the possibility of a nighttime disturbance that was truly terrifying to the bird must be investigated.

Feather Chewing, Shredding, or Fringing

This is the most common form of FDB. It begins with damage to the edge of the barbs of the contour feathers. Both mild and progressive

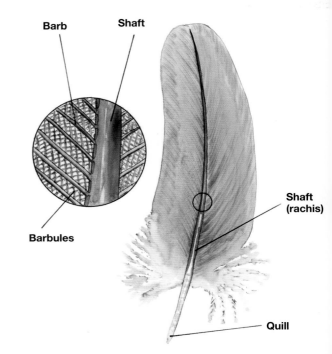

Diagram of a feather

forms of this disorder can exist for years before anyone notices. The first sign of this type of feather damage is often visible as individual floating "fibers" or remnants of the barbs observed in the air or dust in the room. These filaments may be seen floating on the surface of the water dish, on papers in the bottom of the cage, or magnetically attracted to the television screen. This form of damage might be related to soiled feathers, boredom, anxiety, feelings of abandonment, poor diet, or inadequate lighting; but it might be related to slow molt and/or inappropriate preening.

Inappropriate Preening

This is probably related to failure of independence. If a bird perceives that the owner is the one and only fun "toy," then it might not play with even the most carefully designed accessories. It might instead, compulsively preen in anticipation of treasured interactions with the favorite person. As this progresses, the bird is more likely to accidentally or purposefully damage feathers. The bird is working hard to look as beautiful as possible and simply going too far.

Damage to the edge of feathers can also result from slow molt or brittle feathers. If this is ongoing, especially in older overweight Amazons or budgies, work to improve nutrition, exercise, lighting, and showers; and consult an avian veterinarian about adequate nutrition for the thyroid gland. Sometimes improving access to calcium and iodine-rich foods, as well as eliminating or manipulating fat in the diet, especially from peanuts, will help here.

Feather snapping. Feather snapping is a more acute, quickly progressing form of FDB. This involves breaking the feather shaft, which can begin in a small way near the outer end of the feather resulting in a characteristic "Y" shape. In its more acute phase, this might involve snapping the feather off at the base, leaving no contour feather visible outside the down. This is the form most sudden-onset feather damage takes when a bird is apparently in full feather one minute and there's a "naked" bird with a pile of feathers under the perch half an hour later. This, of course, can be emotionally traumatic for new owners.

Feather plucking or pulling. Here, the feather is pulled out, sometimes accompanied by the bird version of an "ouch" sort of sound as it happens. Again, this might be ongoing or it might be a temporary response to dirty or damaged feathers. Feather pulling is especially common around the vent or around the uropygial (preening) gland as well as around the neck where dirty feathers might be annoying the bird. Pulling or chewing off dirty feathers is common behavior in baby parrots that have not yet experienced their first molt. Some birds have been reported to pull cut feathers from the wing, apparently to facilitate faster feather regrowth. These may be feathers that have already molted but have not yet emerged from the tightly held feathers of the wing.

If no health-related issues are present, occasional feather pulling, especially by juveniles, probably resolves spontaneously with the first molt. However, a parrot pulling, snapping, or chewing dirty or damaged feathers should be bathed more often, exercised more, monitored carefully, and carefully *not* reinforced. Frequent drenching showers are absolutely necessary to provide a way to express excess energy (exercise) and to prevent the bird from perceiving that continuation of this activity is necessary. Environmental enrichment can provide distraction from the behavior.

More than any other form of FDB, feather pulling is suspected to have an organic origin. Investigate food, fumes, or allergies when this behavior appears. Examine the possibility of food sensitivities by manipulating the diet. Sometimes eliminating salt or oil and improving calcium consumption helps. Occasionally, radical evaluation of the diet must be made, possibly removing all but one food and then gradually adding one food at a time to observe the effect on the bird.

If one avian veterinarian doesn't find something, then research the possibility of a referral or second opinion from another doctor, as each has different experience and will test for and look for different things. Sometimes just a slightly different perspective can be all that is

necessary to find and eliminate the primary source of stress in a feather-damaging incident. Rely on the veterinarian's experience and testing mechanisms. Avoid treating a problem "in case" it exists. This could make things drastically worse by increasing the bird's stress and setting its body off balance.

Environment and FDB. An underwhelming environment can contribute to feather destruction. Not infrequently, the cage is centered in front of a window; toys hang under rather than beside the bird, and all cage elements including toys are indestructible. Affected birds may be reacting to exclusively horizontal perches made of smooth hardwood dowel, PVC, or, sometimes, slick, too-large manzanita.

Babe: A Case History

The little gray down-covered Mexican redhead (*Amazona viridigenalis*) was not on public display. She was perched quietly in a private area of a friendly, dependable bird store. At the age of seven months, she had seen the veterinarian several times. He had pronounced her healthy and chewing feathers for behavioral reasons. Her head was held high, in spite of two plastic Elizabethan collars stapled in place to prevent her from further damaging her feathers.

Not one to miss an opportunity to work on a behavior problem, I said, "Give me that bird!"

With a twinkle in her eye, the store's owner handed the bird and the cage to me.

That December 9th, Babe was my special Christmas project. I was

determined to help her, and on the way home, while stopped to visit a friend, the plastic collars were removed. Babe responded by immediately, frantically pulling out several beakfuls of down. We misted her gently with warm water, and to our amazement, she stopped pulling down, held out her little fuzzy gray down-covered wings and, in true Amazon fashion, reveled in what might have been her first adult shower. I tucked the moist bird inside my long wool coat and continued on my way.

Arriving at my office, I set up her cage, knowing that she needed a cage both here and at home. Within half an hour, the little bird was dry and pulling feathers again.

"Well," I thought, "if she doesn't chew feathers when she's damp, I guess she'll just have to stay damp until she grows feathers."

That December was not especially cold in Denver, Colorado, but it was chilly enough that wherever I went, I wore my long wool coat with the unusual "accessory" of a damp juvenile Amazon under the coat with me. I found that if she was not left alone and was misted slightly with warm water when her feathers became dry that she did not chew feathers, and she was willing to investigate the various textures of destructible chewables we provided in her cage. Her cage at home was outfitted with branches with soft, peelable bark attached to the sides of the cage in a manner that would allow her great height.

A couple of weeks later, observing that we had made progress in guiding Babe away from feather damage, her veterinarian suggested an unusual operation. Because she had chewed the flight feathers off her wings, and because it would be another six to nine months before she could molt, her avian veterinarian decided to give her a "head start" at regrowing these feathers by pulling every other chewed-off flight feather so that new wing feathers could regrow immediately and the emerging blood feathers would provide mutual support as they grew out. Of course, this procedure is performed only in certain unusual circumstances by a qualified avian veterinarian, and because it is extremely painful, it must be done only under anesthesia. Babe had endured a great deal of bad luck for a bird so young, and the veterinarian wanted her to have every opportunity to recover. On December 18, he anesthetized her and performed her feather-pulling surgery. All went very well, and within another few weeks, there were tiny bright green tips emerging from the even rows of blood feathers on her wings. We were careful at that time not to provide

hanging toys, and to pad the bottom of the cage to prevent injury from rowdy play.

But there wasn't much playing in the beginning. In addition to daily showers, as soon as the blood feathers on her wings had opened, Babe was required to do daily flapping exercises in order to stimulate circulation and metabolism. Gradually, she learned first to chew and then to interact with the various toys and accessories I had provided her. It took weeks for her to get the notion of attacking a surrogate enemy toy, but by January 18, one month after her surgery, she was regularly beating up her Little Birdy Man. She was destroying rope, twine, fabric, straw, and cardboard. She not only had wing feathers, but two tiny contour feathers on her lower left breast. By the end of April, Babe was almost fully feathered and ready to go to her new home.

Exercise and Rainfall

Companion parrots, especially those with trimmed wings, may have very little access to exercise, which can contribute to slow metabolism, slow molt, and poor-quality feathers. Be sure to provide for and encourage daily flapping until the bird is just slightly winded which activates the cardiovascular system, stimulating the bird's metabolism and improving circulation. This strategy should be approved by the avian veterinarian, of course, since it might compromise a preexisting physical or medical condition.

Allowing the bird to dry naturally after bathing, especially if it shivers just a bit, provides similar metabolic and vascular benefits to flapping and climbing exercise. Additionally, frequent showers assist in the completion of molting and remove particle contaminants that might prevent parts of the feather from locking together when preened.

Protective Devices

Plastic Elizabethan collars are sometimes necessary to halt active, acute self-inflicted feather or skin damage. These devices, including the new ball and tube types, are not to be considered cures for feather damage, but rather, are temporary means of prevention. They are especially helpful in the presence of obvious health issues such as a staph infection of the skin that is undeniably stimulating damage. These devices, combined with improved behavioral practice upon removal, are often quite beneficial, even necessary for recovery.

In more behaviorally difficult cases, body stockings or "teaser" bandanna handkerchief devices, designed to encourage the bird to chew on the device rather than to prevent chewing, may also be of great value. These devices are sometimes needed long-term rather than simply as a transition. One Moluccan cockatoo I know never recovered from chewing a hole in its breast when its owner died and it had no access to food for a couple of weeks before the death was discovered. That bird has, however, adjusted very well to wearing a bandanna handkerchief worn (in the manner of a cowboy) over the breast. This induces the bird to chew the fabric rather than its own breast. The bird looks nice when people are present and chews skin only when alone, usually only during sleep times. Because of the danger that these fabric devices might get caught on something, they must be used only with careful supervision.

Resolving Feather-Destructive Behavior

Behavioral feather chewing is a complex issue, and many factors are involved. Appropriate patterning for cooperation, a carefully positioned appropriate cage, gentle handling, full-spectrum lighting, and nutritious diet and eating habits are only a few of the elements needed to raise a happy, independent feathered companion. The bird must have balanced bonding between multiple humans or locations. It must have an understanding of time, of limits of acceptable behavior, and of appropriate relationships. The bird must be encouraged to develop self-rewarding or independent habits to prevent the development of feather chewing, attention demanding, and

Shreddable Fabric

Pure cotton fabric can be provided in configurations intended to replicate the filaments of shredded feathers, but special care must be taken to ensure that the threads peeling off the raw edge of the fabric are not so long that they can wrap around little toes, restricting circulation, and causing the loss of the toe. Woven goods about the weight of quilt or bandanna handkerchief fabric can be cut into strips along the grain of the fabric. Then about every inch, the fabric can be clipped along the edge so that the fibers peeling off the edge are only about an inch long. Tie these fabric "streamers" on toys, perches, or cage bars in places beside where the bird spends time. We are hoping to distract the bird into shredding the fabric rather than shredding its own feathers. Paper pom-poms and paper woven into cage bars or hung from treat holders will make this possible.

other problematic behaviors. The bird must learn that it will never be abandoned, that when people go away they always come back.

Good emotional health starts with confidence, and confidence in parrots develops first with physical coordination. Like all infants, baby parrots are at least occasionally clumsy. A baby bird with an inappropriate wing feather trim, too closely trimmed toenails, and inappropriate perches is surely at risk for the development of FDB related to falling. This is especially true of heavy-bodied birds such as baby African grays. In the wild, where a fallen juvenile would be somebody's dinner, young greys develop extremely sharp toenails as a survival mechanism. In companion parrots, sharp nails can lead to anxiety by irritating the skin of the handler. Failure to allow sharp nails, however, combined with use of smooth, hard, or nail-grooming perches can contribute to frequent falls resulting in damaged or broken feathers. This can, in turn, give rise to feather shredding as the bird learns to "overpreen," first by removing tiny single filaments, then progressing to

removal of larger parts, and eventually chewing off whole feathers. Add a little unintentional reinforcement or a little bad luck, and feather destructive behavior can result and become permanent and ongoing.

Anything contributing to fearfulness or failure of confidence can result in damaged feathers whether or not it was present at the onset of damage. Illness, inadequate diet or light, inactivity, low thyroid, slow molt, perceived abandonment, fearfulness, failure of independence, failure of curiosity, failure to develop natural preening and chewing behaviors, and/or sexual motivation are also often present at the onset of destruction.

Toys, Enemies, and Environmental Enrichment

While the role of toys might seem frivolous to some humans, they provide opportunities for decision making, manipulating parts, chewing, snuggling, talking, masturbating, and dominating and are invaluable in the prevention of FDB. Any companion parrot that is not motivated to chew things other than feathers must be inspired to turn that beak to other things. New, unpainted baskets, grapevine wreaths from the hobby store, clean new little brooms, cardboard, paper, or fabric elements may be introduced to stimulate destructive chewing of external elements rather than feathers. Little plastic whisk brooms can be run through the dishwasher and raw-edge fabric is best cut on the bias.

Diet and FDB

Correcting diet is also usually essential to the resolution of FDB. Be sure that the bird is eating a premium quality diet that has been well tested on this particular type of bird. Salt and fat are often identified as factors contributing to feather damage. There is more salt in processed people food than most people realize, and elimination of processed human foods such as bread or seasoned pasta may be necessary to resolve feather damage. In warm climates, it's even sometimes necessary to advise loving owners to wash sweaty skin before handling their birds because some of the birds will lick salt (or other contaminants) off human skin.

Consult the veterinarian about fat requirements for this particular bird. Most birds benefit from the reduction or elimination of fat from the diet; however, a few birds, probably only the large macaws, may benefit from increasing oil sources in the diet. Peanuts do seem to be problematic, and, like French fries, should be eliminated from the diet of birds engaging in self-inflicted damage to feathers or skin.

The presence or lack of hemp seed in the diet has been observed as an influence in feather chewing. If there is no hemp in the bird's diet, try adding up to 6 percent hemp seed. If there is this much hemp or more in the diet and the bird starts damaging feathers, try eliminating the hemp.

Don't forget the importance of constant access to clean, fresh water, as the stress of dirty water has caused more than one bird to chew feathers or to pick up illness or other health-related problems that cause feather chewing. In many places it may be necessary to use preboiled or bottled water in order to be absolutely certain that the source of the stress causing the feather chewing is not arriving in contaminated water. Vitamins and other additives to the water can be considered contaminants to feather-chewing birds who bathe in the water.

Lighting. Because of the importance of calcium in the development of healthy skin and feathers, and because of the role of vitamin D in the assimilation of calcium, it's absolutely necessary for a bird to have access to full-spectrum lighting. I have seen many birds regrow feathers after the addition of this one additional environmental element.

Chewing skin or feet. While feather damage is often mild and not an outright threat to the bird's health, self-inflicted damage to skin requires immediate professional intervention. The self-destruction of skin, the skin on the feet, or even toes, can be related to poor diet; to inhaled environmental toxins, including nicotine; or to perch size. Cigarettes, especially, must be absolutely eliminated to avoid the danger of progressive damage.

Grooming wings and tail. Inappropriate wing and nail grooming can contribute to self-inflicted feather damage just as correcting grooming can assist in recovery. We have pre-

What to Do: The Feather Destruction Checklist

✔ Go to an experienced avian veterinarian for a "feather" workup.

✔ Examine the environment for stressful elements.

✔ Manipulate the environment to enhance curiosity and confidence (adjust height, cage, location of cage, hiding places, perches, and toys).

✔ Establish a pattern of going away and coming back so that the parrot understands that when people leave, they will come back.

✔ Increase access to face-to-face and side-by-side time with humans.

✔ Increase access to rainfall (frequent drenching showers).

✔ Increase access to exercise, including daily flapping exercises until the bird is slightly winded.

✔ Improve diet, eliminate salt, monitor fat.

✔ Provide full-spectrum lighting at least eight hours daily.

✔ Carefully provide a full 12 hours of uninterrupted sleep nightly.

✔ Consider a better water source and change water more frequently.

✔ Keep an annual journal of the bird's behavior so that it can be distracted to appropriate behaviors before damage incidents have, historically, appeared.

✔ If you're north of the equator or you've seen little or no improvement by July, go to the veterinarian again, perhaps to a second veterinarian. There's only a little more of molting season available to provide easy feather regrowth.

viously discussed how too-short toenails can contribute to falls and to failure of confidence. However, too-long nails can be just as harmful since they might get caught in fabric or in cage parts causing stress as the bird moves around the cage. Sometimes merely grooming the nails can precipitate a recovery from feather chewing. A ragged or too-short wing-feather trim can contribute to falls and to preening disorders. Sometimes a ragged trim can be corrected with very sharp scissors. Many birds recover from an incident of self-inflicted feather damage when wing feathers are allowed to grow out completely, then trimmed only slightly after the bird learns to fly.

Examination, Distraction, and Judgment

Examine the environment for newly added elements that might be stressful to the bird such as new art, light fixtures, carpeting, sound pro-

ducing clocks, other animals, or provocative humans. Consider the possibility that humans or other pets (including birds) may be secretly provoking the parrot.

As with screaming, keep a journal to determine exactly when the bird is chewing feathers and exactly what is happening when feather damage occurs, including the favorite human's reaction. Once you know when the behavior occurs, then distract to other behaviors, such as showering or exercise before the behavior begins.

Of course, at no time should a companion parrot be reinforced for engaging in FDB. Too much attention paid to a feather-chewing bird can reinforce the continuation of the unwanted behaviors.

Likewise, friends of owners and caretakers should be careful not to judge or criticize. Many caring humans have spent hundreds of dollars and thousands of hours working to help their birds recover from self-inflicted feather damage. Owning a feather-chewing parrot is not unlike having a teenager with a habit of nail biting or a fascination with tattoos or piercings. Don't withhold love from anybody or anything merely because you don't approve of that individual's grooming or ornamentation tastes.

Professional Behavioral Intervention

The bird has decided not to allow your significant other into the house, and he or she is only too willing to accommodate. The bird won't let you out of its sight without telling the whole neighborhood about it. You've read every book you can find, and the bird still has you wrapped around a slightly overgrown toenail.

Mere humans can be very anxious about asking someone into their homes to help with their bird's behavior. Could this sort of thing be painful and intimate like psychoanalysis?

An effective behavioral counselor probably works more like a golf or tennis coach than a psychiatrist. There will be more focus on how to change the bird's behavior than on the source of the behavior, but a sensitive consultant will deal compassionately with the owner as well as the bird.

Ask a trusted breeder, bird store employee, avian veterinarian, club, or magazine for a referral to a parrot behavior consultant in your area. Alternatives on the Internet may be wonderful or awful. Look for places where kindness and open minds prevail. Ask for references from others who have actually consulted with a particular professional about a similar problem in a similar type of bird. Expect a professional to expect to be paid for his or her time, and beware of nonprofessionals who profess to know everything and are willing to work for free. You wouldn't hire an amateur dentist.

Expect an initial screening consultation by telephone. Before making an appointment, a companion parrot behavior consultant will, typically, spend a few minutes on the phone asking the age, source, type of bird, nature and duration of the problem. You may then expect a description of what kind of expenditure of time and money might be expected in order to determine how to correct the problem. A professional will also be evaluating your responses and trying to determine whether or not the two of you have a rapport. Expect to be referred to a different consultant if either of you don't feel a good emotional connection or if the consultant is inexperienced in issues affecting your bird.

The consultant might offer group, telephone, or in-home counseling depending upon the location and nature of the problem. Group work must be done carefully for reasons of health and communicable disease. Telephone counseling is attractive for simple problems of short duration, but in-home evaluations remain the most dependable way to solve long-term, enduring problems. While an in-home might appear initially more expensive, it probably offers greater opportunity for success, for sometimes only direct observation by an outsider can reveal what is happening to perpetuate a behavior. In the long run, one-on-one, in-home counseling is usually the most cost-effective option for correcting established behavior problems in companion parrots.

Your parrot's behavior consultant will be examining diet, housing, and handling elements including responses to toweling that might be contributing to the bird's behavior.

- Expect suggestions regarding cooperation practice, diet, and environment. The behavior consultant will examine feather condition and the bird's responses to showering. The easiest way to do this, of course, is to give the bird a bath as a part of the behavioral evaluation. It's not unusual for the consultation to wind up in a waterproof room such as the bathroom. You might want to tidy up a bit if you are shy about strangers in the bathroom, although, a real pro won't care whether the bathroom is sparkling clean, and certainly would be non-judgmental and protect this confidence, anyway.
- Expect confidentiality. A responsible consultant will not reveal your identity or connection to the case without your permission (except to another professional working on the case who should also respect your confidentiality).
- Expect the possibility of a veterinarian referral. Expect a responsible companion bird behavior consultant to refer you to an appropriate avian veterinarian if there is suspicion that health issues may be a factor.
- Expect to enjoy the interaction and to have your life touched in a significant way. It's not unusual for family members to weep with joy when they make a major breakthrough in the rehabilitation of a troubling parrot behavior problem. It is important to like and to trust professionals who work with your

bird—your life and your bird's life may be changed permanently.

Reinforcing Introduced Changes

A parrot behavior consultant seldom encounters birds that completely resist change. Most birds usually respond to predictable environmental or handling manipulations: environmental enrichment, better reward strategies, bathing, eye games, step-up training, petting, etc.

Consultants are often asked to modify what might be described as a "behavioral nightmare" on a bird called Satan, Freddie Kruger, or Dracula. The bird may be said to be so skittish that the owners fear it will thrash about and injure itself. Usually, the animal is "normal," perhaps stubborn but simply giving off incomprehensible messages. The bird may be poorly socialized or slightly socialized—possibly in an inappropriate or understimulating environment.

With professional sensitivity and behavioral techniques that have been around for years, most of the birds I see behave like little angels. Because the behavioral professional seldom sees the bird's worst behavior, the success of the intervention depends upon an effective partnership with owners (who are well aware of how the bird usually acts) serving as the primary mechanism for observing and reporting the bird's true behavior.

A behavior modification session, conducted in a calm but festive manner in the presence of shared food, verbal caresses, mists of water, silliness, and snuggly towel cuddling usually demonstrates, within a very short time, a responsive, cooperative animal. The owners are often stunned, moved to tears and comments that they "don't recognize" or "don't know" that creature responding so compliantly to tried and proven methods.

Are the Changes Permanent?

Possibly. Even step-ups are only a "quick-fix" when practiced solely by the behavior consultant. There is probably a window of opportunity of two to four days to reinforce changes made during the consultant's visit. If the bird returns to exactly the same physical and behavioral environment, its actions will return to what they were before.

For better or worse, few behavioral changes can be described as "permanent," for behavior evolves with time, changing—sometimes subtly, sometimes dramatically—over the years. Even changes in human behavior aren't usually "permanent" and most that become "permanent" start out "temporary."

Any human behavioral counselor, especially an addictions counselor, can tell you that the hardest change to bring about is the first one. A human counselor will also readily admit that just because someone discontinues a well-entrenched habit for one day or one week doesn't mean that behavior is permanently changed. On-going support and reinforcement are necessary to bring about real, long-term behavioral change.

Bird behavior isn't usually immediately "permanently" changed by intervention either, but the benefit of immediate changes being shown can influence humans who monitor and maintain the bird's environment. Because it is difficult to change human behavior, "quick fixes" used to demonstrate what a companion bird is capable of may be the best way to convince people that if they change their ways, the bird's behavior will also change. That's a bigger "IF" than it sounds. It's a real temptation to train the bird and stop, but if humans are not informed, ready, willing, and able; the intervention may be unsuccessful, even though the bird responded perfectly.

Chapter Ten

The Species: How Parrots Both Resemble and Differ from One Another

In the United States it's common to call a particular type of hookbill with a red tail a "Congo African grey" parrot. In other parts of the world, it might be called simply the "African grey parrot" or the "red-tailed" grey. Likewise, many parrots are commonly identified by one name in some countries and a different one in others. Combine that with the evolution of language—a word commonly used to name a particular parrot in 1888 might be uncommon in 2222—and you have a formula for confusion.

During the 1700s, a Swedish botanist named Linnaeus addressed this issue by assigning Latin names to all plants and animals. Since Latin is no longer spoken, Lannaeus' work resolved both the issue of different names in different places and the evolution of usage in a particular language from one century to another. It did not resolve all identification issues, however, for even Latin words may be spelled differently in different places and in different texts.

Linnaeus' system of taxonomy remains the most commonly accepted international method of differentiating living organisms. Plants and animals are grouped according to similarities into kingdom, phylum, subphylum,

African Grey parrot

class, order, family, genus, species, and subspecies.

For example, the African grey parrot is:

Kingdom	*animalia* (animal)
Phylum	*vertebrata* (having a spinal column)
Subphylum	*chordata* (having a spinal cord)
Class	*aves* (birds)
Order	*psittaciformes* (all hookbills, including cockatoos and lories)
Family	*psittacidae* (true parrots, neither cockatoos nor lories)
Genus	*Psittacus*
Species	*erithacus*
Subspecies	*erithacus*

Parrots are birds with a hooked upper beak usually bearing a characteristic notch, a mallet-shaped tongue, and four zygodactyls toes (two opposing two). Parrots with long tails are sometimes called "parakeets." Most parrots, also commonly called hookbills, are opportunistic omnivores, able to eat almost anything and to find food even in severe and limited environments.

Most parrots can survive only in areas in which particular nesting habitats occur. For the larger hookbills, this becomes increasingly difficult with the spread of deforestation. Most parrot species are cavity breeders, laying eggs and raising young inside hollowed-out cavities, usually tree trunks; large parrots need massive trees to accommodate themselves and their growing chicks. Of the full-sized macaws, all species are considered functionally extinct in the wild. Even though many large macaws still fly free, insufficient pairs and too-few nesting sites remain for their continuation into the next century.

Unlike baby chickens and geese, parrots hatch naked, blind, and helpless. Offspring are provided exceptional care and socialization. Mature offspring may delay reproduction to help parents raise younger siblings. This practice enables both those individuals and their younger siblings to access the particular skills required for survival. This characteristic of taking longer to achieve independence, though typical of more intelligent species, contributes to their vulnerability as juveniles, but enables their long-time survival, as past-breeding age elderly individuals are not uncommon.

In or Out?

While parrots remain treasured in art, entertainment, zoological collections, and, of course, our homes; they are usually considered unwelcome competitors for habitat when living wild outdoors. In spite of environmental laws and ecotourism, most species continue to decline. Island species are especially threatened, as most extinct parrots occupied geographically isolated habitats.

The ecological deterioration of islands is a preview of events to come as humans proliferate on this "island" earth. Today, numerous parrots are

CITES: The Washington Convention on International Trade in Exotic Species

While most ongoing threats to wild parrots relate to habitat loss or competition, trapping for the pet trade contributed to declining numbers in the past. In 1973, the Washington Convention on the International Trade of Wild Flora and Fauna negotiated a multinational treaty regulating trade in endangered species. The United States became a part of this group with passage of the Wildlife Conservation Act of October 23, 1992. Many plants and animals listed on CITES are neither endangered nor protected from *anything* except unrestricted trade.

threatened by introduced predators such as rats, cats, snakes, and, of course, humans—the most expansive animal. Most of the planet's resources are committed to benefiting the needs of 6,000,000,000+ humans.

Although many parrot species are threatened, endangered, or functionally extinct, some are simultaneously called "pests." No matter how rare or treasured to the pet owner, ornithologist, aviculturist (parrot breeder), biologist, artist, or naturalist, if a parrot lives wild and eats crops, it exists in conflict with humans. It's a NIMBY (not in my backyard) kind of thing. Even most species protected through CITES can be legally killed by farmers,

home owners, greenskeepers, landscape designers, power companies, or wind farms experiencing damage or interference from parrots.

The problem is especially apparent Down Under. A rose-breasted cockatoo baby might bring well over $2,000 in a North American pet store. Such a bird can expect a rich indoor environment, state-of-the-art diet, toys, medical care, and socialization processes supported by a huge network of humans who love companion parrots. The same baby bird, called a *galah* in Australia, faces a life of privation, untreated injury and illness, possible extermination, and a pest status similar to

Sulphur-crested cockatoo

Rose-breasted cockatoo

that of starlings or pigeons in the United States. While areas of parrot damage are described by scientists as "small and localized," marginal operations experiencing loss may be hard-hit on occasion. Nationally, economic damage caused by parrots is trivial when compared with the effects of weather, insects, disease, and fluctuations in commodity prices. Birds Australia Information Sheet #10 reports that destroying the birds would often be unnecessary if better agricultural policies and practices were implemented.

While Australia controls parrot damage by allowing their extermination, Argentina has taken a different tack. Since the 1980s, when trapping for the pet trade both increased and began to be restricted worldwide,

Argentina has continued to allow exportation of native parrots as a means of managing their numbers. Crop damage by blue-fronted Amazons, tucuman Amazons, and scaly-headed parrots is most commonly reported in citrus plantations where groves occupy valleys surrounded by forested mountains. Grain crops and other types of fruit trees are sometimes damaged by monk parrots,

> ". . . These galahs are going to eat my crop. The drought is bad enough without these bastards eating up the profits."
> Australian Farmer, *Parrots, Look Who's Talking*, Nature Video Library, 1995

blue-crowned conures, and Patagonian conures (also called the burrowing parrot). In Argentina, as in the United States, electrical transmission is said to be occasionally affected by monk parrot nests. Here, as in Australia, damage appears to be localized, often exaggerated, and may be incidental to poor agricultural practices.

Curiously, a few parrot species, including Quakers (*Myiopsitta monachus*), lovebirds (*Agapornis*), canary-winged beebees (*Brotogeris versicoloru*), African ringnecks (*Psittacula krameri*), green-cheeked Amazons (*Amazona viridigenalis*), lilac-crowned Amazons (*Amazona finschi*), and blue-crown (*Aratinga acuticaudata*), cherry-headed (*Aratinga wagleri*), and nanday (*Nandayus*) conures have managed to expand in range with human population. Although these parrots are occasionally introduced to agricultural areas, most are opportunistic inhabitants of urban settings where imported ornamental and tropical plants abound and few native birds remain.

The "Common" Companion Species

Like it or not, species proliferating in aviculture, including companion parrots, are the only parrots with a presumably bright future. Without legal protection, even their continued existence could be threatened. The following chapters list and discuss those birds that have been able to establish a beachhead in our homes. I have tried to define how the behavior as well as appearance of each species might be expected to differ from another.

This is not an easy task. Every parrot is an individual, and anyone wishing to predict a particular bird's actions based on type is wading into deep water. Many experienced aviculturists, veterinarians, pet industry representatives, behavior consultants, scientists, and ordinary pet parrot owners were consulted. If several people reported similar experiences with the same type of bird, then I felt that these events might also be observed by others.

Behavioral issues discussed from my perspective have been influenced by my professional experience. In 30 plus years of experience, I've not usually been invited to work with well-socialized, well-behaved birds, but rather, I'm usually called when something has gone wrong. For this reason, I have solicited contributions from professionals with different perspectives.

Physical characteristics—color, size, feather type, or the presence of a mobile crest—are more easily described than personality, intelligence, and behavior. With little hard science in these areas, I have had to rely on anecdotal reports. While some observations may seem arbitrary, they are usually assembled from the direct personal knowledge of very experienced individuals. I will endeavor to make a distinction between elements contributed by multiple sources and unique or isolated accounts.

Chapter Eleven
Old World Parrots

Parrots from Africa and Asia were, of course, the first to be historically documented, as Alexander the Great is said to have returned from his travels with the large, long-tailed parrot now bearing his name. Indeed, *Psittacula*, the ring-necked parrot or parakeet (so-called for its long tail) is the most widely distributed species, ranging from Africa east even into Pacific islands. Possibly a result of longer habitation by humans, this hemisphere bears fewer species and lesser populations of parrots than the New World and Pacific ranges. Most Old World species also inhabit areas with greater numbers of nonhuman predators, possibly contributing to the well-developed fight-or-flight response so prominent in the behavior of *Poicephalus*, especially.

African Greys

For centuries, the African grey parrot has been known for extreme intelligence, its ability to acquire human speech, and use words and sounds with association to their meaning. Treasured for its shining,

intelligent eyes, pastel gray scallops, and, often, bright red tail, the grey parrot breeds readily and is usually available anywhere parrots are kept as companions.

The larger subspecies called simply the "African grey," Congo, or red-tailed grey differs little from the smaller Timneh African grey parrots except in appaddenceance. Greater size and color variation exist among the red-tailed birds, which may be light silver or almost black depending upon point of origin, as the birds become gradually darker and smaller in ranges to the west of Africa. While they are not considered a separate subspecies, the smallest and darkest of the red-tailed greys is sometimes called the Cameroon or Ghana African grey, indicating its source. The red-tail's beak is solid black; while the usually smaller Timnehs can be easily differentiated by its horn-colored maxilla.

Like other intelligent (K-strategist) species—humans, chimpanzees, elephants, and whales—greys reproduce selectively and require years to reach intellectual and behavioral maturity rather than days, weeks, or months as do other (r-strategist) ani-

Two Indian ringneck parakeets

mals. Likewise, talking skills develop a little more slowly than some other parrots. Juveniles of both subspecies can be identified by their black eyes that fade to silver or yellow as the bird matures.

Both subspecies possess equal talking abilities, with some individuals exhibiting exceptional mimicking and communication skills. As with other parrots, greys achieve human speech without vocal cords. Sounds are produced when the bird forces air across the top of the trachea, a process resembling forced air across the top of a bottle. Sound variations are produced when the bird changes the shape of the trachea. This requires practice. A juvenile grey can be observed quietly muttering or "whispering" until it's confident enough to loudly produce sounds. While a particular youngster might learn a few words before it is weaned, the average grey acquires its first word at about 11–14 months.

Suggested wing trims for African grey parrots. Wing trim (A) is for particularly good flyers. (B) is for adults. (C) is for juveniles.

This might be at about 11–14 months of age, or it might be 11–14 months in a particular home. In my own experience, Timnehs appear to talk earlier than Congos and may be more inclined to do so in front of strangers.

The African grey must be protected from learning unpleasant human sounds such as squeals, squeaks, screeches, burps, belches, and worse. It must be sheltered from learning profanity, for this bird will probably outlive most early human companions and will say in its next home what it heard in the first. Greys must be protected from learning screaming from other parrots and barking from dogs. While they are entirely capable of and often willing to make some very obnoxious, attention-demanding sounds, they simply do not achieve the volume of their larger New World and Pacific Species cousins. An African grey parrot can drive the humans in the home crazy with annoying sounds, but those sounds are seldom loud enough to bother neighbors next door or down the block.

Grey parrots are typically cautious and quiet with strangers or in unfamiliar surroundings. Even a good-talking individual might take a little time—usually a few days or weeks—to begin vocalizing in a new home. As generations of greys are further and further from the wild, this is expected to change, as grey parrots bred for stolid disposition and talking ability appear obviously more interactive in all ways.

The grey's reputation for intelligence might also be linked to the bird's reputation as most "opinionated" birds for even if a particular grey does not talk, it will be exceptionally capable of communicating its preferences. Grey parrots are infamous behavioral martinets and gender chauvinists with a reputation for enforcing many environmental, dietary, and interactive preferences.

Extreme intelligence and sensitive temperament can combine to produce a surprising diversity of both wanted and unwanted behaviors in companion greys. "Creative," neurotic-seeming behaviors can appear suddenly, especially during the Developmental Period. In my three decades plus experience as a behavior consultant, cases involving African greys usually comprise more than half my regular ongoing case load.

Expect to treat a baby grey almost exactly as you would treat a child in the home with this exception: never punish the bird, especially with hitting, squirting, or dropping. Even "the Evil Eye" and "time-outs" can be too frightening for a sensitive grey parrot.

Clumsy and heavy-bodied, juveniles may be sensitive to falling incidents during the period in which personality develops. A newly weaned grey placed immediately into a spacious "adult" cage with slick, large-diameter perches, can easily develop fearfulness rather than coordination, confidence, and independence. Likewise, juvenile greys with sharp toenails and easily gripped perches develop more experimental and exploratory natures.

While tendencies toward aggression are expected, normal, and somewhat desirable, developing extreme and redundant fearfulness must be addressed immediately, as these can contribute to unwelcome stress reactions such as feather shredding.

During the first three to six months in the home, a handfed baby grey should be curious and eager to please. This is the juvenile Developmental Period sometimes called "the Honeymoon" Period. It is the period during which confidence gradually turns from approval seeking to independence and the instinct to dominate. It is an especially good time to avoid corporal punishment, for like human children, the African grey parrot has memory and is perfectly capable of holding a grudge. The bird must be patterned to appropriate behaviors by practice, reward, and repetition.

Green Senegal parrot

Poicephalus: Undiscovered African Treasures

Poicephalus are every bit as enjoyable as their showier relatives, the greys, cockatoos, Amazons, and macaws. These short-tailed African parrots are usually more behaviorally dependable than cockatoos, quieter than most Amazons, and more easily housed and accommodated than large macaws. *Pois* can be an excellent choice for anyone intimidated by larger birds. They are well suited as a "first" bird and usually complicated and interesting enough to retain a place when larger birds are added.

Poicephalus easily develop independence, especially independent play. They enjoy swings and other

acrobatic toys, foot toys, and foraging toys, and may become avid collectors, storing any loose objects in food or water bowls.

Of the ten species, seven can be found as companion parrots in North America. The smaller five *Poi* species—Senegals (*P. senegalus*), Meyers (*P. meyeri*), brown-heads (*P. cryptoxanthus*), red-bellies (*P. rufiventris*), and Jardine's (*P. gulielmi*)—are acrobatic little clowns that might lie on their backs and chew their toenails. They are famous escape artists, breaking out of (or into) even the most "bird-proof" enclosures. They love exploring drawers and snuggling into small spaces where they risk being crushed or suffocated.

Like several other genera, they are easily reinforced with laughter. The favorite human must carefully avoid giggling at unacceptable behavior, no matter how cute it is the first time it appears, for these birds can quickly learn to nip, then curse or squeal in imitation of human pain, followed by mimicking the exact laughter that reinforced the behavior.

Poicephalus have a reputation for developing heightened reactions, behaviors that can be expressed as either fearfulness or fearlessness, as many *Pois* go through both nippy and shy or cautious stages before becoming fully independent. Although they are sometimes totally fearless in the face of grossly larger creatures, they are also often terrified of the most mundane, nonthreatening inanimate objects such as rolled wrapping paper, balloons, or unfamiliar headgear.

The well-developed fight-or-flight response can result in fearfulness as a prominent part of a companion *Poi's* personality. Early patterning, sensitive and consistent handling, positive reinforcement, and planned environmental manipulations can be used to establish controlled, conscious behaviors rather than uncontrolled instinctual responses. Modern, domestic-raised *Poicephalus* parrots, especially red-bellies (*P. rufiventris*), are notably more stolid than the first few clutches raised from newly arrived wild-caught parents only a few decades ago.

Behind the red-tailed grey, the **Senegal** (*P. senegalus*) is the African parrot most commonly bred in captivity. These brightly colored clowns are known for acrobatics, mischevieousness, passion, and panic. They are, perhaps, the most intense in both color and disposition in this occasionally intense family.

The Senegal parrot's head is gray, topping a mostly green body with a breast and belly ranging in color from lime-yellow to deep orange. The body markings form a shallow or deep "V" pierced by a green point running down the breastbone.

Senegal hens seem notably shyer than most cocks. However, aggressive hens are not uncommon, nor are shy cocks. As with many other species, gender differences are often less noticeable than similarities. The safest, most dependable way to identify sex is with DNA sexing.

Pois share a reputation with African greys as the "quietest" (read here, "least loud") of the larger parrots. Their talking ability often outpaces their reputations as modest talkers, with occasional individuals developing large vocabularies. Although these birds speak in adorable little "doll-like" voices, and are well known to lack the volume of most other parrots, the intensity of a Senegal's "whistle/alarm" call can cause pain to some sensitive (especially male) human ears. Indeed, many companion Senegals obviously enjoy making annoying attention-demanding whistles and beeps (the phone, the microwave, the alarm clock).

Senegals may transition through a nippy phase and may also go through a fearful phase before reaching emotional independence at about two years of age. These birds may not form a strong bond with a permanent favorite human until after both nippy and fearful stages pass.

The **Meyer's parrot** (*P. meyeri*) has a reputation for docility, although they are probably not as uniform in behavior from bird to bird as the

cockatiel. Mostly taupe brown or warm gray tinged with yellow at the crown, thighs, bend of wing, and underwing coverts, it can also be strikingly beautiful as belly, rump, and underparts may range from vivid bluish green to almost pure blue. The beak is gray. The adult's eyes are bright red-orange; juveniles have brown eyes.

The **brown-head** (*P. cryptoxanthus*) has a grayish brown head and a mostly green body with bright yellow under the wings. The upper mandible is gray; the lower mandible is pale beige. The adult bird's eyes are yellow, but not always bright yellow. The juvenile's eyes are brown; the change to yellow is sometimes subtle. This bird looks a little like a Meyer's parrot without the yellow or turquoise and also shares its disposition. Both are said to be more exploratory and more experimental

than the Senegal parrot. Where Senegals have a tendency to favor a person, Meyer's and brown-heads may more easily maintain balanced interactions between multiple individuals. They're more interested in and willing to meet new people and explore new things. They're less likely to stay on or in the cage when unsupervised.

Both the brown-head and Meyer's moods are said to be more constant, usually showing less extremity in either aggression or shyness than the Senegal, Jardine's, or red-belly. Either can be an excellent choice for homes with sensitive, trainable children.

Neither the Meyer's nor the brown-head is known for exceptional talking ability, although they will pick up a few words and quite a few other sounds. With the Jardine's and red-bellies, they share a notable predisposition for whistling rather than talking. These birds make almost exclusively pleasant sounds.

Although they remain rare as companions, the **Jardine's parrot** (*P. gulielmi*) has enjoyed a steady rise in popularity along with a reputation for intelligence and congenial temperament. These birds are said to be capable of large vocabularies and of grey parrot-like accuracy in mimicry. Jardines are gifted whistlers and share the Senegal's reputation for a fascination with annoying sounds.

Famous for motionless calm, the Jardine's play has been described as lorie-like or caique-like. The Jardine's mood can turn in an instant from absolutely still (except perhaps a subtlely pinpointing iris) to tumbling rowdiness.

Jardines are enthusiastic bathers, easily learning to enjoy human-provided mist showers. Although the "real" human shower is usually too forceful and scary for any *Poicephalus*, including the Jardine, almost any *Poi* might enjoy sitting on a high perch or shower rod and being misted with a water bottle as humans shower.

Jardines enjoy a reputation as most stolid of temperament, being reportedly less inclined to the fight-or-flight response than some of their cousins, notably the red-bellied parrot. However, the Jardine's parrot can learn to bite with enthusiasm. They can be stubborn and extremely focused.

Most *Pois*, but especially Jardines, are said to go through a "teething" or nipping stage (during the first year in the home), during which the beak-on-skin activity has sometimes been described as mild "beaking" and sometimes "excruciatingly painful." However, even one bird that was called a "monster" during its nippy phase, ultimately learned more productive "love sponge" behavior.

Senegals, Jardines, and red-bellies are given mixed reviews regarding their suitability for children. Some children do extremely well with them; some do not. It might be best to separate bird and children if either are going through difficult transitions.

African red-bellied parrot

The **red-bellied parrot** (*P. rufiventris*) possesses brownish gray upper parts with green lower parts and a wash of blue over the rump. They are sexually dimorphic, with cocks having a deep orange breast, abdomen, and underwing coverts. Hens have a delightful tinge of iridescent red highlights over green in these parts. The beak is completely black. Cocks have a wash of orange on the cheeks. The adult bird's eyes are bright red-orange; the juvenile's eyes are brown. Some juvenile red-bellies resemble hens, the majority resemble cocks, while some juveniles have dimorphic colors in their fledging feathers.

With the widespread use of modern hand-feeding techniques, the red-belly's popularity has skyrocketed, as wild-caught pairs have adjusted to captivity and produced calmer, bolder, and more interactive offspring. Hen red-bellies, especially, enjoy a loud, vocal following of loyal fans; however, Jean Pattison and

"Uncape" parrot

other experienced aviculturists report little difference between male and female red-bellies as companions.

Poicephalus, especially red-bellies and shyer individuals of any subspecies, are reported to appreciate the advantages of a hide box. This might be simply a towel over one end of the cage; it might be one of those little fabric tents; or it might mean cage placement behind a plant.

Red-bellies and Jardines share a reputation as best talkers of the *Poicephalus* family.

Uncommon as companions at this writing, the golden-headed **Cape** (*P. robustis*) and brownish gray-headed **"uncape"** (*P. fuscicollis*) parrots are the largest of the *Poicephalus* parrots. Although they are only 7 to 14 ounces (250 to 400 grams), they can seem as large as an African grey parrot. The more-common *fuscicollis* head is tinged sometimes with silver,

sometimes with red. A wash of red over the neck gives the bird its common name, the brown-necked parrot. Hens are slightly brighter with a well-defined area of poppy on the forehead. Cocks may have some less-defined poppy on the forehead. Both adult and juvenile eyes are dark brown.

In captivity, these birds share much behavior with their smaller *Poicephalus* cousins, but because of their size, shape, and unique gait may seem more "goofy" than "acrobatic." They love playing upside down, both hanging and swinging and on their backs in owner's hands and on the floor. Both Capes and uns are sometimes fascinated by their feet. They are crazy for nuts, may be prone to caution, and enjoy hiding behind a bird-safe plant where they can see but not be seen. These larger *Pois* can be very loud, but dependable of disposition, with individuals rarely forming problematic bonds.

Agapornis: The Lovebirds

Three of the species of lovebirds (*Agapornis*), the smallest of the short-tailed African parrots, have long been bred in captivity both in Europe and in the United States, developing numerous color mutations. However, their role and suitability as human companions has been less thoroughly studied. Unlike an aviary pair, a companion lovebird bonds to humans rather than to its own kind. In many respects this arrangement works out very well, because the relationship between two lovebirds can turn hostile in a blink. In fact, even their common name, "lovebird," could be called an oxymoron, a word that contradicts its own true meaning.

The development of strong bonding behaviors in lovebirds is often accompanied by the development of aggression, abandonment anxiety, breeding stress, and other difficult behavioral issues. In pairs these tiny parrots seem to exaggerate their larger cousins' behavior. They are exceptionally territorial and able to inflict painful damage to both human and avian skin. Especially, lovebirds seem to become easily fixated on an individual, object, or location and to defend them with excessive devotion. This tendency to extreme bonding can also work to the disadvantage of a pair, for bonding or attempts to bond are sometimes accompanied by "spousal" abuse.

The difference between a solitary companion lovebird and a breeding pair can be striking. Keeping pairs and facilitating their reproduction — aviculture — is a bona fide hobby. Keeping a single lovebird is more like a love affair between human and bird, for no other parrot seems to bond as strongly to a person, a toy, a location, a toaster, a hair dryer, a stapler, or any other shiny object, as *Agapornis*.

Peach-faced lovebird

There's a huge difference between breeding lovebirds and companion lovebirds. Their socialization is different. Their behavior is different. Companion lovebirds cannot be expected to retain any companionability if another lovebird is introduced. They must be kept individually. A human bonded lovebird can turn murderous if a lovebird intruder enters the scene.

Genetics, too, as well as environment and socialization, are significant in the development of companion or avicultural lovebird behavior. Aviculturists specialize in producing birds for particular genetic goals: some lovebirds are produced for color, some (companion) lovebirds are produced for genetic predisposition to

good disposition. The former lovebirds are parent raised; the latter are usually hand-fed by humans.

Many breeders believe that companion lovebirds are best removed from parents before their eyes open. Sensitive hand-feeding is a must. Ideally, babies are kept singly both during hand-feeding and after weaning. When purchasing a baby lovebird and waiting for it to wean, resist the temptation to ask that weaning be hurried along. As with larger parrots, careful, bird-paced weaning is more likely to produce a bird that stays tame. Healthy, well-handled lovebirds usually wean between six and ten weeks old. Birds requiring longer to wean appear to have a better chance of remaining tame as adults. Hand-fed lovebirds probably have the best chance to remain tame if they go to their new homes within a month after weaning.

Toys are not optional. If the bird is to remain tame, it must fill its hours with appropriate activities, not sit around storing up energy to make everybody nuts. A generous number of diverse, appropriately sized toys, both destructible and indestructible, provide opportunities to "blow off steam" (express energy that might otherwise come out as aggression). Lovebirds provided with tiny foot toys before weaning are more likely to develop both foot toy play and foot food holding.

The bird must have opportunities to play alone, developing confidence by engaging in self-rewarding behaviors. If a human is the only

"toy" a lovebird plays with, expect to see escalating territorialism, bonding-related aggression, and other unwanted behavioral issues. Especially, the lovebird must have something to "beat up," preferably a toy. Often a bell or other noise-generating device, this can become both a surrogate enemy and mate, being the object of the bird's most hostile and most intimate aggressions.

Maintaining tameness in a solitary, hand-raised lovebird is no different than it is with most other types of solitary hand-raised parrots. However, taming a lovebird is more difficult, and retaming a lovebird that has been allowed to go wild is very, very difficult.

As with larger parrots, daily practice of the interactive routines maintains cooperation, although step-up practice is unnecessary for the maintenance of confidence, as most lovebirds are bold beyond all understanding. Step-up practice should meticulously include handling with perches, for many devoted, long-time lovebird humans pick up their mature lovebirds with hand-held perches only, not hands.

Prevent the bird from developing chasing behaviors by removing it from the cage to service the cage. That is, whenever feeding, cleaning, or changing accessories, first remove the bird to a chair back or play perch. If a lovebird learns that hands will "jump" or "run away" when they are bitten and chased, it might learn to create drama by chasing other pets and humans. If a lovebird charges, with head feathers ruffled and beak open, with obvious intent to bite, it must be distracted from the attack, possibly with a loud "HEY!" clapping, slapping a rolled newspaper on a table, or creating a barrier between the bird and victim. Then some appropriate behavior may be stimulated, possibly step-ups with verbal reminders to "Be a good bird."

As with all parrots, positive reinforcement rather than punishment is the only effective means of ensuring long-term cooperation. While yelling *"No," "Don't,"* or *"Stop"* can momentarily interrupt an activity or intended action, reminding a bird to *"Be a good bird!"* more effectively prompts for appropriate behavior that can then be reinforced.

If a lovebird is becoming too territorial at home, try rearranging and moving the cage and play areas. Occasional outings where the bird is handled by sensitive, astute strangers can be used to manipulate bonding behaviors, improve patterning, and lower territorialism.

Trick training is an excellent means for continuing to reinforce cooperative behavior and preventing the development of inappropriate behavior. Any activities that are not annoying to humans, unsafe, or unhealthy for the bird may be reinforced to "fill" the behavioral environment with appropriate behaviors. Bathing, searching for hidden food (foraging), and chewing wood and paper can approximate some of what the bird would be doing in the wild.

Lovebirds *love* water and have been observed to drink more than other small parrots such as parakeets. They like to bathe and "play" in water and often fill the water bowl with trash. Because of their extreme curiosity and activity, lovebirds are inordinately vulnerable to accidents involving water: drowning in a toilet, half-full glass, or undrained tub.

They are fascinated by any tiny space they can crawl into, so they are also prone to accidents involving enclosed spaces such as drawers, dryers, and microwaves. They are especially happy to crawl inside heavy sleeves, and more than one hapless lovebird has been taken home from a party in a coat left in a pile on a bed.

Fisher's and peach-faced lovebirds

As with many other small companion parrots, adult lovebirds die more often in household accidents, especially those related to flying, than illness. Meticulous, up-to-date wing feather trims are an absolute necessity if a companion lovebird is to live to a ripe old age. A bonded companion lovebird wants nothing more than to be absolutely next to that favorite human. They have a tendency to "follow too closely," making them easy to step on, sit on, roll over on, or slam in a door or drawer. Flighted lovebirds are often struck down by ceiling fans and also suffer danger of escape as well as danger of being fried, flushed, "nuked," or yoga'd.

There is no cavity too small for a lovebird to try to explore, no enemy too large to be challenged. These are definitive behaviors of this incredible little feathered dragon. They are a major part of the mystery and enchantment of the lovebird. Discerning owners of companion lovebirds both correct for and exploit these behaviors daily for happy effect.

Peach-faced lovebirds (*Agapornis roseicollis*) are the largest, heartiest, and usually the easiest to keep tame. They seem obsessed with puncturing the edges of any paper they can reach, ripping off the edge as a strip, then stuffing it like streamers into their rump feathers. This is a remnant of wild behavior, for like Monk parakeets (*Myopsyttia monachus*), the peach-faced lovebird is a builder, although its nests are assembled inside cavities rather than free standing.

Brilliantly colored **Fisher's lovebird** (*Agapornis fischeri*) are differentiated by their white eyerings and bright red beaks. Fisher's are neither as hearty, nor as large as peach-faced lovebirds. They have a reputation for being more aggressive, and in companion settings have been known to kill intruding lovebirds, especially peach-faced ones.

The popular blue-masked lovebird is a mutation of the **black-masked lovebird** (*Agapornis personatus*) with a reputation for being both more docile and more fragile than the normal-colored bird. Both have a light horn-colored beak and breed well in captivity.

The Regal Ringnecks

Another of the birds previously considered "aviary" birds, ringneck parakeets have gradually worked their way indoors. In the last 20 years, we have seen an amazing influx of these elegant birds hand-fed and introduced to the living room. From the beginning, reports of companion ringnecks were glowing, with a surprising number of even first-generation hand-feds learning huge vocabularies. Their voices are clear; they are beautiful, and charming, and breed readily in captivity. Although they are not yet exactly common in most parts of the country, with proper management, ringnecks just might turn out to be one of the most popular companion birds of the next millennium.

Although the rose-ringed species, the most common, have a reputation for easily changeable personalities, we hear more uniform stories about

Mustached and ringneck parakeets

other members of the family. Especially common these days are stories of Alexandrine ringnecks, and their mostly gentle nature and uniform treatment of humans. This is not a bird that will attack all but the chosen human. While it will exhibit an obvious preference for a particular human, this nonpair bond species easily develops relationships with multiple humans, making it an excellent family bird.

A ringneck may not be a good choice for someone with little time for interaction, as most ringnecks must be handled frequently in order to remain trusting of humans. Although ringnecks do not typically enjoy petting, they often greatly enjoy hugging and enthusiastic face-to-face interactions. Most ringnecks don't like to have anybody or anything touch their

Cochise

Cochise, an Indian ringneck hen, came to us in 1998. Her favorite toys are those little cat toy balls with bells in them. She not only loves them; she worships them!

After arranging her balls along the edge of her playgym and properly bowing, cooing, and clucking at them, she ambushes them like a child knocking off toy soldiers! She then jumps up onto the edge of the gym and looks down to make sure she "killed" the ball.

When given those "dead" balls back, she picks them up with either foot or beak and beats them into submission before placing them on the edge of her playgym to start the "worship-and-kill" game all over!

Betsy Lott

long, elegant tails. Indeed, it can make a ringneck quite skittish for people to be constantly trying to touch its tail. (Unlike macaws that actually seem to like some types of tail play.)

With their long graceful tails, smooth, glossy feathers, and delicate markings, ringnecks can be called the most elegant of parrots. Well, "elegant" is a relative term when applied to a bird, for even these most ornamental of parrots can be goofy, too.

Lutino ringneck parakeet

Ringnecks like dancing and "mugging" and communicating with body language rather than with actual physical contact. They will posture and stretch and crane their necks in approximate mimicry of humans playing passive posture games with them.

Ringnecks usually develop neither bonding nor territorial aggression, though they may be "fear nippers" or "annoyance nippers" that apply beak to flesh only with the intention of getting the flesh to go away. Indeed, the ringneck personality can be cautious to the point of skittishness. Most companion ringnecks prefer some kind of readily available shelter, whether that accessible "safe place" is a cage with the door open, a little tent or hide box, the favorite person's shoulder, or maybe a plant or huge toy to hide behind. A ringneck might consistently turn its back or keep a visual barrier between it and a person or situation it dislikes.

Ringnecks are swift and agile flyers; they are especially sensitive to loud sounds such as firecrackers, and must have wing feathers trimmed to prevent household accidents. It's a good idea to keep the windows and curtains nearest the ringneck's cage closed during times when fireworks might be expected. Ringnecks have occasional night frights like cockatiels and benefit from being covered and having a night light.

Ringnecks are visually dimorphic at sexual maturity, usually two to three years. Nancy Newman reports that both sexes make good compan-

Ringneck parakeet

ions, although I see these birds as sort of resembling eclectus and lovebirds in that females can be expected to be at least as aggressive as males.

Ringnecks can be accomplished talkers, developing large, understandable vocabularies. They will more easily talk in public and around strangers than many other types of parrots, especially the red-tailed African greys.

The ringneck's long tail makes it necessary to have a larger cage than might otherwise be given to a bird of this weight. The bird must be able to avoid hitting the tail on the side of the cage every time it turns around. Also, a ringneck should have enough room to comfortably sit on the bottom perch without its tail touching the bottom of the cage.

Suggested wing trim for ringnecks. (A) is for adults. (B) is for juveniles.

(A)
(B)

The **rose-ringed African** and **Indian ringnecks** (*Psittacula krameri kermeri* and *P. k. manillensis*) are best known for their bright red beaks and for the ring of red or pink edged in black and pale blue that encircles the mature male's neck. The rose-ringed species has a reputation for being the most difficult in which to maintain human interactive behaviors.

The **Alexandrine ringneck** (*Psittacula eupatria*) is a generally considered docile bird with the potential to develop a large vocabulary. While this bird can make very loud noises, this is usually in indication that the bird's need are not being met; Alexandrines are not prone to screaming for the joy of it. They are large for a parakeet and have extremely long tails. They need a large cage; a cage that is at least 24 inches wide by 24 inches deep (61 × 61 cm) is necessary to comfortably house this bird.

The **plum-headed parakeet** (*Psittacula cyanocephala*) is about the size of a cockatiel. The male has a purplish red head while the female and juveniles have a gray/violet head. This bird has a reputation for staying more easily tame than the rose-ringed parakeets. The plum-head's voice is pleasant, chattery. This species is not as loud as the larger members of this group.

Chapter Twelve
New World Parrots

Perhaps because of humans' "recent" arrival to the "New" world, more parrot species populate the Western Hemisphere than either the "Old" World or Pacific Islands. Likewise, lesser predation as well as greater nutritional and nesting opportunities have resulted in species that are, for the most part, bolder, louder, and more colorful than their African "cousins." Even one Western species—*Myiopsittia monachus* (the monk parakeet)—repeatedly adapts to new habitat, while so many others falter, flourishing world-wide in human cities.

The Magnificent Macaws

With elegantly elongated wing and tail feathers, macaws may be accurately called both majestic and goofy, as few creatures come close either to their beauty or comical natures. Part of that description relates to their distinctive facial markings not unlike the exaggerated tracery of grease paint on the face of an opera star. Like human fingerprints,

the patterns of tiny remnant facial feathers along lines of circulation are unique to each macaw. Bare facial areas, usually white, leatherlike patches, probably evolved to keep oil from damaging feathers resulting from the birds' opportunistic, sometimes carnivorous, eating habits. This unique feature also allows a glimpse into the birds' emotions as the skin can be seen to blush red with physical stimulation, excitement, or possibly even "embarassment."

Infamously adaptable, macaws are well known for learning or improvising new behaviors and teaching them to successive generations. This serves them well both outdoors and in the living room.

Macaws reproduce in greater numbers in captivity than in the wild where nest sites are increasingly unavailable. Some species such as hyacinth and Buffon's macaws exist in greater numbers indoors than in the wild. Because of availability, prices have never been (relative to the economy) lower. Although some macaws discussed here are relatively uncommon as companions at this time, they have been included

Beyond *Ara*

Although all macaws were once labled *Ara*, they are now divided into six genera:

Ara, including the blue-and-gold, scarlet, and greenwing,

Prophyrrhura, the yellow-collar,

Diopsittaca, the red-shoulder or noble,

Anodorhynchus, the hyacinth and nearly extinct Lear's,

Orthopsittaca, the red-belly, and

Cyanopsitta, the extremely rare spix macaw.

because they appear exceptionally prolific in captivity. If present trends continue, red-bellies, red-fronted, and hyacinth macaws will become increasingly available.

While wild flocks are usually limited to relatively small family groups, these birds are extremely social and, as companions, macaws will seek out humans in the home if possible. Wing-trimmed birds simply go to the floor and walk around looking for people or other pets. This can be dangerous if other pets are larger and predatory. Many macaws love cuddling and snuggling, and because they are such adorable babies, it's easy for a young macaw to develop attention-demanding behaviors if it misses the window-of-opportunity for the development of independence. Step-ups, fetch, and active play involving wing flapping rather than constant snuggling will help the bird to develop confidence rather than obnoxious attention-demanding behaviors.

Macaws are nothing if not dramatic, as many love to lunge at new acquaintances, rarely biting, but rather bluffing to observe human responses and finding great enjoyment in flamboyant reactions. If a macaw that doesn't bite is rewarded with drama: an "ouch," an "eek," and a jump, when it lunges or pretends to bite, it will continue *not* biting. Likewise, a bird biting for a drama reward can be trained not to bite by disallowing opportunities to bite and providing drama rewards for behaviors other than biting.

Chewing is both an exercise and a natural expression of sexual behavior to the macaw, a cavity breeder. This is not optional. If a macaw is denied access to destructible, appropriate chewables, it will chew anything it can reach: perches, cage bars, picture frames, woodwork, computer keyboards, cables, or even its own feathers. Interesting appropriate objects to chew should be within ready reach. Objects that should not be chewed must be well out of reach.

Use special care when introducing branches with bark to macaws, as these birds may be extremely sensitive, especially to both the fruit (acorns) and bark of oak trees. Kashmir Csaky reports that oak sensitivity is common in hyacinth macaws and Dave Flom has reported it in blue-and-golds. Allergic reactions by macaws to dust (including cockatoo feather dust), pollen, and potent fragrances have also been documented.

Large macaws (and cockatoos) have the longest potential life span of all companion parrots. It's a mixed blessing. A bird that lives almost 100 years will certainly require multiple homes during that lifetime. Fortunately, also like cockatoos, macaws easily adjust to appropriate new environments and can often be effectively resocialized at well-advanced ages. I have seen very old macaws that had not interacted with humans in decades settle in to become treasured household companions. The macaw is the epitome of that oft-repeated adage: "You can teach an old bird new tricks."

Except for longevity, loudness is the quality most often associated with home changes. The larger birds, the hyacinth and the green-wing, have booming voices that have been described as able to "wake the dead." However, some of the larger macaws are less frequent and less annoying screamers than many smaller parrots, especially *Aratinga* and nanday conures.

Flapping is extremely important to healthy companion macaws. This is surely a replacement behavior for their wild activity of flying many, many miles to forage far away from nest sites. In companion settings where household dangers lurk at

Facial "Baldness"

Exercise is especially beneficial in maintaining skin health. I have seen facial feathers regrow on older macaws placed on conditioning programs that included daily flapping exercises. The birds were encouraged to hold onto human hands and flap until they were just slightly winded, a condition that in macaws is accompanied by blushing. As endurance improved with practice, tiny new feathers began to reline the once almost bare face patches. Facial feathers on scarlet macaws are usually white or very pale red and not as noticeable as those of other macaws. Illger's, nobles, and yellow-collar macaws have bare face patches.

every turn, wing feathers are best kept trimmed and absolutely up to date.

The **hyacinth macaw** (*Anodorhynchus hyacinthinus*) is the largest of the companion macaws. At this time, I would not call the hyacinth a "common" companion parrot, however, as it is still extremely expensive, both to purchase and to maintain. Hyacinths as well as the rarer members of the genius *Ancorohynchus*, the almost extinct Lear's and glaucus macaws, are the only macaws that have neither a bare face patch nor a uropygial gland.

Hyacinths are natural acrobats, with a reported love of running, hopping, and even somersaults. Kashmir Csaky even reports seeing one of her baby hyacinths chase her own tail. Like greys, hyacinths are sometimes seen to dig in corners. Because of their extreme size and strength, hyacinths need specially fabricated caging (be sure a particular cage is guaranteed for a hyacinth, not just for a macaw) and a veterinarian with hyacinth experience.

The **greenwing macaw** (*Ara cholroptera*) is the largest macaw that can reasonably be called "common." The greenwing has a reputation for easy disposition, good-talking ability, great beauty, and for being mechanically inclined (they can completely dismantle some cages). Especially appealing are the delicately traced lines in tiny red feathers on the white face patch. So appealing are these lines that in art, especially commercial and product art, when we can often see from the facial feathers that what is supposed to be a scarlet macaw, is often a greenwing macaw with the green patch on the wing depicted in yellow.

This giant bird needs lots of exercise, lots of handling, and lots of chewing materials to maintain good disposition. The greenwing macaw can be a surprisingly active bird as well as a willing talker. It has an extremely loud voice, and will use it when necessary. Disposition may be maintained with little difficulty in young birds and during the breeding years, but these birds have a reputation for being really, really nice when they are much older.

Scarlet and greenwing macaws

While Dianalee Deter jokingly calls the **scarlet macaw** (*Ara macao*) "the only bird worth having," it is also one of the most maligned and misunderstood parrots. Whether the bird's highly debated disposition is a matter of nature or nurture, it is infamously sensitive, and sensitivity evokes response. Liz Wilson reports that many people so fear scarlets that they "react differently" in their presence. Understimulation, especially an understimulating environment, combined with a love of drama and of watching humans scream and jump, easily produces a bird that nips or even bites for the fun of it. My own scarlet macaw is sweet, dependable, and 100 percent predictable.

The **blue-and-gold macaw** (*Ara ararauna*) is the most common and, perhaps, the most evenly disposed of all macaws. With a reputation for clear speech, more than one blue-and-gold has been said to learn and use a word, sound, or phrase with association after hearing it on only one occasion. They adapt easily to their surroundings and become comfortable enough to breed. The blue-and-gold macaw has a reputation for being easy to socialize or resocialize at almost any age.

My personal favorite, the **military macaws** (*Ara militaris*) are surely the most underappreciated of the readily available macaws. While their colors may appear unexciting from the front, one glimpse from the other direction reveals a breathtaking brilliant turquoise rump and burgundy wing and tail feathers accentuating the bright green body. Amazingly inexpensive and easily available, both as babies and second-hand adults—an especially favorable situation for a first-time would-be macaw owner, militaries can be physically interactive, even when not actually touching.

Military macaw

Red-fronted macaw

Look for a characteristic goofy craning head maneuver ending with one eye prominently and expressively advanced. Like the scarlet macaw, militaries love drama, and can go through (apparent) nippy phases if boredom is allowed to persist or if minimal needs for interaction are unmet.

The great green or **Buffon's macaw** (*Ara ambigua*) is extremely rare and frequently mistaken for the (smaller) military macaw, which it resembles. Both greens and blues are notably lighter than the military, with tail tending to predominant red-orange rather than burgundy.

The **red-fronted macaw** (*Ara rubogenys*) remains uncommon, but breeds well in captivity. While other neonatal macaws usually just slump over and sleep wherever they are, whether near a sibling or not, gregarious nestling red-fronts reportedly wrap their little bodies around each other like yin and yang.

Only slightly smaller, the **red-bellied macaw** (*Orthopsittaca manilata*) is known generally for its pleasing disposition. Although still unusual in companion settings, this macaw remains well populated in the wild. The natural calls of the red-bellied macaw sound a little like a small child. They have sweet voices and are great talkers. Cuddly and not so rowdy as some other macaws, survivability was poor in early captive populations because of misunderstandings about nutritional needs. With a natural diet exclusively of palm fruit, red-bellies have a greater need for vitamin A (beta carotene) and a lesser need for oil than other macaws.

The **severe** or **chestnut-fronted macaw** (*Ara severa*) is a most easily accommodated size, maybe 12 to 16 ounces (350–450 grams), but retains the glamour, fun, and excitement of its larger "cousins." With a reputation resembling a scarlet, this intelligent little bird needs lots of exercise (including showers), environmental stimulation, and consistent handling to remain a good companion. In spite of its small size, this bird has a shrill voice that may be perceived by some as more annoying than a larger macaw, and because it may express extreme bonding preferences, may not be the best choice for families with children.

Yellow-collar macaw

The popular **yellow-collar macaw** (*Prophyrrhura auricollis*) is a fine choice for anyone craving the qualities of a full-sized macaw without the huge space and maintenance demands. They can be good talkers, acquiring a ready variety of understandable words. Although they tend to develop strong bonds with favorite people, places, and things, they can easily be taught to talk for attention rather than scream for it. Also often highly underrated macaws, these birds are famously adaptable and able to learn new things, including words used with association at almost any age.

In spite of its small size, the **Hahn's** or **noble macaw** (*Diopsittaca nobilis*) enjoys a reputation for

extremely good, possibly the best, talking of the group. Except for its definitive bare face patch, this bird physically resembles the blue-crowned conure (*Aratinga acuticaudata*). In fact, when imports were allowed into the United States, unsuspecting tourists had been sold

Hahn's macaw

blue-crowned conures with plucked facial patches as Hahn's macaws. Quite a con, considering that a typical Hahn's usually costs at least twice as much as a blue-crowned conure.

The Amazing Amazons

These short-tailed, heavy-bodied birds are what most people think of when they hear the word "parrot." Intelligent, beautiful, mischevious, they are well suited to those who like a little "vinegar" in their greens. They are behaviorally predictable (sometimes predictably unpredictable), with expressive mannerisms enabling a reasonably observant human to know exactly what to expect.

These primarily green birds are talkative, adaptable, and rarely shy. Few birds relish "rainfall" (provided indoors by caring humans) more than Amazons, as an Amazon enjoying a shower gets sillier as it gets wetter. Indeed, Amazons denied access to rainfall frequently become truculent, as disposition and feather quality decline.

Amazons are recreational eaters, being plagued by problems related to obesity probably more than any other health issues. Overweight older Amazons risk cardiovascular, foot, and feather disorders as they become increasingly sedentary. Amazons, more than any other companion parrot should not be free fed; rather, they must be fed limited amounts on a schedule and learn other activities for daily entertainment.

Amazons are famous mimics, with an attraction to high-pitched "feminine" voices, including singing voices, and words said with great enthusiasm. President Andrew Jackson's yellow-headed Amazon, Poll, was removed from his funeral for cussing.

An Amazon will usually let humans know, in no uncertain terms, when something is wrong, either with their voices or with their disposition. A bored Amazon might scream for attention and then bite when it is picked up. This may not be aggression, but rather simply little "punishments" for "neglect." While hand-fed baby Amazons usually arrive in their first homes tame, their Developmental Period may be more noticeable than that of any other parrot, as even well-patterned juveniles may transition through a nippy phase somewhere around 9–12 months of age. With careful socialization including prepatterning to step-ups, handheld perches, and towel games, this

Suggested wing trims for Amazons. (A) is for adults. (B) is for juveniles.

The "African" Amazon

When asked to provide a parrot for the opera "Amahl and the Night Visitors," I ran into an unexpected casting complication. Although I had provided a choice of African parrots, the director insisted on *his notion* of a parrot—a stocky green bird. I was unable to convince him that an Amazon parrot, from Central or South America, could not have participated in an event that took place more than a century before Europeans knew of the existence of the New World. My yellow-naped Amazon, Portia, played the part of a parrot attending the birth of Jesus.

White-fronted Amazon

"terrible-twos"-like behavior may be virtually unnoticeable or might pass quickly.

The **orange-wing** (*Amazona amazonica*)—most common of all Amazons in the wild—was once called "the poor man's Amazon," being the least expensive and most easily accessible of the Amazons imported into the United States. They are charming characters with unique, adorable mannerisms, especially "shadow boxing," in which the feathers of the neck and cheeks are held erect in a "hawk-headlike" position while the bird stabs at a shadow on the wall or other imaginary enemy. During the times that these birds were imported, they were not known as great talkers, and since the 1992 ban in avian imports, the availability

has plummeted as aviculturists preferred to facilitate breeding of more expensive parrots. Domestic birds should be both good talkers and evenly disposed although they are parrots, and all parrots pursue their own agenda from time to time. The orange-winged Amazon has a reputation for being especially good with children.

The smallest of the common companion Amazons, the **white-front** (*Amazona albifrons*) is sometimes erroneously called the "spectacled" Amazon in the United States. This unusual Amazon is sexually dimorphic, with a small patch of wing feathers known as the alula being red in mature males and green in mature females and most juvenile birds.

White-fronts share a reputation with yellow-napes for mischief, noise, and a willingness to nip. Like the

cise provided by a larger than usual cage or flight. Males may be nippier from time to time, mostly during breeding season. Females seem generally less extroverted and quieter than males. Except for the occasional development of loud calls, behavioral complaints are unusual.

The brilliantly colored **blue-fronted** (*Amazona aestiva xanthopteryx* and *A.a. aestiva*) Amazon's reputation probably resembles that of the little girl with the curl in the middle of her forehead, for when they're good, they're very, very good, and when they're bad, they're horrid. I have seen docile mature adults, and aggressive neonates in this species. Most, however, seem to resemble their African relatives, *Poicephalus* and *Psittacus*, with an observable degree of cautiousness sometimes contributing to aggression in some birds' personalities. Hens are probably slightly less likely to develop extreme terratorialism than cocks, but extremely territorial hens are sometimes observed.

blue-fronts, the white-fronts have a reputation for being a little more reactionary than larger Amazons. They are active and benefit from the exer-

Yellow-headed Amazons (*Amazona ochrocephala oratrix*) are known for their great beauty and talking ability. Though highly prized, prices should remain relatively low, for these Amazons reproduce most readily of all Amazons incaptivity, adjust easily to new homes, and can remain problem free for years. I have seen birds that were confined to the same small cage for decades blossom under the efforts of new owners who began to include the birds more extensively in daily activities.

Famous for their vocal abilities, these birds love operatic voices, especially soprano and tenor. They easily learn arias, though both words and melody may be improvised and much poetic license taken.

Most common behavioral issues are screaming and biting, usually seasonal. Good behavior can be best maintained by patterning to hand-held perches so that the birds can be handled during seasonal phases. Yellow-heads can become extremely overbonded and territorial, sometimes attacking all but the most-favored human. Females can be as excitable and protective of their mate/human as males. This tendency is much more easily controlled than the same tendency in yellow-napes, but the birds should be considered dangerous on the shoulder.

The intelligent, feisty **yellow-naped Amazon** (*Amazona ochrocephala auropalliata*) is sometimes called the "créme de la créme" of this very desirable family. This bird is the epitome of the feathered "dragon," as most yellow-napes need to "breathe a little fire" every now and again. Both males and females can be extremely territorial. Like yellow-heads, napes love to sing opera.

The large **mealy Amazons** (*Amazona farinosa*) are sometimes called "gentle giants," although their giant beaks can deliver giant bites. Like cockatoos and African greys, a healthy mealy will have powder on its feathers. They are both the loudest and the mellowest of this behaviorally varied family. The five sub-

Red-lored Amazon

species are mostly green with some being plain, some with red, yellow, blue, or a wash of lavender on the head. These birds can be louder than cockatoos. Calls are occasionally punctuated with a mulelike bray.

The stocky **red-lored** or **yellow-cheeked Amazon** (*Amazona autumnalis*) is known for loyalty and are very loyal to humans in their "flock," although the number of humans accepted by the bird may be limited. Curious and energetic, these birds can be good talkers, but they can be very loud and territorial. As with mealys, the red-lored's disposition is often so good that volume is readily tolerated by doting owners. Deter suggests that domestically raised red-loreds are not as noisy as their imported predecessors. Both male and female birds may be cuddly,

issue occurring primarily during breeding season.

The small, slender-bodied **green-cheeked Amazon** (*Amazona virigenalis*) is sometimes called the "Mexican Red-head," a name indicating source. More active than the similarly colored lilac crowns, these birds can be extremely affectionate and interactive but have a reputation for overbonding and for dominating younger or shorter family members. However, in my experience, a green-cheeked Amazon is just as likely to favor the youngest, smallest child and treat everybody else like a rival. Dispositions and personalities can be extremely variable.

The achingly beautiful **lilac-crowned Amazon** (*Amazona finschi*) is generally considered quieter, gentler, and less exuberant than the green-cheek it resembles so much. Their voices are described as "softer" all around, including both calls and occasional language.

Unexpectedly prolific in captivity, the **festive Amazon** (*Amazona festiva festiva*) is a mid-sized, mostly green parrot with bright, blue-edged wings, red lores, and a wash of iridescent lavender atop the head. The more colorful **Bodini** subspecies (*Amazona festiva bodini*)—also called the red-backed Amazon—is increasingly available in the United States. These amusing beauties are active, acrobatic, and talkative, but they can be loud if they excessively demand human attention as a result of failure to develop independent self-rewarding behaviors.

almost never refusing a head rub. Males are more territorial in the spring. Red-loreds sometimes require more beak maintenance as this is the only common companion Amazon with a tendency to malocclusion of the upper and lower beak called "scissor beak." This may be a genetic predisposition or may be a cyclical

The Comical Conures

From an agricultural pest that generated little interest to a star of the pet trade, these long-tailed parrots are the epitome of the slogan, "You've come a long way, baby." Since the banning of imports into the United States in 1992, few other parrots have so demonstrated such improved adjustment to living room life as the conure. From the large, loud Patagonian to the thin, quiet pyhurras, there is, quite obviously, great variety in this group. Sometimes underestimated, these birds are surely at greater danger of becoming bored than overstimulated.

If farmers could exterminate them, these birds would surely be wiped out as quickly as possible. Developing Central and South American nations could easily follow our model in eliminating these parrots. Captive conure populations might join captive populations of some macaws, Amazons, cockatoos, and lories as species more numerous in captivity than in the wild.

Blue-crowned conures (*Aritinga acuticaudata*) have a reputation for being extremely affectionate and loving when properly nurtured and socialized as babies. They are extremely intelligent and learn to talk easily. They are personable little birds that suffered in the past from a reputation for being extremely loud. Hand-fed domestic babies don't have nearly the loud learned language of their wild-caught ances-

tors, but they can still get the message across when their needs aren't being met.

Like all conures, blue-crowns relish bathtime. They will bathe in their own water dish if humans don't provide showers or other water for bathing.

Newman reports that, "In my experience, most blue-crowned conures seem reluctant to bite hard and will, instead, either push your hand away with their beak or take it gently in their beak and move it away—but seldom will they bite hard. This anomaly has been confirmed with other breeders and owners. Even parent-raised blue-crowned conures will usually tame quite easily."

The **cherry-headed conure** (*Aritinga acuticaudata*) has a reputation as the best talker in this group. Even imported birds often develop large vocabularies. Unfortunately, the cherry-headed conures also have a reputation as frequently tending to

Cherry-headed conure

bonding and territorial-related aggression.

Beautiful little **sun conures** (*Aritinga auricapillus solstitialis*) have more than once gotten themselves into situations where an appreciation for visual beauty far overrides humans' abilities to tolerate their voices. This is the domestic conure most likely to wind up homeless, for even though the wild-caught nandays had a worse reputation for noxious sounds, the domestic sun conures carry a heavy reputation for making far more noise than anyone would imagine from such a small bird.

Years ago, lovely imported **mitred conures** (*Aratinga mitrata*) were very inexpensive, but they didn't seem to be especially interactive, especially

The Carolina Conure: Born in the USA

Once upon a time, a small parrot enjoyed a huge habitat exclusively in the United States. The Carolina conure resembled the Jenday conure in coloring and the mitred conure in shape. Like many parrots, the bird was not sexually dimorphic. Like most parrots, it probably reproduced selectively and infrequently in comparison to songbirds and mammals. Although they preferred cockleburs, if there were none, Carolina conures would also eat corn.

The birds suffered from the expansion of agriculture, the introduction of European honeybees, habitat loss to large hydroelectric projects, collection for fashion, and, of course, shooting contests.

The Carolina conure was the first bird that biologists knew in advance would become extinct. Even efforts by naturalists to collect skins for museums and research contributed to the bird's demise. Last-minute attempts by primitive aviculturists to save our only parrot were unsuccessful. Both the smaller southern subspecies and the larger one that ranged as far north and west as Colorado were extinct by 1917.

Denver's Museum of Natural History has a large collection of skins of this beautiful little parrot. On a "back stacks" tour, I once held one in my gloved hand.

vocally. New parrot owners often seemed to have expectations that the mitred would be "Amazon-like" or "macaw-like" and they were often disappointed. Things have changed. Today's hand-fed domestic mitreds are talkative, interactive, bright-eyed, and beautiful. Hand-fed mitreds need lots of hands-on interaction to maintain their sweetness.

Nanday conures (*Nandayus nenday*) have a reputation for being very beautiful and very sociable, and if sociable means "communicative," then nandays are certainly that. Few birds this size can make anywhere near this much noise. They are unsuited to apartments or condos or for persons with sensitive hearing. However, if noise is not an issue, these are beautiful and amusing birds for a tiny price. Because of their natural sociability, nandays make a good choice for multi-bird households.

Few birds have such a well-deserved reputation for screaming as the **Patagonian conure** (*Cyanoliseus patagonus*). This bird's voice can even make other birds uncomfortable. This is a bird for a person with an estate. But if you have a good deal of insulation between you and your neighbors, and if you crave an amazingly beautiful, unbelievably intelligent, loyal companion bird for a relatively low price, this just might be the bird for you. Not unlike macaws in their intelligence, the Patagonian conure even has a shaped eyering slightly reminiscent of the macaw's bare face patch.

Suggested wing trims for conures. (A) is for adults. (B) is for juveniles.

Blue-crowned conure

181

and the maroon-belly's is mostly green.

Often called the quiet conures, this *Phyrrhura* family is highly treasured among conure lovers. Don't forget that "quiet" is relative and that even a quiet conure makes noise. This bird is reported to have a lower volume call than a cockatiel.

The Quakers: Nature's Most Adaptable Parrot

When naming the best talking parrots, African greys and yellow-naped Amazons often head the lists. But these are pricey, long-lived species involving a large initial investment and a couple of generations of planning and commitment. For a sturdy bird with a more reasonable price and life expectancy, many who fancy a talking bird are now turning to the Quaker parrot.

At first glance, the **Quaker** or **monk parrot** (*Myiopsytta monachus*) does not appear to be particularly compelling, but its plain colors and unimpressive size mask a truly exciting personality. Among other things, it's not unusual for this intelligent little bundle of energy to use human words with understanding before it's six months old. In my study of talking Quaker parrots, published in *Bird Talk*, October 1998, I found that it is not unusual for baby Quakers to learn human speech at six weeks of age. While talking by ten months, it's

Cliff-dwellers, Patagonians are known to dive down rather than up when frightened indoors. Companion birds learn tricks and are famous for being tricksters, playing "jokes" on humans and pets in the home. Newman suggests that their cliff-dwelling habits also influence their living room play, which tends to games like hide-and-seek and peek-a-boo.

Beautifully marked **maroon-belly** (*Phyrrhura frontalis*) and **green-cheeked** (*Phyrrhura molinae*) **conures** might be called "ideal" conures, since their size and quiet natures makes them well suited even for small living spaces. These birds are just about identical in almost every way, except that the green-cheeked conure's tail is mostly red

not unusual for a Quaker parrot to learn to say its first human word after it is one year old.

No baby parrot, including the Quaker parrot, can be guaranteed to talk merely because it is of a particular species. One of the most exciting aspects of the talking capabilities of the Quaker parrot is the sheer number of words these birds can acquire. In my studies, Quaker parrots over one year old averaged between 50 and 60 words. On the other hand, Quaker parrots are not known for being especially easy to understand.

Note: Many of these birds had learned both to use words with understanding and to sing word songs. The latter use of language probably more accurately resembles bird song, and for the purpose of my work, the number of words in songs was not included in the total number of spoken words.

Many Quaker parrot owners reported that their birds used an average of 15–16 words in ways consistent with their meanings, and some owners of talking Quaker parrots report that their birds speak only with apparent understanding. That is, these birds do not merely repeat any old word at any old time, they use *all* words *only* with the apparent intent of conveying appropriate meaning at the appropriate moment. Most of the birds in this group spoke an average of about eight words.

Quaker parrots are especially prone to accidents in the home,

including flying away. Wing feathers must be trimmed at least a couple of times yearly to prevent drowning in the toilet, burning up in the skillet, or crashing into the ceiling fan. Tame Quakers that fly away in urban areas are usually easily recovered.

Because they are famously territorial, Quakers have special behavioral needs. Like humans, if Quakers do not learn cooperative habits and limits of acceptable behavior by the time they reach sexual maturity, they may be completely out of control. It's best for Quaker parrots to learn cooperative behavior just after weaning in order to prevent the development of early aggressive behaviors

Quaker parrots

during the Developmental Period called the "Terrible Twos" (which usually appears sometime between 9 and 18 months in Quakers).

Most behavior is comprised of a series of habits that are routinely reenacted. A bird that learns to habitually cooperate will be less likely to try to dominate humans in the environment. In order to create good habits and to establish a pattern of cooperation in the bird's behavior, we practice a couple of interactive exercises—step-ups and the towel game—most days in neutral territory.

Because of the Quaker parrot's instinct for territorial aggression, it's important not to service the cage with the bird in it. Just open the door, let the bird come out to the top of the door, then step the well-practiced bird up to a hand or hand-held perch and put it in a playpen. Then food, water, toys, or perches can be safely changed, and the bird will not learn how much fun it is to chase hands and other human parts.

A well-adjusted Quaker parrot is too busy to be noisy. If the bird is making lots of unpleasant sounds, it may be unhappy. Try to find out why. Much chronic noisemaking is a habit, like any other. First assess and improve the environment, then guide the bird to replace habitual noisemaking behaviors with more-appropriate behaviors.

These little green "feathered dragons" are never spayed or neutered for behavioral reasons, and therefore, they may be expected to demonstrate several diverse forms of sexually related behaviors. In this group, approximately half of the birds over one year old masturbated. While a little more than half of those birds seemed to prefer the pleasure of a toy, a little less than half seemed to prefer their favorite person's hand. One of the birds in this study was reported to pleasure itself frequently "with anything handy," while saying "peek-a-boo" the whole time.

In the past it was feared that escaped Quaker parrots could represent a threat as potential agricultural pests. Several states reacted by banning or otherwise regulating the ownership of Quaker parrots. Because so many modern Quaker parrots are hand-feds that could probably not survive outdoors, it would not be surprising to see a little easing of these regulations.

Actually, Quaker parrots might be the first birds we see with permanent ID requirements such as microchips. And, because a Quaker that could not reproduce would not threaten the local environment, Quaker parrots might be the first parrots spayed. While this may seem hard on the bird and not at all ideal, if safe, humane spaying techniques could be developed, they could help a Quaker parrot remain with its long-time family. It just might be worthwhile.

Clownish Caiques

Described by some as a single species, **black-capped caiques**

(*Pionites melanocephala*) and **white-bellied caiques** (*Pionites leuco-gaster*) are so close in appearance and range that they have been known to interbreed even in the wild. Playful and exhuberant, they are animated little clowns, sometimes called "the New World lories," for, like lories, caiques develop extremely strong feet and legs. Even healthy caiques with full wings might appear to prefer to hop and climb around rather than to fly.

Also like lories, the caique's love of bathing is well reported; and like lories, they will sometimes play their water away. Because they love to play in it, caiques benefit from having water changed more than once daily and benefit from a tube as well as a bowl if they are left for long periods.

Whether they're hopping in enthusiastic display, making a beeline across a table to examine an unfamiliar object, screaming in anger and disbelief as you put them back into the cage, or leaf bathing in a visiting politician's hair, the clownish caiques are more than strutting little Napoleons. Caiques love hugging and towel games and are at special danger of suffocation as they often seek out the folds of quilts and afghans just for the "fun" of it.

The caique's personality can be extremely complex, with the same bird sometimes exhibiting both aggression and fearfulness. A caique might suddenly exhibit fear of an inanimate object, especially a new one. Like the scarlet macaw, a

caique might be sweet as pie when picked up, only to bite fiercely when being put down. A caique can react intensely to a new hat, hair color, or garment.

Like the scarlet macaw, caiques are known for extreme intelligence. It's always a challenge to stay one step ahead of these smart little birds. Each day will differ, as these birds will always be looking for new ways to have fun by frequently improvising new behaviors.

Caiques are not known for exceptional talking ability, nor are they known for great volume. They probably prefer mimicking sounds to mimicking words. With this lesser volume, a caique will seldom get you kicked out of your neighborhood, but its voice can be very annoying inside the home. Then again, some owners report that they have *never* heard that shrill alarm call which some caiques are said to "abuse."

They can be stubborn and difficult to distract from whatever quest they're currently pursuing. Caiques can bond strongly to one person and have been seen to stalk family members disfavored by their favorite person. Frequent outings and handling by multiple individuals is especially beneficial to the gregarious caique personality. Especially, if one family member is often attacked by the bird, then that family member will probably benefit the most from being the means by which the bird goes to the veterinarian or groomer. Even if the less-favored human never actually handles the bird, sometimes being hoisted about in a carrier in strange places by the less-favored person will restore at least some harmony to a disharmonious caique/human relationship.

As with Quakers, cockatoos, and other parrots with a tendency to develop chasing, it's important not to allow poorly socialized humans to intentionally or unintentionally provoke a caique. It's a good idea, both for immediate practical reasons and for long-term behavioral benefit, to remove the bird before servicing the cage so that it doesn't develop hand-chasing behaviors.

Plucky, Puckish Pionus

The pionus parrot family are wonderful birds, like *Poicephalus*, that is often overlooked in favor of larger, showier birds. Pionus babies are not as flashy as some other birds in the medium parrot family; the adults develop colors ranging from the muted white front to delicate pastel shades of the bronze-wing, to the dazzling cornflower blue and pink of the mature blue-headed pionus. Companion pionus have a reputation as cautiously calm, graciously interactive, and with normally subdued volume.

Pionus usually tolerate the presence of humans, pets, and other types of birds in the home well. Indeed, pionus are known more for ignoring disliked humans than for attacking them. If a pionus doesn't like someone or something it will often sit with its back to the offending party.

Pionus love baths and are vigorous bathers. Because they are not as high energy as the *Poicephalus* family members, many older humans enjoy pionus for the noninvasive companionship they can usually provide. Pionus learn to play with toys easily, may even tolerate servicing the cage without being removed, and love interaction just as much as any other parrot.

Pionus are known more for their stolid dispositions, undemanding personalities, and subtle beauty than for their talking ability, although they can pick up a few words in a little robot, computer-like voice. Pionus parrots are not typically loud birds and often do well in apartments where noise can be a factor. These little birds, especially the hens, have shrill calls and can use them, although there is usually something wrong in the environment when this kind of behavior appears. The pionus' fear response sounds a little like it might be asthma, but this must not be confused with a health problem; look for something that the bird is afraid of.

"Cautious" is the word that best describes young pionus babies, who would rather snuggle than explore. After three months, however, these inquisitive youngsters begin exploring and can be in danger of household accidents like being stepped on if they are not properly contained.

At around two years old, a pionus will begin testing the limits of the behavioral environment. This is typical behavior and an expected developmental phase that passes with consistent handling and continued interactions. Strong flyers and strong-willed individuals benefit from well-maintained wing trims. A flighted pionus can develop extreme territorial tendencies and might decide not to let people into the house at all. To prevent the development of adverse reactions to grooming, these sensitive little birds should be groomed early and frequently throughout their lifetimes, as they can come to fear towels excessively

Blue-headed pionus

if they are a part of the birds' ongoing experience.

The **blue-headed pionus** (*Pionus menstruus*) has a very dependable disposition. Although it may bond exclusively to a favorite person to the exclusion of all others, it will seldom abuse others because of the strength of that bond.

The **white-crowned pionus** (*Pionus senilis*) is not so brightly colored as some other members of the family, but this bird's personality is far from colorless. They are beautiful and this may be the most active of this generally placid family. Hen white-crowns are especially treasured companions, but that doesn't

mean that the males can't be really sweet also. White-crowns have a reputation for being both the most aggressive and most territorial of the pionus species.

Stunning and subtly colored, the **bronze-winged pionus** (*Pionus chalcopterus*) is usually a noninvasive addition to even the smallest living room. I seldom see unwanted behavioral issues in these birds, although they can be sensitive to grooming and exhibit a great deal of towel stress. Young birds should be well acclimated to the towel and towel games continued throughout the birds' lifetimes.

The **scaly-headed** or **Maximilian's pionus** (*Pionus maximiliani*) is, perhaps, the most docile of this generally docile group and is even more subtly colored than the others. With proper socialization on both sides, these birds often adjust easily to children.

The "Pocket Parrots": *Brotogeris* and *Forpus*

Two families of New World parrots are often referred to as the "pocket parrots." *Brotogeris*—a sturdy little bird with a reputation for being "born tame"—and *Forpus* (parrotlets).

During the 1980s, when **gray-cheeked parakeets** (*Brotegeris pyrrhopterus*) were frequently imported, they had an almost universal reputation for gentleness. Exceptionally popular as imports, their prices first doubled, then trebled. Sold by the thousands through chain stores, **canary** and **white-winged beebees** (*Brotigeris versicoloris versicoloris* and *B. v. chiriri*) had a loyal and very vocal following through the 1970s and 1980s. Even wild-caught birds were known for very easy, very successful long-term human/parrot relationships, especially with children.

These birds were, for centuries, harvested in the manner of a renewable resource by indigenous peoples like those seen in the "Spirits of the Rain Forest," a Discovery Channel video. Machiguenga girls of Yomuibato, Manu are shown feeding neonates by spitting chewed banana into the beaks of baby **golden-winged parakeets** (*Brotegeris crysopterus*). Although the gray-cheeked parakeet had the best reputation of the group, even the most common beebees seemed to come tame, and while practically every bird came tame, they weren't always easy to keep that way. Because of their small size and relatively modest chewing habits, it was easy to allow a gray-cheeked parakeet to live at liberty in the home. However, these little guys easily develop *extremely* territorial behavior. Especially, gray-cheeks and beebees may form excessively strong bonds with chrome appliances. Quite a few of these little characters became so territorial they wouldn't let anyone, sometimes even the favorite person, into the kitchen or bathroom. I have worked with several cases of overbonding to a toaster or hair dryer in this family.

These birds require just as much careful patterning and maintenance of behavioral limits as a larger bird such as caique. They might even be called caique-like or lory-like in their ability to focus, chase, and stalk. They are pugnacious and known to attack other companion animals, for one of the leading causes of *Brotogeris* death in the home is the bird harassing a dog until the dog turns on it.

The second most common behavioral complaint, behind inappropriate territorialism, is noise. In spite of their small size, the *Brotogeris* voice can be both loud and shrill. Prevent the development of screaming behaviors carefully, providing for the development of independence during the window of opportunity between weaning and sexual maturity.

If you have an older *Brotogeris* parrot and want to switch it to pellets, proceed cautiously. See the veterinarian first. If the bird has a weak liver or kidneys, a diet change might be too hard on the bird. Also, be careful supplementing vitamins for *Brotogeris*, especially if pelleted diet is fed, as the little birds can be sensitive to vitamin D-3. Feed whole fresh foods instead of supplementing vitamins for *Brotogeris*.

Forpus, those very tiny parrotlets, are sometimes called the "South American lovebird" or "blue-winged lovebird." Sandee Molenda likes to say, "Although they are the smallest

parrot, they don't know it." They are everything one would expect of a "real" parrot. There are seven species in the *forpus* family: the **spectacled parrotlet** (*F. conspiciliatus*), the **Mexican parrotlet** (*F. cyanopygius*), the **blue-winged parrotlet** (*F. xanthopterygius*), the **Pacific parrotlet** (*F. coelestis*), the **yellow-faced parrotlet** (*F. xanthops*), the **green-rumped parrotlet** (*F. passerinus*), and the **dusky-billed parrotlet** (*F. sclateri*).

The most common companion parrotlets in the United States at this writing are the green-rumped, Pacific (celestial), and spectacled parrotlets. These birds cannot quite be called common and are not yet produced in numbers enabling them to be found in a "normal" pet store. The best places to find parrotlets are parrotlet breeders, specialty bird stores, and bird shows.

Parrotlets don't require daily handling in order to remain tame. Matthew Vriends reports that they seem naturally tame, are quiet, and not messy. The "quiet" part is extremely charming, for the parrotlet's voice is chattery and seldom invasive in the slightest. Even the scream of an angry parrotlet usually falls way short of obnoxious.

Molenda also reports that they may be temporarily angry after you've gone away for a while. They have obvious memory and are loyal to favorites from the past. Parrotlets bond strongly to their favorite person, sometimes abusing spouses. They can be extremely cage-territorial and, like a Quaker, benefit from being removed from the cage to change toys, food, and water so that they do not develop chasing behaviors. It's important to keep the parrotlets well socialized to towels and to handheld perches for handling when they're in a cranky mood.

Molenda also suggests that the companion parrotlet's wing feathers be kept consistently trimmed. In the parrotlet personality, feelings of power stimulated by flight can create playful and territorial aggression. Well-maintained wing trims help to ensure safety, for these little birds are so curious and exploratory that they frequently die in accidents rather than of illness.

The **Pacific** or **celestial parrotlet** (*Forpus coelestis*) had a head start in the pet trade over the other species of *Forpus*, but they can be more aggressive. They might take any opportunity to dominate anybody. If someone backs off, the bird may become convinced it can chase them and will try harder the next time. This might actually be playful behavior, as these birds, like other parrots, love to improvise interactive games. Pacific parrotlets breed readily in captivity. Several color mutations are now available.

Chapter Thirteen
Pacific Distribution Parrots

Australia and the Pacific islands are well populated with parrot species, mostly rain forest birds peculiar to both separate and overlapping ranges. While pet trade is sometimes blamed for declining numbers of birds in the Old and New Worlds, many Pacific distribution parrots have been introduced into trade for quite another reason. Huge numbers of lories and island cockatoos were captured and sold not because they are so well suited as pets (some adjust poorly), but rather, because they were simply in the way, "harvested" as byproducts of logging or agricultural development occasionally involving entire islands.

Budgies: The Most Popular Parrot

The common parakeet or budgie (short for budgerigar, a native Australian word meaning "good to eat") is the most popular pet bird in the world. Its size, ease of reproduction, modest physical requirements, and predictable disposition have earned *Melopsittacus undulatus* respect in all sectors of aviculture. From homemakers to Ph.D. geneticists, budgies are beloved of rich and poor, old and young owners of all religious and social persuasions. Except for the cat (and not counting fish) they are surely the most numerous pet.

These tiny bundles of energy are everything one might expect from larger parrots, and, in some ways more, because they do everything twice as fast. They are fabulous talkers, but since they double the speed of everything they say, unless they were taught at half-speed, they might not be understandable. They mature quickly, so careful attention must be paid to training during the time of rapid behavioral development (two to six months).

Age is a very important factor when selecting a pet budgie. Usually parent-raised, these birds don't come tame, so younger is better. Ask the breeder or dealer for an immature bird still retaining characteristics of a nestling—perhaps some dark spots still on the beak, lines on the forehead coming all the way down to the cere (area around nostrils), and a very smooth, pale

cere. I prefer buying from a dealer who allows me to handle or tame the bird in the store.

Start by having the wing feathers trimmed so that the bird can get to know you without being hurt flying into a wall or window. Ask for a "training clip" with no long feathers left at the end of the wing to be bumped or caught in cage bars. This temporary procedure must be maintained three or four times yearly if the bird is allowed liberty in the home. A budgie flying indoors risks death from cooking pots, toilets, ceiling fans, and common poisonous plants, among many other hazards.

Find a quiet enclosed area, perhaps a closet or bathroom, and sit on the floor with the baby budgie nestled loosely in your hands, clothing, or a towel. Be very still and speak continuously, quietly (not whispering, for they have a natural aversion to hiss-ing sounds made by their predators, snakes) perhaps humming directly into the bird's head. Slowly, gently, place the baby bird on an index finger, and speak soothingly until it remains still on the finger, expressing interest in what you are doing. Since you are sitting on the floor in a small, contained space, if the bird flutters off, it has only a very short way to go. Don't chase a retreating bird, but once it becomes still, gently pick it up and place it back on the finger.

After the bird has become accustomed to sitting on your finger, begin slowly approaching the feet from below (not the front) with the opposite index finger. Slowly, gently, lift the tip of the toe or toes nearest the tip of the finger the bird is sitting on with your opposite index finger. When the foot is lifted successfully off the finger, slowly, gently, push back with the "top hand," and lower the (back) hand (the one the bird is sitting on). As the bird transfers weight to the new finger, say "*Step up*" so that it associates the words with the action.

Within a very few minutes, a young, untraumatized bird should easily understand what you expect and cheerfully step from finger to finger. This interaction will become a daily part of your routine; a good rapport with any parrot is maintained with daily practice of this exercise. Daily step-up practice is similar to prayer or meditation in that it gives the bird (and owner) a behavioral and emotional "baseline," an understanding of what is expected and what happens next.

The cage is the bird's retreat, not its prison. If the bird is to spend a great deal of time there be sure to purchase a big one with at least three dishes, one for the regular diet, one for water, and one for daily soft foods such as hard-boiled egg (mashed with shell on), broccoli (they like the little balls on the tops), toast (without butter), grated cheese, and carrots, or whatever healthy fare you regularly consume. Budgies are especially fond of warm cooked rice, quinoa, and pasta. Avoid avocado, chocolate, coffee, and Teflon cookware.

The only disadvantage to loving a budgie is the possibility of the bird's short lifetime. Smaller American budgies or parakeets can be expected to outlive their large-breasted English cousins, but both birds are fragile. A five-year life span is possible, ten years unusual.

The Charming Cockatiels

Genus *Nymphicus* is so specialized that it has only one species, *Nymphicus hollandicus*.

This is, in fact, a **miniature cockatoo**, including the mobile crest and facial fan, in a small, easy-to-accommodate body. Almost universally regarded as the most docile of all parrots, cockatiels are swift fliers and require wing trimming as a matter of routine safety. Grounding these light-bodied birds with a wing trim is absolutely impossible, so no cockatiel, even one with every primary feather trimmed, can be trusted outdoors without a harness or carrier.

Grey pied cockatoo

Suggested wing trims for cockatiels. (A) is for adults.
(B) is for juveniles.

(A)
(B)

feminine call most of the time. The single exception is when she masturbates. Pearl likes to back up into the corner of her cage, with her tail straight up; she demonstrates to me that the hen cockatiel's language use is by choice. When Pearl masturbates, she whistles what I consider to be the second most common male cockatiel courtship song. It must be her favorite tune.

Those Confounding Cockatoos

"Night frights"—thrashing in the darkness—trouble cockatiels and almost no other birds. It's not unusual for these sensitive birds to thrash in apparent fear in the darkness. A small night light can help provide a sense of safety. These incidents are more common in lutinos and newer color mutations than in normal gray cockatiels.

The male cockatiel's song can be achingly beautiful. At about four months old, even before developing adult feathers, a little boy 'tiel starts strutting, hopping, and whistling. It's the easiest way to tell the girls from the boys. Listen before you look. Female cockatiels will, for the most part, retain the monosyllabic chirp of the juvenile bird rather than acquiring words, songs, or whistles, while males may acquire multiple songs and words. My own cinnamon pearl cockatiel, Pearl, is quite the lady, never uttering a sound except her

With would-be descriptive names such as Sugar, Honey, Peaches, Angel Baby, and YumYum, or Kaiser, Napoleon, Caesar, Alexander, and Hillary, little wonder that cockatoos can be as unpredictable as springtime in the Rockies. While I occasionally encounter birds named Sarge, Killer, Dikembe Mutumbu, Dracula, and Nosferatoo, the most common companion cockatoo name is, undoubtedly, Houdini for its incredible talent as escape artist.

Cockatoos have the most expressive faces of any bird. Rather than simply denoting species or gender, their mobile crests, facial fans, and auricular feathers (around the ears) can be used to convey extremely complex emotions. Indeed, a cockatoo can completely cover its beak with the facial fan feathers. This is no small matter, as the head display (obviously the most important part of the show) of a Moluccan cockatoo

The "Rival"

Charity, a 12-year-old sulphur-crested cockatoo, was well cared for and adored in her first home. Her beloved owner used a walker, but got by just fine until illness forced her to board Charity at a pet shop. She promised the bird that she would return, but she was never able to do so.

Luckily, Charity found another loving home. A few years later, when knee replacement surgery rendered her new favorite human dependent upon a walker, the bird went just a little nuts. She began biting, leaving painful bruises and deep puncture wounds. Soon Charity's new family realized that these episodes occurred only when the walker was nearby. The little cockatoo obviously remembered a similar obnoxious metal "rival" from the past and didn't intend to lose this "mate" to a walker.

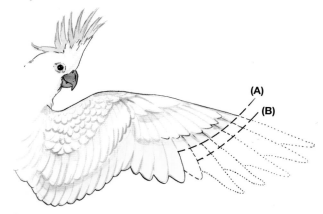

Suggested wing trims for cockatoos. (A) is for adults. (B) is for juveniles.

cockatoo (*Cacatua goffini*) lies flat on the head when not in use. The more unusual recurved crest, like that of **sulphur-crested cockatoos** (*Cocatua sulphurea*) sweeps back, then up and away from the head. The recurved crest is considered to have more signaling capacity than the recumbent type.

can be fully one half of the bird's total height!

Common companion cockatoos come mostly in white or white with pastels, most commonly various shades of yellow. Breaking from the mold are pink cockatoos: the rose-breasted, Goffin's, and Moluccan. Rarer cockatoos also come in black, some with red or yellow markings.

The crests of the various species of cockatoos are described as recumbent or recurved. The common recumbent crest of the **Goffin's**

Cockatoos have soft body feathers covered with powder (an indication of good health), large, strong feet, and large, strong beaks to compliment those sensitive, expressive faces. Most companion cockatoos love bathing, including human-supplied showers. Cockatoos have been observed to make and use tools such as sticks for scratching and for tapping displays for mates.

No parrots demonstrate a greater love of chewing. A cockatoo reducing the clock or Queen Anne chair to toothpicks is not expressing anger or discontent. It is demonstrating nesting skill, proudly showing favorite humans and anyone else who will notice, "Look what a good mate I would be. I could carve a darling nest cavity for you and our babies!"

Cockatoos possess some of the most "human" of all characteristics found in parrot-type birds. They are (serially) monogamous, although apparently not sexually exclusive. They copulate for reasons other than procreation. They access "birth control" when needed by refusing to raise chicks that can't be supported by the environment. The male parent takes an active part in the rearing of offspring. And, also like some humans, cockatoos suffer from a tendency toward spousal abuse. Cockatoos obviously have memory.

Cockatoos might be called the most (domestic) "catlike" of all parrots. A cockatoo might suddenly decide that it wants to be held by the only person in the room who doesn't want to touch it. One companion cockatoo might be inclined to absolutely smother you to death whenever possible, or another might become positively apoplectic if forced by chance or circumstance to have any physical contact with a human. Of course, there is also a great deal of middle ground.

Imported cockatoos were generally less talkative than their imported New World cousins, Amazons and macaws, being more inclined to mimic movement than sound. Now that all new baby cockatoos in the United States are domestically raised, we hear many exciting and amusing stories of cockatoo talking ability. More and more often, cockatoos become outstanding talkers. Common expressions for cockatoos to pick up early and easily are *What 'choo doin'?,*"

The Bridge

One evening I watched a friend's cockatoo boarding in my living room as she worked a perch out of the cage, inch by inch. First she pushed the barkless branch from inside the cage, gradually wiggling it between tight cage bars. Then she would go outside the cage and pull the branch, gnawing briefly if it became stuck between the bars, before returning to push again from inside.

For ten or fifteen minutes, I sat mesmerized, believing that the bird wanted nothing more than to get that branch out of her cage. At one point, however, I realized that she was *way* ahead of me. She didn't *just* want the branch out of the cage. She wasn't *simply* discarding trash. She had another goal in mind!

When the chewed, bare limb protruded about a foot from the cage and was tightly wedged between bars so that it did not wobble, Kaku suddenly jumped onto it, scrambled out to the end, and proudly hopped across a previously unattainable chasm to a bookshelf she had been eyeballing for weeks!

The bridge she had been building was complete, and if I hadn't immediately removed it, my books would have been history!

"Step-up," "Gimme a kiss," "I love you," and *"Night, night."* Although they are not generally extremely vocal, many cockatoos, perhaps most, can be, at least occasionally, loud. Cockatoos are known sometimes even to scream in the dark, which is very unusual in most parrots.

Even though we can only occasionally see outstanding talking ability, we can always expect an incredible penchant for acrobatics and mechanical ability. If lories are the "puppies" of the parrot family, then cockatoos are the "monkeys." Cockatoos love all kinds of simple mechanical devices: nuts, bolts, and carabiners, including many cage door fastening devices.

The cockatoo bite has the potential to be the most penetrating of all parrot bites, since many cockatoo beaks possess three very pronounced points: one on the maxilla (upper beak) and two points on each side of a razor-sharp chisel-shaped cutting edge on the mandible (lower beak). Not only are the beaks relatively large; they can be very sharp. A cockatoo beak can puncture and slash the skin in three places all in one movement. Fortunately, most domestic cockatoos are lovers, not fighters. However, even the most ardent "Romeo" may occasionally attack a perceived rival or try to browbeat a beloved companion to get his way. This aspect of their personality is probably the most problematic aspect of a long-term relationship with a cockatoo. The occasional tendency to sudden aggression is managed with vigilance and step-up practice, the towel game, and other cooperation routines continuing throughout the bird's lifetime.

Although some cockatoos may be absolutely trustworthy regarding bites, this varies with age and with individuals. This family has been called "emotionally incontinent." A truly "trustworthy" teenage cockatoo may be unusual; in my experience perhaps no more than 10–15 percent of mature companion cockatoos could be called "completely trustworthy." Like many exotics, most sexually mature cockatoos can be dispositionally uneven and may exhibit frequent or occasional aggression. When this appears, it will usually be cyclical or seasonal, usually twice yearly, spring and fall. This may or may not be gender-related, with male 'toos being most combative in most, but not all, species. I have seen some very

aggressive cockatoo hens and some very docile cocks, but watch those crests and facial feathers for clues that the bird's mood is about to change.

A cockatoo is not an impulse purchase. I do not recommend cockatoos to individuals with antiques, respiratory allergies (because of their abundant powder), sensitivity to loud noises, to homes with extremely active or irrepressible children, or to individuals of quick and fiery temper (the bird might provoke anger in such a human).

Caging requirements for a cockatoo are great. The larger species must have especially strong welds and bars, as these birds love to exercise those huge, strong beaks on the cage, and an insubstantial cage will simply be dismantled. Because of their extreme curiosity and mechanical ability, cockatoos cannot be left alone outside a well-designed cage or bird-proofed environment. Colorado avian veterinarian, Dr. Jerry LaBonde, says, "If it's been in an accident, it's probably a cockatoo."

Cockatoos do well with humans who are fully capable of setting limits early *and* enforcing them. I recommend cockatoos to people with a great appreciation for playfulness, a love of nature, and a tolerance for destructible possessions. I recommend cockatoos to those who are willing to take great care designing their bird's environment for behavioral effect. Most of all, cockatoos do well with people who long for great beauty in their lives. A cockatoo is like a special child to cherish and protect from its own very emotional nature. If you think you would enjoy living with a gorgeous "flower" with an occasional "temper," chances are you would treasure a 'too.

When buying or adopting a cockatoo, be sure to check for powder by rubbing a broad feather between thumb and forefinger. If a particular cockatoo has no easily observable powder on the feathers, don't buy it without a full veterinary workup to ensure that it does not have Psittacine Beak and Feather Disease (PBFD), an incurable illness that can be communicated to other birds.

There are many wonderful opportunities to adopt older cockatoos. These birds probably come with a behavioral issue or two, but older cockatoos can often be relatively easily and effectively resocialized. This ease of readjusting later in life is one of the cockatoo's most attractive traits, for these are among the most long-lived of parrots.

The sulphur-crested cockatoos, including **lesser**, **greater**, **eleanora**, and **citron** (*Cacatua sulphurea, C. galerita, C. eleanora,* and *C. sulphurea citrinocristata*) are known by their bright cab-yellow recurved crests and white bodies with occasional touches of yellow. These birds are comical, acrobatic, and mechanical, and often highly prized in companion settings even though they are exterminated as agricultural pests in their outdoor ranges.

The **rose-breasted cockatoo** (*Eolophus roseicapillus*) is known for its cautious nature, often with a well-developed fight-or-flight response. This bird is often called "quietest" of the companion cockatoos. Calls can be loud but are usually infrequent, limited to dusk and dawn or when disturbed. They are high-energy creatures needing a larger cage than some of the larger cockatoos. Rosies don't need extremely strong cage bars and welds like a Moluccan or umbrella cockatoo, but they can outsmart some of the most sophisticated door-locking mechanisms. Wing trims are extremely important, as a full-flighted rosie may develop a stronger fear response than other cockatoos and will be, therefore, more difficult to maintain as a companion. Rosies are more prone to obesity than their larger cockatoo "cousins."

Major Mitchell's or **Leadbeater's cockatoo** (*Cacatua leadbeatri*) remains uncommon but is highly prized in companion settings. A cautious bird, the Leadbeater's is known for great beauty and for loud, infrequent calls. These birds have a reputation for being ill suited as pets for all but the most patient and educated of owners, although occasional individuals, including hand-fed, handicapped, or imperfect birds, may more easily maintain companionability.

Salmon-crested or **Moluccan cockatoo** (*Cacatua moluccensis*) are surely the loudest and most long lived of the companion cockatoos. These birds have magnificently resounding voices and a reputation for using them with great frequency. This bird might scream even in the dark. Moluccans are gorgeous and showy, but can be more difficult to accommodate than any other parrot. Because they are so long-lived, Moluccans are often available through adoption programs.

The **umbrella cockatoo** (*Cacatua alba*) may be the best talker of the group, but can also be loud, especially in breeding settings. Males have a reputation for becoming aggressive and behaviorally uneven during breeding cycles, whether there's a mate present or not. This behavior is seldom seen in the hens, and I believe, therefore, that the hen umbrella cockatoo is the most desirable pet of the companion cockatoos. Like many parrots, the umbrella cockatoo can become obsessed with floor control, including attacking human toes, feet, and other body parts encountered on the floor. Limits and watchfulness are necessary when a cockatoo shares the floor with children or even adults who are unfamiliar with the need to block cockatoo toe attacks.

As a result of human expansion into its habitat, the **Goffin's cockatoo** (*Cacatua goffini*) is probably more numerous in our living rooms than in the wild. Smaller than most other cockatoos, they are extremely active and need a cage at least as large as that required by an umbrella or Moluccan. Also known to scream in the dark, this is a cautious, reactionary bird with a tendency to form extreme bonds. The Goffin's cockatoo is not for everyone, but the ones who do adjust well are among the

most beloved of all companion parrots. When these birds were still imported in huge numbers, they had a reputation as a poor pet with a huge failure rate as a companion; even handfed Goffin's can be difficult.

The **DuCorp's cockatoo** (*Cacatua ducorps*), another island cockatoo, remains rare, but is increasingly available in aviculture. The DuCorp's might be called a "white Goffin's" though it is usually a little more behaviorally stolid than the Goffin's.

The little **corella** or **bare-eyed cockatoo** (*Cacatua sanguine*) with its bare, puffy eye rings, looks a little like a "depressed" Goffin's. Don't be fooled by appearances as this mischievous bird is known as a charming companion with excellent ability to mimic human speech. It has been called the "most intelligent of the white cockatoos."

Long-billed corella or **slender-billed cockatoo** (*Cacatua tenuirostris*) shares the bare-eye's reputation for talking and the rosie's reputation for becoming overweight (a pudgy slender-bill is quite the "star" of the popular video, "*Parrots, Look Who's Talking*"). Probably a little more stolid than the bare-eye, slender-bills love to dig, and companions benefit from having a sandbox where toys can be buried and found.

The Exotic Eclectus Parrots

This beautiful bird is called "eclectic" for the unusual nature of its coloration and behavior, as both vary significantly from other parrots. Female and male eclectus parrots share little coloration in common, with hens being mostly red and purple with black beaks, and cocks mostly green and blue with a light or bright orange upper beak. The sexes are so dissimilar that early attempts to label the bird resulted in males and females being considered different species. While the female eclectus has been called more "brightly" colored than the male, this can be misleading, as hen colors are more difficult to see in dark spaces (nest cavities) where they spend most of their time, while males are very bright, almost "electric" greens and

blues that blend well with new foliage. Chimeras, or birds showing coloration of both genders, occur occasionally, although this is usually a juvenile issue, with colors settling in as the bird matures.

Eclectus have a reputation for tending to reverse the gender-related personality traits commonly associated with sex in other parrots, with females said to be generally more aggressive than males. This can be seen even in very young birds, with males tending toward caution and females tending toward boldness, although most eclectus parrots tend toward caution and may be sensitive to unfamiliar colors, people, and places. When confronted this bird can, and often does, remain completely motionless for quite some time, as it appears to be processing information.

These birds do not pair-bond like other species as bonding is neither rigid nor exclusive in eclectus as in other parrots. Although a companion eclectus will usually express an obvious preference for one human over all others, it will rarely attack non-favorite humans. Disposition can vary greatly from bird to bird and season to season. Expect nippy phases in either sex to be seasonal and/or transitional. I have seen both males and females of all species be exceptionally gentle with everyone including small children. I have seen apparently identical birds that would readily bite any human flesh within reach.

Feather structure resembles that of other parrots, but barbules do not

cling as tightly to each other, leaving each filament coming off the central shaft or rachis in an individual strand resulting in a "hairlike" or "furlike" appearance. Eclectus molt more gradually than other parrots that shed large numbers of feathers only in warm months. Possibly because of this feather peculiarity, electus appear to prefer petting in the direction of the feathers as a furred pet would, rather than within the feathers as other parrots do. Eclectus can be a good choice for anyone with dust sensitivity, since they produce and shed less feather dust than many other parrot species, especially cockatoos and African greys.

Even the diet of the eclectus parrot must differ, for this bird's intestines are much longer than those of any other parrot. Eclectus have a greater need for vitamin A and show benefit from greater than normal amounts of fruit. Many eclectus take great delight in eating an occasional mealworm. Also, like African greys, eclectus are sensitive to low calcium levels. This can have a behavioral component, as irritability has been observed in calcium-deficient eclectus.

While eclectus are known for soft, gentle speaking voices, their screams can be deafening. Although not known for frequent screaming, alarm calls can resemble a siren.

The **grand eclectus** (*Eclectus roratus roratus*) is not the largest of the group, but derives its name from perceived demeanor. It is said to be both well established in aviculture and thriving in the wild.

The **vosmarie eclectus** (*Eclectus roratus vosmarie*) is the largest species, with males said to be very evenly disposed.

Red-sided eclectus (*Eclectus roratus polychloros*) are the most colorful of this vibrant group. Also well represented in U.S. aviculture, hens can be recognized by the dazzling periwinkle blue eye ring and cocks by their very orange beaks shading to yellow tip.

Solomon Island eclectus (*Eclectus roratus solomonensis*) hens are said to be as evenly disposed as males.

Lories

There is no more vibrantly active and amusing creature than a lory. The most colorful of parrots, they are exceptionally athletic and possessing extraordinarily strong feet in order to climb out to the ends of very tiny, flexible branches to eat the nectar, pollen, and buds of flowers that sustain them in the wild. Fast flyers and talented escape artists, they are accident-prone in the home. With their eye popping jewel-toned feathers and frantic, mind-boggling antics, lories are sometimes called "feathered puppies" for their exuberant, playful natures. It's not unusual to see two lorries on the floor locked together, rolling over and over like growling puppies in mock battle.

Lories are bold in more than color: behaviorally, they are among the most expressive of parrots, with astute owners easily interpreting a lory's mood from body language. Special care must be taken to build in behavioral controls for their extreme bonding-related behaviors, for more than almost any other type of parrot, a companion lory has a reputation for abusing all but its favorite companion. Their domineering ways and fearless attitudes have been often painfully endured by their significant others' significant others, including significant other people, birds, and pets. These reports are increasingly less common, however, as advances in breeding and behavioral practice are coming to the fore.

Just as a hyperactive child becomes increasingly excited at a picnic, a lory can get "wound up" with much escalating hissing, swaying, and pinpointing. Because this excitement is sexual and sexual means territorial, it can be accompanied by biting. A well-practiced owner can see overload coming and replace the behavior with step-up practice or grab a towel to calm the bird or return it to its cage before biting begins.

In addition, lories can be domineering to the point of harassing literally every living creature in a household except one (or maybe even everyone). Usually, however, if the bird is well handled during the "Honeymoon" Period just after weaning, its interactive behavior can be carefully maintained. It's very difficult to resocialize a lory that has decided it is intended to stalk anything that breathes except the primary person. While lory beaks are softer than the beaks of other parrots and don't often draw blood, their nips can be incredibly painful. A lory must not learn that it can get its way by intentionally causing pain.

Lories can become excellent talkers with voices sometimes described as being as accurate as the African grey, mimicking voices so perfectly that you can tell exactly who it is the bird is copying. Like African parrots, they are less loud in general than their New World cousins. Also like Africans, they are gifted mimics of electronic devices, sometimes learning an electronic phone ring so accurately that humans in the home don't know whether to answer the phone or to tell the bird to be quiet.

Lories have a characteristic smell, which is strong in breeding season and is quite different from that of macaws and Amazons. The family Eos, which includes the now nearly common blue-streak, has the strongest odor, an almost fetid floral scent not unlike some sweet jungle flower.

Lories do a lot of hissing, swaying, and hopping as part of their neverending displays and postures. I remember seeing a blue-streaked lory courting a small statuary on "America's Funniest Home Videos"; I think it won. I was once accused of becoming a hermit when two blue-streaked lories, Heckle and Jeckle, took up residence in my living room. These birds were unbelievably amusing to watch, even for a jaded old bird person like me. For quite some time, I fought an irresistible urge to do nothing except sit and watch them.

The lory's reputation for ease of handfeeding and early weaning is unquestionably related to the bird's natural diet and to its unique tongue. The brushlike structure of the tongue helps the bird to eat liquid nectar and powdered pollen of flowers, the basis of their diet in the wild. It's a significant advantage in the hand-feeding and weaning process.

Dietary needs of lories have been long cussed and discussed; they differ significantly from other parrots', and seed diets can be especially harmful. While some immature and sprouted seeds are tolerated, even relished, avoid, especially, dry, hard seeds found in old-fashioned parrot mixes.

The way lories eat is more like squashing something. Each piece of moist food is systematically smashed until there's only a flat piece of pulp left. Then the bird shakes its head and throws the piece of pulp out of the beak before starting on the next piece. This leaves sort of "pre-dried" cementlike fruit and vegetable residue stuck to anything it reaches. For this reason, it's a good idea to have Plexiglas lining the areas of the cage where the bird eats and waterproof walls and accessories nearby.

Dr. Jerry LaBonde reminds us to avoid honey, reporting that while honey itself is fine for lories, it can carry harmful microorganisms, and lories can develop various health-related problems if they are fed honey.

Because they will play with anything that isn't tied down, including

Rainbow lorikeet

food, lories must be fed in dump-proof bowls, and because they are known for frequent water games, if they are to be left alone all day lories should also be provided with water in a tube so that when they play away all water in the bowl, there will still be water to drink. Lories also frequently contaminate their water as they love to dunk toys and food and then "fish" for them.

The **multi-species genus** (*Trichoglossus*) or rainbow lorikeet is known for its "million dollar colors at a pauper's price." This bird is the most inexpensive, most colorful, and most high-strung of the common companion lories. Although Matthew Vriends reports that there are more than 30 subspecies of this dazzling animal, we most commonly see the **green-naped rainbow lorikeet** (*Trichoglossus haemodatus*) in companion settings in the United States. This bird is a well-known nomad that benefits behaviorally from safe, contained outings with both favored and less-favored humans.

The **red lory** (*Eos bornea bornea*) was probably the first lory seen as a common companion in the United States. This bird is only slightly less high-strung than the blue-streaked lory, which is usually a little less high-strung than the rainbow lories. Easily tamed as wild-caughts, hand-feds seem more docile than most hand-fed rainbows. *Eos* lories respond well to food rewards.

In spite of the implications of their name, the **chattering lory** (*Lorus garrulus garrulus*) is perceived as the "quietest" of the common companion lories except, possibly Duivenbode's. It's not that the chattering lories can't be loud. They can be, and their voices are at least as shrill and piercing as any other lory, but the companion chattering lory is less high-strung than its *Eos* and *Trichoglossus* cousins and doesn't usually choose to use that shrill call so often. The chattering lory, like the red lorry, has a reputation as an excellent talker.

The **blue-streaked lory** (*Eos reticulata*), a subspecies of the red lory, is a relatively recent arrival in the U.S. marketplace. Its beauty, ease of reproduction, ease of transitioning to new homes, and relatively low price have made it probably the most accessible lory available to the public at this writing.

I had never seen blue-streaked lories until I was given a couple of charming young imported cocks in about 1985. Why had we not seen these birds before? Why were they suddenly available everywhere? Rosemary Low explains: "Beginning in the 1980s we started seeing more unusual lories in the pet trade than ever before. Logging roads were being bored into the jungles of Indonesia, and these previously inaccessible sites were yielding up previously untraded types of lories. Several glorious birds like the blue-streaked lory were suddenly available at the corner pet store."

Blue-streaks may be the hissingest, swayingest, sexiest of this group. These birds can hardly be called secretive copulators, with some birds becoming obviously excited and sexually active when numerous humans are present—the more the merrier. As mentioned, a sexually excited blue-streaked lory really "wowed" the whole country on "America's Funniest Home Videos" in about 1993 as it actively courted a tiny statue.

Admittedly uncommon, **Duivenbode's lory** (*Chalcopsitta duivenbodei*) has a reputation as the best companion in this group. This species is called the "glossy lories" and is an exquisite treat for the eye. Duivenbode's lory is unbelievably gorgeous and is usually absolutely meticulous about maintaining perfect feathers. In captivity, we might see a baby tail and, occasionally, cage fray in adult tail feathers, but in most adults, every golden brown, yellow, and violet feather will be clean and tight.

Duivenbode's lory must be kept at human room temperature, as it is known to be intolerant of cold. Although not exactly common, Duivenbode's are occasionally available in Florida, California, and Oregon, and rarely in other parts of the United States.

The Grass Parakeets

Kakarikis, rosellas, and Bourke's parakeets, long-time residents of the aviary, have also begun appearing in living rooms around the United States.

Each of these birds is characterized by great beauty, especially the rosellas and Bourke's. While they don't always learn human words, they have truly lovely natural songs.

These birds are generally considered peaceful but have a reputation for being high-strung. Many who keep them expect more side-by-side interaction, with birds and humans enjoying independent activities rather than face-to-face interaction. A grass 'keet that likes you will want to sit as close to you as possible. Active and curious, these birds love to play whistling games and non-contact peek-a-boo.

Fast flyers every one, these birds must have spacious cages or flights and must be wing feather-trimmed if allowed liberty in the home. They can startle easily and take flight suddenly, sometimes causing injury even in familiar rooms. They should be well socialized to step-ups both with hands and handheld perches from a very early age.

Active little **kakarikis** (*Cyanormphus novaezelandaie*) look a little like miniature conures. They love to climb and benefit from horizontal cage bars. Because of high activity levels and constant movement, this bird is very difficult to keep tame as a pet. What is missing in personal interaction is gained in entertainment, however, for kakarikis are tremendously interesting to watch. Even full flight kakarikis seem to prefer climbing to flying. These birds love leaf bathing. Males tend to aggression.

The **Eastern rosella** (*Platycercus eximius*) is a strong, beautiful bird. Males tend to aggression when kept in pairs. While these birds can have a really beautiful song, they can also be loud. They may prefer to interact without touching, but may enjoy whistling back and forth, peek-a-boo, eye games, and other types of nontactile interplay.

The **pale-headed rosella** (*Platycercus adscitus*) is a stunning bird well-suited to humans who love to look and whistle and sing with their birds, but not necessarily touch them. Maintaining this bird on a physically interactive level with humans is difficult, but a good rapport can easily be maintained for side-by-side interactions.

Bourke's parakeets (*Neopsephotus bourkii*) are known in the wild for activity on bright moonlit nights. As companions, they are said to be trusting and agreeable when not breeding. They are charming companions with little tendency to chew or scream. The voice is a pleasant chirp.

Chapter Fourteen
Stories About Companion Parrots

Dolley Madison and Uncle Willy

If you've heard the overture, you know there must have been some scary war in 1812. Actually, there were several wars in 1812, and to make matters even scarier, one of them was not fought on foreign soil (unless you happened to be British). It was a "civilized" war in which our Presidential Parrot—between bouts of entertaining at parties and traipsing through valuable state documents—received diplomatic immunity. Uncle Willy, the First Lady's blue and gold macaw, resided safely in the home of the French Consulate when the presidential mansion and much of Washington, D.C. was burned to the ground during the War of 1812.

Uncle Willy's owner, the socially astute, usually turbaned Dolley Madison enjoyed numerous loyal friendships with persons of different political persuasions, races, and genders. As a close friend of the "Bachelor President," Thomas Jefferson, she served as surrogate First Lady for social functions in the sparsely furnished (but paid-for) presidential mansion in which she resided. By the age of 40, during her husband's presidency, Dolley Madison was called the "Queen of Washington." Not unlike First Ladies today, in addition to being extremely popular, she was also insulted on the streets, defamed, and ridiculed in the newspapers.

According to Rita Mae Brown's meticulously researched novel, *Dolley*, we know that during the Madison presidency Uncle Willy slept in a cage in the presidential bedroom, that he was covered at night, and that he engaged in occasional scuffles with King George, the presidential cat. We know that Uncle Willy ate sunflower seeds and stayed up late for parties, that he could be noisy, and that he sometimes ran to his mistress with wings outstretched for a hug. Uncle Willy was also hawk wary, exhibiting great noise and excitement when observing hawks in the fields of Montpelier, the Madison family's country home.

During the war, Uncle Willy's survival depended upon Jean Souioussant, who served as Dolley Madison's majordomo and lifetime friend, for "French John" often provided assistance with Dolley's animals. This "cosmopolitan Frenchman," well remembered for his many tattoos, also later saved Mrs. Madison's cow. In those days, there were no pensions for widowed First Ladies. The financially challenged Widow Madison once had to decide whether to give up her carriage or her cow. True to her reputation as a lover of dairy products, there was little question that Dolley would keep the cow even though it was difficult to find accommodations for a cow in the city.

Mrs. Madison doted on her intelligent talking bird. Uncle Willy was often the center of attention and was "...as colorful and entertaining as the First Lady." It is also reported that the president and First Lady, in spite of strict religious backgrounds, would laugh when the bird used "bad language."

In August 1814 when U.S. troops were defeated at Bladensburg, Maryland, President Madison sent word to his wife to leave Washington quickly. She received his message at about 1:15 P.M. as she sat down to a lunch of cold cuts. With the smell of smoke in the air, Uncle Willy screeched at approaching artillery fire and British soldiers within sight of the presidential mansion, while our devoted First Lady worked quickly to remove the important papers of state. In one hour and fifteen minutes, Dolley Madison would save the letters of President George

Washington, the Constitution, and the Declaration of Independence from the fires that soon engulfed the presidential mansion. One particularly problematic rescue was the full-length portrait of George Washington, which was screwed to the wall. Mrs. Madison borrowed a knife and cut the canvas from the stretcher, departing in her carriage less than 30 minutes before British soldiers ate her lunch. The presidential mansion was burned at 3:00 P.M.

There was no way to take her precious macaw in the carriage. Mrs. Madison asked French John to take Uncle Willy three blocks away to the "Quadrangle," temporary home of the French Minister, Serurier, where the bird resided for the duration of the British occupation of Washington.

By September 1814, the Madisons had moved back to Washington and into the Quadrangle for a time before moving "for political reasons" into a row house, the end dwelling on the "Corner of the Seven Buildings at Pennsylvania Avenue and Nineteenth Street." Here, it is said that the president and First Lady lived happily with plain rugs and secondhand furniture in a house whose windows opened directly onto the street. The tiny house was frequently so packed with Washington society that parties were called "Squeezes." When there were so many people at the parties that there was no room for lighting, Dolley Madison arranged for servants to hold torches outside the windows for light. This social tradition of "Night Parades" of lighted torches, carried south by another presidential parrot owner, Andrew Jackson, survives today in New Orleans as Mardi Gras and in San Antonio as the Parade of Lights.

At this time in her life Dolley took great delight in her parrot. Schoolchildren gathered daily to look into those street-level windows to watch Mrs. Madison and her bird. She would feed Uncle Willy, enticing him to talk for the children. One Washington resident, remembering his childhood, said, "She, as well as her pet, was very engaging. I can clearly recall her as she appeared in her inevitable turban."

Mrs. Madison's macaw is known to have outlived President James Madison, who died in 1836. On Dolley's 70th birthday, it is recorded that Uncle Willy was still entertaining his remarkable mistress.

Lolita Lowers the Volume

Lolita spent the winter in a trendy ski resort. She and her mate lived with more than 30 large macaws in an unheated dog run. Most of the birds survived through March on a diet of seed and water in unwashed bowls. The kennel owner—who had no previous aviculture experience and incomplete care information—eventually realized there was trouble. By that time four birds were dead, and several had lost toes to frostbite or to animal bites. Twenty-four birds required extensive veterinary treatment and fourteen were adopted by a group of individuals paying into a pool to reimburse their medical expenses.

It's a dismal tale, but not the one I want to tell here. Lolita was one of the lucky ones, the only surviving Amazon. I'm told that her mate bled to death after having his leg torn off by a wolf/dog hybrid. Lolita was there, watching and screaming, no doubt. I wonder how much of that she remembers.

She's one of those odd, probably wild-caught members of the *Farinosa* group, probably *Amazona farinosa guatemalae*. In California, she might be called a "lilac-crowned mealy." In Colorado, she's usually called a "blue-crowned" Amazon, with the speaker then making a distinction between this subspecies and the one with the totally blue head. They are unusual birds in captivity. They are also unusually large. My living room companion, Saucey, weighed 740 grams the last time he went to the veterinarian, and I'm sure he's put on weight since Lolita moved in just a month ago.

She arrived on the last Thursday night of last month. Lolita quietly ate most of my Good Times hamburger on the way home, but she was immediately vocal when she saw the handsome Saucey sitting there in perfect feather.

In a bleating, Amazon wail, she began calling out, "*Elllll Greckkkkkkko, Ellll Greckkkkkkko, Ellll Greckkkkkkko,*" and would not be silenced until the light was turned off.

Since Lolita had already been quarantined, the next day both birds were allowed to sit in the bathroom while I bathed. Lolita looked squarely at Saucey and said in a sweet, sincere voice that tore my heart out, "*El Greco, El Greco, how are you?*"

Looking up, I corrected her, "*No, Lolita, that isn't El Greco; that's Saucey.*"

Regarding me with an odd expression that seemed to be a mixture of puzzlement and concern, Lolita first paused, then replied, "*Bummer!*"

Saucey was even less happy with her than she was with him. He was especially offended by her behavior. While I'm not suggesting that he would have been any more receptive if she had been prettier, I feel that Lolita's appearance and condition must be mentioned here. Her feet remain always cold to the touch. All of the toes were still attached, but each had multiple cracks and erosions in the peeling skin as a result of vitamin A deficiency and having been repeatedly frozen. Her feathers showed obvious effects of the severe Alpine winter the birds endured.

Lolita looked a little like something to be used to mop the floor. Instead of "flour"-covered pale apple green feathers with iridescent undercolors, her contour feathers were dull, broken, chewed, and tattered with multiple patches of gray down poking through. She had only one whole tail feather with all other remaining tail quills being less than an inch (2.5 cm) long.

I kept telling Saucey that she should be beautiful in only six months. This feather problem will take care of itself with time, good diet, and a stimulating environment.

One thing that had remained quite thoroughly intact was Lolita's libido. Saucey was very offended each time Lolita pleasured herself loudly in his presence, doing what one of my online buddies calls "the cluck dance." The first couple of days, this was a very frequent occurrence, and to make matters worse, she continued calling Saucey "El Greco" during those intense moments. He would lean as far over as possible trying to get around the "barriers" provided by his cage to get to her cage to bite her.

Another thing that remained intact was Lolita's big farinosa Amazon voice, which occasionally lapsed into a donkey-like bray (the infamous mealy bray). In Lolita's case, it also occasionally lapsed into something resembling the Madeline Kahn "note"—you know the one—the "happiness song" from Mel Brooks' movie, *Young Frankenstein*.

From her very first day here, when Lolita was happy, she sang out a loud soprano "*Ahhhhhhhhhhhh!*"

But most of the time Lolita talked or warbled a noisy Amazon call with all its clucks, honks, trills, yells, and downright screams. I had been working on a "noise problem" with my other Amazons and felt that my neighbors should be informed that the bird noise might escalate for a little while. I felt it was important to let these very understanding neighbors know right away that she was not an impulse purchase, that this new loud bird was an adoption born of necessity. Fortunately, all I spoke with were sympathetic about Lolita's recent emergence from concentration camplike circumstances as well as Saucey's 15-year isolation from his own kind.

Most invasive was Lolita's tendency to express excitement on the balcony. My first efforts to soften her loud Amazon voice, as well as her learned barking and macaw calls, consisted largely of timeouts combined with modeling (setting an example of) lower volume. Many times, I would say to her, "*Say 'Hello', Lolita. Talk, don't squawk!*"

This quick-fix effort was modestly successful, lowering her volume maybe 30 to 50 percent in the first couple of weeks. While timeouts did not alter frequency, the loudest screams were temporarily silenced, giving my neighbors a little relief. We also lined the wooden balcony (which seemed to amplify sounds) completely with Astroturf, instantly reducing noise levels.

We made further strides by manipulating environmental distractions before the onset of screaming combined with verbal and food rewards for improved behavior. One month after her arrival, I believe both volume and frequency are less than half of what they were the first week. And then, last night we had what can only be described as a Helen Keller-and-teacher-at-the-pump moment in which Lolita finally figured out what I expect of her (quiet) when she's out on the balcony.

About an hour before dusk, Lolita was in a pattern of escalating volume, which usually prefaces yelling sessions. This evening, unlike previous times, my well-behaved Saucey was getting into the act, actually attaining loud volume well before Lolita did. Although silence had often been achieved by removing only Lolita from the balcony, this evening I was able to remove only Saucey, much to Lolita's surprise and delight. Walking away from the balcony with my male bird, I paused to model that operatic "*Ahhhhhhhhh-hhhh*" at very modest volume.

Something must have clicked in that ratty-looking gray-green head, for Lolita stopped, eyes all awhirl, and broke into her own happiness note, "*Ahhhhhhhhhhhh*," over and over and over again, at very modest volume. She seemed to be trying to tell me that, well, of course, she could do that if it meant she could stay outside!

Lolita has not yet figured out that she can also talk rather than scream, or chew or eat or play rather than scream, or practically anything else except scream; but she now knows that "*Ahhhhhhhhhhhh*" is OK. It's a welcome insight and one that I hope will reward my neighbors with many peaceful afternoons.

But even if we can get Lolita's volume down to acceptable levels, there is no guarantee that she is a permanent addition to our home. My first loyalty in this matter is to Saucey; and if Saucey doesn't like her, she will not stay.

Things might be warming up between them, however. Sometimes I see him preening her head; and once, I caught him with a big, wet string of masticated food running from his beak to hers. (It was very romantic!)

He's waited 15 years for this first friend. She is looking prettier every day.

The Slightly Unsaintly Bernadette

I was contacted by a representative of the Catholic Church advising me that there was a large white bird, apparently a parrot, living wild on the grounds of the seminary near my home.

"It seems," he said, "that the bird has been living there all summer and is waking up the seminarians very early in the morning."

("Hmmm," I thought, "aren't seminarians supposed to get up early?")

"Besides," he continued, "they say that a hawk is stalking the white bird. They say that it caught the white bird once."

Taking Joey, a friend's umbrella cockatoo (*Cockatua alba*) as a lure bird, my assistant and I set out for the seminary. The grounds proved lavish that September, with fruit trees bearing apples, crabapples, plums, and peaches in surrounding neighborhoods and large locust tree bean pods present in great abundance on the seminary grounds. The spacious landscape was also rich in wildlife, including a large eastern fox with black legs that we saw duck into a den under the sign at the main entrance.

Arriving on that first afternoon, we placed our lure bird, with well-trimmed wings, in a clearing on top of his traveling cage while we hid in a group of huge bushes and waited. Within minutes we noticed a change

Leadbeater's cockatoo

She flew almost immediately to the cage top where Joey was bouncing, dancing, crest erect in the manner of a bird who would fly to her if he could. We watched as she landed on the opposite side of the Preview Hendrix 125 cage. Her immediate posture indicated that she could be a bird of easy virtue. She was obviously soliciting Joey's sexual attentions. There was much crest flinging and hopping about, but what was it? There was something else. Something was awry.

Examining the bird through binoculars, we could see that one leg stuck out from her body at a right angle. She couldn't exactly walk, though she tried; it was the hopping gate of a biped with one limb half the length of the other.

Amazingly, it appeared that Joey (what a guy!) was mimicking her gate. He was responding to her as though the jerky, hobbled movements were part of her dance of solicitation. When she hopped, he hopped, bowing and throwing his crest in a mirror image of her display. He was a most gracious suitor.

"*Ahhh*," my assistant whispered, "this should be easy. She looks tame."

"Wait here," I instructed.

Stepping into the clearing, I approached them, hands clasped behind my back.

"Hey, Joey, who's your friend?" I called in my softest, most soothing tones.

The birds regarded me for a nanosecond and then returned to

in Joey's behavior and heard the loud call of a cockatoo from a nearby rooftop.

The buildings were exquisite examples of Gothic style featuring lots of arches, larger than life-sized art nouveau statuary, ornate carvings, and red-tiled roofs. There on the wrought iron cross atop the library building was a lovely lesser sulphur-crested cockatoo (*Cockatua sulphurea sulphurea*), a hen. Her bright, terra cotta eyes were clearly visible from 50 yards or more.

their posturing. Approaching at a pace of no more than a few feet every 20 or 30 seconds, I was within an arm's length before she flew to a nearby locust tree.

Retreating to my shrubbery hide-a-way, I rejoined my assistant. After only a few minutes, the cockatoo with the red eyes swooped down toward the lure cage. But just as she was about to land on the cage, she executed a sharp turn to the west, landing in a different, more fully foliated tree. She was screaming frantically at Joey, and in truth, he looked worried. We waited for half an hour in ignorance of the danger. As the last rays of sunlight left the area, the hen cockatoo flew over the huge tile-roofed building to the east. Defeated for the day, we collected Joey and went home.

The Quest Continues

For the next few days, we frequented the seminary for a few hours after sunrise and a few hours before sunset, usually enjoying the company of the red-eyed bird that we had christened "Bernadette, the Less-than-Saintly," We learned that she liked to spend her mornings in the area near the Grotto of the Virgin on the east of the library, and her afternoons in the locust bean trees west of the library. Sometimes we could find her; sometimes, we could not.

On Saturday morning, Joey and I were working alone. Situating Joey on top of his cage in the clearing beside the grotto, I walked around the south end of the library to see if Bernadette was in her customary evening foraging area. Returning to the grotto, I rounded the library, maybe 50 or 60 yards from Joey's perch, to see the shadow of a bird circling over him. Drawing closer, I realized that a huge brown and white raptor was preparing to eat Joey for breakfast. The white cockatoo was sitting like a virgin sacrifice with trimmed wing feathers on top of his cage.

Running, waving my arms, and screaming like a banshee, I watched in horror as a Swainson's hawk in partial winter colors began the dive to grab Joey. While I was still at least 30 or 40 yards away, and the hawk was halfway into the dive, I saw the bird slow, slow, braking with huge beats pushing forward the broad feathers on the bottom of the wing. The hawk apparently realized that this was a larger bird, a different white bird, than the one he had hunted before. In mid-dive, the hawk realized that Joey would be way too much work for a hawk with a field full of rabbits and prairie dogs only a stone's throw away.

Realizing my age and my mortality (and Joey's), we stepped into the grotto for a few moments of thankfulness. It was the last time Joey would function as a lure bird without the protection of a cage.

The Trap

I decided that Bernadette was not physically capable of stepping up, no matter how much time we spent with her. We began a new recapture strategy: we would establish a food dependency and trap her. I laid Joey's PH125 cage on its back and tied the grate inside the front of the cage, making a wire "bridge" or shelf across the opening formed by the open door. I attached one end of a long string to the door, threaded it through the cage bars so that it could be used to pull the door closed, and waited. Of course, I did not intend to pull the door closed since the grate was blocking the opening, but I wanted Bernadette to get used to the string being there before we needed to use it.

We put Joey into the cage through the bottom. That very first afternoon, Bernadette landed on the cage and shared a little bit of an ear of corn with Joey. But before she helped herself to the ripe fresh corn, Bernadette did something else. The first thing she did when she landed on the cage was chew the string off the door. On the next visit, we replaced the string with wire.

Leaving the corn and the cage in place, we did not return to the site until late the next day. By that time, the ear of corn was crumbles. We lowered the cage grate, wiring it about three or four inches below the opening of the door. At this point, Bernadette would have to stick her head into the cage to get to the corn. We "hid" in the car and watched as Bernadette immediately ate the refreshed supply of corn. Driving off into the sunset, we made plans for the next morning.

At sunrise on Tuesday, I lowered the grate about a foot into the cage below the door opening. Placing both fresh corn and a few bright red slices of apple, I slipped back to my hiding place and waited with wire in hand. In only minutes, Bernadette was there, climbing confidently into the cage with one good leg and her beak used as a hand. I pulled the door shut behind her and took her immediately to the veterinarian.

Rehabilitation

The bird in the cage was sweet. She was obviously thrilled to have the option of fresh water from a bowl. As we drove to the veterinarian's office, she helped herself to a vitamin-enriched seed mix. She seemed oblivious to her injury.

Dr. LaBonde pronounced Bernadette fit and surgery was scheduled for two weeks hence. During that time, as well as her brief recovery period, she lived in my living room on a freestanding tree perch, sleeping in the cage she was trapped in. She loved to fly across the room to whoever was sitting on the sofa. We didn't trim her wings because she couldn't really quite walk.

Her leg had been pulled so far out of the socket, that when it snapped back, it went inside her pelvis. The head of the femor had grown adhered to the inside of the pelvis. In a 45-minute surgical procedure, Dr. Jerry LaBonde scraped off the bone that had attached itself, amputated the damaged top end of the bone, pulled a flap of muscle over the hip joint, and sewed the end of the femur into a "pocket" in the muscle.

Within hours, Bernadette was scratching herself with that newly functioning foot, holding food with it, and even doing just a little limping around.

At about that time, Bernadette was adopted into a home where the other pet birds also flew free. Bucy's dining room was an avian fantasy of freestanding trees in Christmas tree stands. The adjoining living room had been appropriately bird-proofed with a "halo" of 18-inch streamers encircling the ceiling fan. Bernadette could fly and would not have to depend on that damaged leg for lots of walking and climbing.

I visit Bernadette a couple of times a year to trim her toenails. She's a happy, well adjusted, indoor bird that usually insists that all persons occupying the sofa must perform cockatoo petting duty every moment they're there.

Frankly, Scarlet

A circus of concerned neighbors parades in the street, looking up at the red-, yellow-, and blue-feathered apparition, gawking, crook-necked, shielding their eyes against the slanted light, sometimes pointing, gnawing their fingers with worry, and sidestepping to allow cars to pass. They're waiting for me, the bird recapture specialist, to tell them what to do.

The parrot's calls are loud, bleating, goatlike. It hangs first upside down, then sideways like an acrobat in a huge golden aspen tree, obviously a lost pet looking for a friendly face.

As daylight fades, the giant bird takes wing. Spectacular in flight, the floating crimson cross looks tired, gaunt. It crashes into a dense tree, an easy-to-climb tree. With a little coaching, a teenage volunteer starts carefully up. When he can go no farther, stretching high with legs spread on different branches, the boy pounds on the trunk near the branch where the bird sits. The bird puts beak to limb, climbing one foot over another, and steps onto the boy's arm. The trembling bird looks obviously delighted to reconnect with human flesh. Sharp toenails clench into the young man's biceps as he carefully descends. When they can make no lower progress, I step-up the bird onto a long branch and pull it from the tree.

The young scarlet macaw is nervous on my unfamiliar arm. I endure a couple of punctures and a slashing bite, hold tight, and walk into the nearest garage, thinking that this is the home of one of those helpful neighbors in the street. No one pushes a button to slide the huge door down behind me. I walk through the unlocked door into the house. An old man on a tweed recliner watches football on television.

"Edna," he says, hardly looking up, "somebody just walked in with a macaw."

"Sorry." I'm trying not to bleed on the shining floor. "Your neighbors called me to help recover this bird.

Scarlet macaw

a tissue for my bleeding wounds, then follows me outside to the meeting in the street.

The man who called me has gone home to supper. The boy who climbed the tree doesn't want the bird. The man who owns the tree the bird was caught in is shocked when I suggest that he keep it, and Edna's beginning to look nervous.

Until now, no one has admitted knowing whose bird it is. Finally, from the shadows, a man with small round eyeglasses speaks.

"The bird lives on the block behind the house you left it in." He's so pale he looks like a spaceman in the alien-pink circle of street light. "The owners don't want the bird."

I stare at him, nose-to-nose, stunned.

The other neighbors exchange knowing looks.

"What do you mean? How can that be?"

"I saw a streak of red fly by the window the other day and asked my neighbor's kids about it. They said the bird flew away. Said their dad told them not to go after it."

"The bird's beautiful, and very valuable." I'm amazed, incredulous. "Why would anyone want to abandon such a huge investment?"

More looks and raised eyebrows recede into the growing darkness. The group dwindles from a dozen or so to Edna, the boy who climbed the tree, and the man with the strange eyeglasses.

I'm shivering, suddenly aware of the chill. I want to go home.

Can I leave it here while we decide what to do?"

They reply in one voice, "Sure."

There's something I don't like about the way they look at each other.

I perch the bird on a chair back in an enclosed patio room. Edna offers

"So, this is the way it works," I say. "If I take the bird to my house where there are other birds, I'll have to take it to a veterinarian. It'll cost a hundred bucks or more for tests, maybe treatment, if it's sick. If I leave the bird with someone who has no birds, it can be returned with no charges."

Dark silence congeals the air.

"Well," it's the guy with the glasses again, "I'm pretty sure I know where the bird came from. I could leave your card on the door."

The hair on my arms stands straight up. My shiver turns into a shudder.

"If the bird stays with me only tonight, I won't charge my full fee, I'll drive all the way back here to return it for the cost of gas, maybe 20 bucks."

More skeptical looks.

"Or maybe I just won't charge 'em."

The strange man arches one eyebrow. "You'll never hear from them."

What a curious allegation! How inhumane this man must think his neighbors are. I've never seen anyone who wasn't heartbroken when their bird flew away.

All the neighbors turn to go. I can tell Edna wants me to follow her.

* * * * *

I wind up with a scarlet macaw perched on the back of my passenger seat. In the darkness, the bird says, "*What's up!*" once, quietly, then nips off a bit of cording from the edge of the seat. Guess I'll need that cage stored in Mom's garage. Don't have the energy to pick it up tonight.

The bird spends the night on the back of an old chair beside a wooden TV tray with water, parrot food, and a few blueberries. I toss and turn, worrying, thinking about a sensitive scarlet macaw separated from its rightful humans. When I see the sun coming up, I pull on my striped robe, then scurry barefoot across wet grass and cold concrete for the newspaper.

No, there's a couple of lost budgies, a 'tiel, and a Quaker. No lost macaw. I call police, animal control, state wildlife and agriculture departments. They're amused, disinterested, absolutely unhelpful.

I'm outraged! This amazing feathered vision has been abandoned! Just thrown out the window!

She loves saying "*Hello*" and "*I ruvvv roooo,*" and, frequently, and with great enthusiasm, "*Scarlet!*" In my living room she's stretching that long neck over to the side, one wing up, flashing one yellow eye in my direction, then "*Hunh?*" and "*What's up!*", and, with head switching quickly to the other side, "*Scarlet!*"

She chews on everything but won't eat anything but blueberries. She carefully examines food, first with one eye and then turning her head to look with the other, and says, "*What's up?*," cocking her head and listening to the way the words resonate in the metal bowl. Then she dumps anything but blueberries on the carpet. My wiener dogs rush to gobble up whatever drops to the floor, no matter which end of the bird it comes from.

I wait past noon for the phone to ring, cleaning and refilling dumped bowls and trying to get blue parrot poop stains out of the carpet. I put the food and water bowls on a large cardboard box and throw what remains of the TV tray away.

Walking out the door to go get that cage from Mom's garage, I hear the bird talking, repeating over and over the same words in different voices, "*Ouch*" and "*No*" and "*Don't*" and "*Stop it!*" And laughing manically.

* * * * *

"Wow! A scarlet macaw!" Mom looks a little envious as she helps load the cage from her garage.

"Maybe you'd like to buy her something to play with," I say. I'm irritable, all ready feeling a financial pinch. "She chewed up $35 worth of toys in an hour."

When I get home, Scarlet's not on the chair back anymore. She's peeking out of a large hole chewed in the cardboard box I left her dishes on. My antique African mask is a pile of toothpicks under the coffee table. Turning the corner to my dining room/office, there are little beige cubes everywhere. Computer keys, some whole, some not, form a minefield between my bare feet and the carpet. Every cable is chewed through, and my office chair is

beginning to look more than a little like the passenger seat in my van. How could she do so much damage in just two hours?

I chase the red bird out from under the box, but she stabs at my hand and arm when I try to pick her up. When she finally does step up, she reaches down with that giant beak, pinches my forearm, screams "*Ouch!*," and then laughs that maniacal laugh.

It's an unendearing game. I know those lumps will bruise.

She stabs at my face, grabs for my eyeglasses, achieves her goal with amazing swiftness.

"Give me those glasses!" I grab them away. That's the second time she's gotten them today. I have duct-tape repairs to the plastic bridge across my nose. My glasses rest lower on the left side of my face than the right.

* * * * *

Sunrise the second morning, I'm awakened to something like bagpipes in death throes at several times the usual bagpipe volume. Drooling, half asleep, I stumble into the living room, and pick up the bird. The bone-numbing sounds subside. Angry pounding explodes from the front door. Hurrying down the hall with Scarlet on my arm, something hard hits the floor and bounces. A few more feet along, something else drops. Opening the door, my pajama top hangs open. A trail of broken buttons leads from the bird cage, across the living room, down the hall to the front door. Scarlet holds the last button in her enormous beak. I pull my pajamas closed.

My neighbor doesn't notice. She's clutching her head, hung over, pitiful, wincing through gritted teeth. "What on earth is that!?"

"It's a macaw. I'm really sorry. It's temporary; she'll be out of here in a day or two." I apologize as eloquently and sensitively as possible.

The trip to the veterinarian is uneventful except for $65 for the giant macaw-sized carrier and the bruises I get putting the bird into it. Scarlet is a little dehydrated, otherwise OK. Dr. Greene charges a mere $192, suggests hand feeding since the bird won't eat anything but berries. I stop to buy parrot hand-feeding formula and supplies and a few more toys (only one from yesterday survives).

The big bird loves being hand fed. That is, she loves the Organic Baby Parrot Diet if it's exactly 104°F (40°C). As the warm formula gets cold, she refuses it, shaking her head, slinging big green globs on me and everything else in the kitchen. Feeding her takes half an hour; cleaning up takes longer.

* * * * *

On the third day Mom stops by to see the bird.

"She's beautiful!" My mother can't suppress a huge sigh as she caresses shining feathers with her eyes.

"She's a pain in the tush!" I say.

Scarlet is also smitten; maybe something about Mom's red blazer. Seizing the moment, the big bird climbs up Mom's arm to her shoulder, jerks her head up and down a few times, beak open, regurgitating blueberries into Mom's ear. Then Scarlet lifts her tail straight up and starts masturbating on Mom's head.

Suddenly realizing what that erect red tail moving back and forth is doing to her head, my mother reaches up, grabs the long feathers, and pulls them down. Scarlet screams, turns around, and stabs wildly. With a couple of tugs, a twist, and a jerk, the massive beak rips a cultured pearl earring through my mother's earlobe.

Mom screams. The bloody bauble drops. Reaching down, there's a flash of brown, and the earring disappears.

Oh, my God! Kirby's got it. He's under the bird cage coughing, choking.

Mom's in the bathroom screaming.

I pick up the dog, trying to accomplish something like a Dachshund Heimlich maneuver.

No, no. It doesn't work.

Mom staggers out of the bathroom, down the hall to the front door holding a blood stained towel to the side of her head. I grip Kirby by the hind legs, one in each hand, and shake him like a salt shaker. Nothing. I hold my convulsing dog tight against my chest, run up two flights. My neighbor Mary's a nurse. She'll know what to do! We wrap my struggling wiener in a beach towel, wedge his mouth open with a wooden spoon, and extract the earring with a long hemostat. Most of the blood on the dog appears to be Mom's. I drop Kirby off at the veterinarian's for observation.

Back home, Scarlet's out, roaming again. Oh, God, *all* the birds are out. The red macaw's been on another excursion, opening cage doors. Where is everybody?

I can hear Kiwi, but can't find him. There's Pearl on top of the curio. Sammie-Jo's on the lamp. It takes almost an hour to restore my little flock to their respective places, then clean up Mom's blood in the bathroom and entry hall.

My cuticles are bleeding, and I've started leaving tiny curved hairs beside wherever I sit. What is that?

When Scarlet screams, when she really blasts one, my other birds get upset. They're noisier than usual now. Kiwi, a green Quaker parrot, has gray down showing in a couple of places. Is he chewing his own feathers?

What's that hammering? There's an eviction notice tacked to my door. I'm going to lose my home if I don't find a way to return the red bird!

* * * * *

Looking for the place she flew from, on the next street over from where we pulled Scarlet out of a tree, I look for signs of a macaw. There's a huge cage sitting empty on a side patio. I can see a vase of red tail feathers through one window. The house is behind and only one number lower than Edna's on the other side of the alley. This must be Scarlet's true home.

I ring the bell and knock repeatedly, peeking through dusty windows. There's lots of normal family clutter, no people. Two cars in the driveway, but nobody comes to the door.

I sit on the front step for half an hour, then decide to leave a note:

"Hello, I am a bird recapture specialist who was able to recover your lost macaw. She's fine now, but wanting to come home. I would very much like to return your bird. Related expenses include:

Recovery	$200.00
Carrier	65.25
Veterinarian	192.00
Handfeeding supplies	20.00
4 toys	72.57
	$549.82

I can deliver your bird at your convenience and will gladly accept a check to reimburse expenses."

I chew split, bleeding cuticles as I drive the freeway home. My head's exploding. I'm kicking myself for not adding medical expenses for Mom and Kirby to the statement I left for Scarlet's owners. Looking in the visor mirror, there's bare skin above my eyes, those little curved hairs I've been leaving all around are my former brows and lashes. By the time I get home, the birds are screaming bloody murder. There's another eviction notice on my door, and a phone message, at last, from Scarlet's owners.

"Hello, thanks for finding our bird. We are willing to accept her return if you bring $500 cash in compensation for our pain and suffering. We will be available this evening, but will require a higher cash payment if she is not returned by tomorrow.

Be sure to come after dark, as we can't be held responsible for what the neighbors will do if they see you return the bird."

Their pain and suffering! I'm incredulous, looking at my buttonless shirt and bruised, punctured forearms. And what about the neighbors!

Standing in the shambles of my living room, clutching the eviction notice, thinking about being homeless with five birds, two dogs, and a cat, I'm hyperventilating. I know what has to be done. I load the bird into the carrier, stopping at two teller machines and a grocery store to cash $500 in after-hours checks.

I approach the door with the red bird on the same hand as the envelope with the money inside. Reluctantly, suspiciously, with growing impatience, I pass the envelope to the man inside. The pale man with the tiny round eyeglasses! The door closes, then opens again.

"Well," he says, "looks like it's all here."

I sigh a huge sigh and hand the bird over to the wicked man.

As I turn to walk away, he calls out, "Scarlet. Hey, Scarlet, com'mere."

"What?" There's a muffled response in a curious voice. A familiar voice. It sounds just like the macaw!

A red-headed woman in a T-shirt under a buttonless blouse walks around the corner. Duct tape binds the bridge of her glasses. Remnants of yellow bruises gild her forearms.

"Hey, Scarlet, look who's home!" The man fairly glows as he lofts the blissful, flapping bird to the center of the foyer.

"Wow, that was quick!"

The woman's voice is exactly like the bird's! Her eyes expose both fatigue and satisfaction as she regards the beating red wings and screaming, happy parrot.

"It's our working bird! Good job!" She speaks through a tight-lipped smile. "What's up, Red Chief?"

Author's note: Of all materials in this book, this alone is fiction. Parrot behaviors described herein are accurate, however, and the story itself is based on actual events.

Glossary

Please note that the following definitions set forth the meanings of these words as they are used specifically in this text. These definitions are not intended to be full and complete definitions.

abandonment: the feeling of being left behind and out of the flock. To a parrot, this can mean death.

adaptive behaviors: learned behaviors that increase the bird's chances of surviving by producing more offspring.

adapted: having adjusted to the environment in a positive manner.

aggression: nipping, biting, or chasing, causing damage to human skin.

ailanthus: "trees of heaven," so named for a Moluccan word meaning, "tree that grows up to the sky"; weed tree common in older urban cities in the United States. Soft, easy to grip branches well suited as African grey parrot perches.

allofeeding: mutual feeding or simulated mutual feeding. One of several behaviors related to breeding.

allopreening: mutual preening or simulated mutual preening, as in a human scratching a parrot's neck.

altricial: a bird that is helpless upon hatching and must be cared for by its parents.

alula: the triangular shape formed by four feathers above the coverts at the shoulder of the wing.

anthropomorphic: ascribing human attributes to a nonhuman being.

aviary birds: birds that live in captivity, but in a bird-identified setting in which they do not interact on a regular basis with humans.

Avitrol: name brand of birth-control seed soon available (at this writing) for feeding unwanted "pest" parrots, squirrels, and other "invasive" species.

baby days: a young parrot's first, impressionable weeks in the new home, an idyllic period before the baby bird's instincts for independence, dominance, and exploration develop. *See also:* honeymoon.

baby tail: frayed or broken tail feathers typical of extremely playful juvenile parrots usually under two years old.

band: coded metal device placed around a bird's leg for identification purposes.

beaking: benign testing of the feel of the beak on various substances, including skin, by a parrot.

behavioral environment: behavioral conditions, especially redundant behaviors, including habits, present in the bird and in individuals around the bird.

bite: use of the parrot's beak in a manner intended to cause damage or injury.

blood feather: unopened immature feather, which is completely or partially covered by a bluish/white membrane, indicating that the feather is currently supplied with blood.

body language: nonvocal communication involving posturing, displaying, or otherwise signaling an individual's feelings or intentions.

bond: the connection with another bird, a human, an object, or a location, which a bird exhibits and defends.

boredom: stress caused in companion parrots by a lack of access to activities that they would be instinctually suited to experience, including wild and self-rewarding companion pastimes.

breeding-related behaviors: behaviors with a source related to breeding habits in the wild, such as chewing, emptying cavities, hiding in dark places, allopreening, allofeeding, masturbating, copulating, and aggression at the nest site (cage).

cage bound: so fixated on an unchanging environment that any change stimulates either aggression or fearfulness in a captive bird.

cage fray: damage done to feathers usually of the tail, head, or wing, by frequent contact with cage toys or other accessories.

cavity-breeding behaviors: breeding-related behaviors of parrots, including chewing, emptying cavities, fondness for small spaces, peeking out, and aggression at the nest site.

chasing: to drive away by pursuing.

chewing: breeding-related behavior involving destruction of wood or other shredable environmental elements.

cloaca: also called the vent. Part of the bird's anatomy where waste materials are collected for excretion. Also opening where sperm is deposited.

clutch: siblings hatching from the same group of eggs.

command: a prompt or instruction given to stimulate a behavior.

companion parrot: a parrot that lives as a companion to humans.

contour: a layer of covering feathers, as in the gray and green feathers covering the bird's down.

counterintuitive: going against intuition or common reason.

crest: a set of feathers on the head used for expression of emotions in the cockatoo.

cue: a word or group of words established to stimulate certain behaviors.

dander: powder formed when discarded sheaths are removed from new feathers, or powder that is contained in certain down feathers that is released when the bird preens.

developmental period: a period of rapid behavioral development wherein a parrot may demonstrate tendencies for dominance, independence, aggression, and panic. *See also:* terrible twos.

diarrhea: abnormal droppings that include undigested food in the feces or do not have three distinct parts. True diarrhea is usually accompanied by weight loss in the bird.

dominance: control, enforcing individual will over others.

down: the small fuzzy feathers next to the body that are normally covered by coverts.

drama: any activity that brings an exciting response, either positive or negative.

evert: sticking out, as in the hen everts her cloaca during copulation then pulls semen deposited there inside when the cloaca returns to its normal shape.

"evil eye": a behavioral technique, first described by Sally Blanchard, in which the bird is stopped from unwanted behavior by a stern, predatorlike two-eyed gaze.

eye contact: the act of maintaining eye-to-eye gaze.

family: category ranking above genus. The order of parrots, *Psittaciformes*.

feather cyst: one or more feathers growing under the skin, causing an uncomfortable abscess.

feather destructive behavior: self-inflicted feather damage involving damaging any part of the feather including the edges or the center shaft or rachis.

feather picking: used here to refer to any kind of self-inflicted feather damage including shredding, snapping, or plucking feathers from the follicles.

feather plucking: pulling feathers from the follicles.

feather shredding: self-inflicted damage to the edge of the barbs of the contour feathers, sometimes giving the feathers a hair-like appearance.

feather snapping: self-inflicted feather damage involving breaking off the center shaft, or rachis.

feather tracts: symmetrical lines on the bird's body where feathers grow in along lines of circulation; especially visible on neonatal parrots.

feces: excreted solid waste, usually "wormlike," which can be differentiated from urates and liquid urine.

fight-or-flight response: instinctual, automatic reaction to real or perceived danger.

fledge: the act of learning to fly in order to leave the nest.

flock/flock members: as it applies to a companion bird, human companions sharing a home with a captive parrot.

forage: the search for and consumption of food.

free feeding: allowing access to food at all times.

genus (pl., genera): a group of related species, usually sharing basic morphological and behavioral characteristics.

grooming: the process of having the companion parrot's wing feathers trimmed, nails cut or filed, and beak shaped, if necessary.

group: a set of related species sharing basic morphological and behavioral characteristics, such as the group Amazona. Also commonly called "genus."

habit: redundant behavior that has become a fixed part of the bird's behavior.

hand-fed: a parrot that as a neonate was fed by humans rather than birds.

handling techniques: methods used by humans to stimulate and maintain successful tactile interactions with companion parrots.

honeymoon period: a young parrot's first, impressionable weeks in the new home; an idyllic period before the baby bird's instinct for dominance and exploration develop. *See also:* baby days.

hookbill: a parrot.

human/mate: the human companion chosen by the bird to fill the role of mate. The bird will perform courtship displays for this person and protect this person as it would a mate of the same species.

imperfect: a bird with an obvious physical defect resulting from congenital anomaly or injury.

independence: improvising and enjoying self-rewarding behaviors.

juvenile: fully weaned, but immature grey parrots. Also, behaviors unrelated to nesting or breeding.

keel bone: the flat bone below the bird's crop that is attached perpendicular to the sternum.

language: vocal communication wherein multiple individuals use the same groups of sounds to convey the same meaning.

maladaptive: behaviors that decrease the bird's ability to function in its environment.

mandible: the lower beak, or horny protuberance, with which the bird bites against the inside of the maxilla.

mantling: wing outstretching happiness behavior as described in falconry.

manzanita: commercially available hardwood branches usually best used with larger parrots because of their size and smoothness, but which, in small sizes, are suitable as perches for smaller parrots with no gripping or perching problems.

masticate: to chew, as in this case, with the beak.

mate: the individual to whom the parrot is primarily bonded. *See also:* human/mate.

maxilla: the upper beak; the notched protuberance that gives the hookbill its name.

mimicking: to copy modeled behavior, especially vocalizations.

model: a learning process by which one individual demonstrates behavior for another.

molt: the cyclical shedding and replacing of feathers.

neonate: a baby parrot that cannot yet sustain itself by eating food independently. In the case of baby greys, these birds are usually being hand-fed.

nest/nesting: the act of constructing a structure for the purpose of reproduction.

nest box: a human-constructed box for bird nesting.

night frights: unexplained thrashing in the night that is sometimes seen in cockatiels and a few other species of companion parrots.

nipping: an accidental, unintentional, or nonaggressive pinch not intended to cause damage.

normal: the original animal that occurs wild. Not a color mutation (pied, lutino, or albino).

overload: episodes of excitement resulting in feather displays indicating sexual interest or aggression. Especially common in Amazons and cockatoos.

parrot: a hookbill; a bird with a notched maxilla, a mallet-shaped tongue, and four toes (two facing front and two facing back).

patterning: stimulating an individual to repeat behaviors through the process of repeatedly drilling the behavior.

phobic: irrational or unexplainable fear.

pinch: a behavior designed to get a human's attention where the bird takes that person's skin in its beak and squeezes hard enough to cause pain, but not hard enough to break the skin.

polymer fume fever: the condition that can kill a bird that is exposed to fumes from Teflon heated to 500°F (1060°C).

preen: to groom the feathers, as with "combing" and "zipping" them with the beak.

prompt: a cue; here used for the physical cue to cause the bird to step-up.

Psittaciformes or **psittacine:** any parrot.

quarantine: enforced isolation for the prevention of disease transmission.

reactive: to quickly revert to instinctual reactions, such as aggression or fear.

recapture: to apprehend or recover possession of a parrot that has flown away.

recumbent: a cockatoo crest that tops off with a backward curve, such as that of an umbrella or Goffin's cockatoo.

recurve: a cockatoo crest that tops off with a forward curve, such as that of a cockatiel or sulphur-crested cockatoo.

regurgitate: voluntary or involuntary production of partially digested food from the crop. *See also:* allofeeding.

reinforce: process of rewarding a behavior that we wish to become habitual.

reprimand: punishment; action intended to discourage a behavior.

rescue: fortuitous removal from frightening circumstances.

rival: a competitor; one who competes for territory, reinforcement, or reward.

roaming: unsupervised explorations away from approved cage or play areas.

roost: the place where a bird usually sleeps.

scissor beak: condition wherein the mandible overgrows the edge of the maxilla on one side.

self-mutilation: self-induced damage to the skin.

self-rewarding behavior: an activity that is enacted solely for the pleasure of doing it.

sexual behavior: self-rewarding, breeding-related behavior.

sexual maturity: the period during which breeding-related behaviors become prominent in the bird's overall behavior.

signaling: anything — vocalization, tapping, or other body language — that warns, alerts, or telegraphs an intention or apparent impending behavior. A vocalization that falls short of true language.

species: subgenus; related groups of individuals that share common biological characteristics.

spraddle leg: a deformity that prevents normal use of any of the joints of the leg, usually causing the leg to bend outward.

status: positioning related to dominance within the pecking order.

step-up: practice of giving the step-up command with the expectation that the bird will perform the behavior.

sternum: the breastbone from which the keel bone protrudes.

stress: any stimulus, especially fear or pain, that inhibits normal psychological, physical, or behavioral balance.

submission: allowing another creature to demonstrate dominant status.

subspecies: a subdivision of species, especially by color or geographical characteristics.

substratum: material placed in the bottom of the bird's cage or play area to contain mess and droppings; plural, substrata.

teaser: a skin or feather-protection device worn by the parrot designed to attract chewing behaviors to itself rather than in addition to or as a means of preventing feather-destructive behavior.

terrible twos: a behavioral period wherein the bird's instincts for dominance, independence, and aggression are first manifest. *See also:* developmental period.

tool: an implement that is manipulated to accomplish a particular function.

toxin: any substance that causes illness or death through exposure to it.

toy: any tool for producing self-rewarding behavior.

trap: a device used to recapture a free-flying bird.

treading: style of mounted copulation used by most parrots during mating.

urates: nitrogenous wastes; the solid "white" part of a bird's excrement.

urine: clear, colorless liquid part of the bird's excrement.

vent: cloaca.

vocabulary: words or elements comprising a language.

weaned: capable of eating a variety of foods independent of help or supervision.

window of opportunity: a finite period during which something can be accomplished; a period of time during which behavior can be changed.

winking: a form of masturbation involving opening and closing the cloaca, especially in Amazon behavior.

wobble distraction: a gentle wobble intended to distract from unwanted behavior just as that behavior is signaled and before it occurs.

Resources

Books

A Guide To Eclectus Parrots, Their Management, Care & Breeding, Australia: Australian Birdkeeper, 1991.

Athan, Mattie Sue, *Guide to a Well-Behaved Parrot*, Hauppauge, NY: Barron's Educational Series, 2007.

Athan, Mattie Sue, *Guide To The Quaker Parrot,* Hauppauge, NY: Barron's Educational Series, 2007.

Athan, Mattie Sue, and Deter, Dianalee, *Guide to the Senegal Parrot And Its Family,* Hauppauge, NY: Barron's Educational Series, 2008.

Forshaw, Joseph M., *Parrots Of The World*, Neptune, NJ: T.F.H. Publications, Inc., 1977.

Freud, Arthur, *The Complete Parrot,* New York: McMillan, 1995.

Greeson, Linda, *Parrot Personalities*, Fruillend Park, FL: Greeson's Baby Parrots, 1993.

Harrison, Greg J. and Harrison, Linda R., *Clinical Avian Medicine and Surgery*, Philadelphia: W. B. Saunders Company, 1986.

Jupiter, Tony and Parr, Mike, *Parrots: A Guide to Parrots of the World,* New Haven, CT: Yale University Press, 1998.

Lantermann, Werner and Susanne, *Amazon Parrots*, Hauppauge, NY: Barron's Educational Series, 1988.

Lantermann, Werner and Susanne, *Cockatoos,* Hauppauge, NY: Barron's Educational Series, 1989.

Low, Rosemary, *Encyclopedia of the Lories*, Blaine, WA: Hancock House, 1998.

Marquez, Garbriel Garcia, *Love in the Time of Cholera*, New York: Viking Penguin, 1989.

McWatters, Alicia, *A Guide to a Naturally Healthy Bird*, East Canaan, CT: Safe Goods, 1997.

Murphy, Kevin, *Training Your Parrot*, Neptune, NJ: T.F.H. Publications, Inc., 1983.

Ritchie, Harrison, and Harrison, *Avian Medicine: Principles and Application,* Lake Worth, FL: Wingers Publishing, Inc. 1994.

Sweeney, Roger G., *The Eclectus*, Perry, ON: Silvio Mattacchione & Co, 1993.

Sweeney, Roger G., *Macaws,* Hauppauge, NY: Barron's Educational Series, 1992.

Vriends, Matthew, *Conures,* Hauppauge, NY: Barron's Educational Series, 1993.

Vriends, Matthew, *Lories and Lorikeets*, Hauppauge, NY: Barron's Educational Series, 1993.

Vriends, Matthew, *The New Australian Parakeet Handbook*, Hauppauge, NY: Barron's Educational Series, 1992.

Vriends, Matthew, *Parrotlets,* Hauppauge, NY: Barron's Educational Series, 1998.

Wolter, Anette, *African Gray Parrots*, Hauppauge, NY: Barron's Educational Series, 1987.

Wolter, Anette, *The Long Tailed Parakeets,* Hauppauge, NY: Barron's Educational Series, 1992.

Contributors

Sally Blanchard is the editor and publisher of *Companion Parrot Quarterly.* She was first published in *Bird Talk* in 1988. Interviews: 1998 and before.

Kashmir Csaky has studied behavior in companion parrots since 1965. She is a well-respected breeder specializing in hyacinth and scarlet macaws. She frequently lectures and writes, and is a regular contributor to *Companion Parrot Quarterly* and other avian publications. Correspondence: October, 1998. Interviews: 1998–2009.

Dianalee Deter studied Zoology and Animal Behavior at the University of Florida. She is the co-author of *Guide to the Senegal Parrot and Its Family, The African Gray Parrot Handbook, The Second-Hand Parrot,* and consulting editor of this book. Consultations: 1998 and before.

Sybil Erden is founder and director of Oasis Sanctuary Foundation, established in 1994. Oasis is one of a very few nonprofit sanctuaries that neither breed nor adopt out birds, but rather provide lifetime care for unwanted parrots and other exotic birds. Interview and correspondence: 1998.

Dave Flom is a long-time breeder of companion, trick-trained, and free-flying macaws. Interviews: 2008.

Linda Greeson is a breeder of Quaker Parrots and numerous other species. She has authored several well-known booklets and has been an important influence on avian publishing, including electronic publishing, for many years. Correspondence: October, 1998.

Diane Grindol is the author of *The Complete Book of Cockatiels.* She writes *Bird Talk's* "Small Talk," which features news and information about birds, research, conservation programs, and birds in the media. Interviews and correspondence: 1998.

Mary Karlquist is a well-respected breeder and lecturer specializing in macaws and cockatoos. Interviews: 1998–2008.

Betsy Lott works in parrot rescue and adoption in the south San Francisco Bay Area. She is networked with other rescue programs and individuals all over the United States and Canada, and serves on the Board of Directors for the Oasis Sanctuary Foundation. Interviews and correspondence: 1998.

Rosemary Low is the author of more than 20 books and hundreds of articles on parrots spanning more than 30 years. She is the former curator of two of the world's largest parrot collections, Loro Parque and Palmitos Park. Correspondence: 1998.

Sandee Molenda has bred parrotlets for 15 years, producing six of the seven species including color mutations. She founded the International Parrotlet Society. Interviews: 1998–2009.

James J. Murphy was a biologist specializing in the behavioral biology of birds and mammals. Interviews, correspondence, and publications: 1998.

Nancy Newman is the owner of SkyDancers Aviary. She is a breeder of conures and cockatiels. Correspondence: 1998.

Jean Pattison is president of the African Parrot Society, a frequent lecturer, writer, and a well-respected breeder of African parrots. She is sometimes called "The African Queen." Interviews and correspondence: 1998–2009.

Tani Robar is a long time professional animal trainer who turned her attention to birds and revolutionized the world of avian trick training with small birds never before used in shows, including, astonishingly, a trick-trained, public performing African grey parrot. Interviews: 1998 and videos: 1994.

Tom Roudybush is a nutritionist, writer, founder, and president of Roudybush, Inc. A pioneer in his field, Tom has studied the nutrient requirements of birds for more than 25 years. Interviews and correspondence: 1998.

Rita Shimniok is a small breeder of primarily African parrots, operating Oakridge Feather Farm in Cross Plains, Wisconsin. Rita writes for several national avian magazines, and is most known for her research and articles on the Jardine's parrots. Correspondence and interviews: 1997–1998.

Michele I. Traugutt has owned and bred various hookbills including lories, her favorites, for over fifteen years. Deter interview: 1998.

Matthew Vriends, a Dutch-born biologist/ornithologist who holds a collection of advanced degrees, has written more than 80 books in three languages. He has achieved many first-time breeding results in his extensive aviaries. Interviews, correspondence, and publications: 1998 and before.

Liz Wilson is one of the most experienced bird behavior consultants in the world. Correspondence and interviews: 1998 and before.

Dr. Margaret Wissman is an extremely experienced and respected avian veterinarian practicing in Florida where large collections of parrots abound. She authors a regular *Bird Talk* column and has been published in other professional journals and textbooks. Correspondence and interviews: 1998.

Organizations

The Amazona Society
P.O. Box 73547
Puyallup, WA 98373-4016

The African Parrot Society
P.O. Box 204
Clarinda, IA 51632-2731

American Federation of Aviculture
P.O. Box 56218
Phoenix, AZ 85079

Association of Avian Veterinarians
(556) 393-8901

British Columbia Avicultural Society
11784 9th Avenue
North Delta, B.C. V4C 3H6

Canadian Avicultural Society
32 Dronmore Court
Willlowdale, Ontario M2R 2H5

Canadian Parrot Association
Pine Oaks R.R. #3
Catherines, Ontario L2R 6P9

International Aviculturists Society
P.O. Box 2232
LaBelle, FL 33975

International Loriidae Society
17704 S. Tapps Drive East
Summer, WA 98390-9172

International Parrotlet Society
P.O. Box 2428,
Santa Cruz, CA 95063

World Parrot Trust
P. O. Box 34114
Memphis, TN 38184

Videos

Fantastic Performing Parrots, Robar Productions, 1994.

Parrots Look Who's Talking, Thirteen/WNET and BBC-TV, 1995.

Paulie, Dream Works Pictures, 1998.

Pyrruhas the Quiet Conures, The Feather Tree, 1997.

Spirits Of The Rainforest, Discovery Communications, Inc., 1993.

Vanishing Birds Of The Amazon, Audubon Productions and Turner Original Productions, 1996.

Index